THE AGE OF

THE AGE OF FITNESS

HOW THE BODY CAME TO SYMBOLIZE SUCCESS AND ACHIEVEMENT

JÜRGEN MARTSCHUKAT

TRANSLATED BY ALEX SKINNER

polity

Originally published in German as *Das Zeitalter der Fitness*. Copyright © 2019 S. Fischer Verlag GmbH, Frankfurt am Main

This English edition © 2021 by Polity Press

Polity Press
65 Bridge Street
Cambridge CB2 1UR, UK

Polity Press
101 Station Landing
Suite 300
Medford, MA 02155, USA

ISBN-13: 978-1-5095-4563-6

A catalogue record for this book is available from the British Library.

Library of Congress Cataloging-in-Publication Data

Names: Martschukat, Jürgen, author. | Skinner, Alex, translator.
Title: The age of fitness : how the body came to symbolize success and
achievement / Jürgen Martschukat ; translated by Alex Skinner.
Other titles: Zeitalter der Fitness. English
Description: Medford : Polity Press, 2021. | Includes bibliographical
references and index. | Summary: "Why the pursuit of fitness has become
a central preoccupation of modern life"-- Provided by publisher.
Identifiers: LCCN 2020033791 (print) | LCCN 2020033792 (ebook) | ISBN
9781509545636 (hardback) | ISBN 9781509545650 (epub)
Subjects: LCSH: Body image. | Physical fitness. | Success. | Performance.
Classification: LCC BF697.5.B63 M37713 2021 (print) | LCC BF697.5.B63
(ebook) | DDC 306.4/613--dc23
LC record available at https://lccn.loc.gov/2020033791
LC ebook record available at https://lccn.loc.gov/2020033792

Typeset in 10.75 on 14 Adobe Janson by
Servis Filmsetting Ltd, Stockport, Cheshire
Printed and bound in Great Britain by CPI Group (UK) Ltd, Croydon

For further information on Polity, visit our website:
politybooks.com

CONTENTS

FIGURES

ACKNOWLEDGMENTS

This book took shape over many years and in the context of a number of research projects. Between 2012 and 2015, the Fritz Thyssen Foundation funded our project on "Das essende Subjekt" ("The Eating Subject"). I am as indebted to that institution as I am to the Volkswagen Foundation for generously funding the project on "Ernährung, Gesundheit und soziale Ordnung in der Moderne: Deutschland und die USA" ("Nutrition, Health, and Social Order in Modernity: Germany and the United States") from 2015 to 2019, as part of the funding stream *Schlüsselthemen für Wissenschaft und Gesellschaft* (Key Issues for Science and Society). Without the research professorship that formed part of this key issues project in the summer semester of 2018, I would not have been able to complete this book.

While working on the manuscript I received valuable feedback from numerous colleagues and friends. The North American History colloquium at the University of Erfurt and various seminars, from Charlottesville in Virginia to Dunedin in New Zealand, were a great source of inspiration. Through a William Evans Fellowship in the spring of 2017, the University of Otago enabled me to carry out research at its School of Physical Education, Sport and Exercise Sciences, which in turn allowed me to discuss the project intensively and advance it greatly. My thanks go to Doug Booth for his tremendous support, his wonderful hospitality, and his input at various workshops and over numerous coffees. My thanks also go to Stefanie Büttner, Katharina Dahl, Paula Dahl, Tristan Dohnt, Norbert Finzsch, Laura-Elena Keck, Tae-Jun Kim, Olaf von dem Knesebeck, Nina Mackert, Irene Martschukat, Maren Möhring, Stefan Offermann, Tanja Robnik, Olaf Stieglitz, Heiko Stoff, Paula-Irene Villa and Simon Wendt, who read various parts and versions of the text and discussed them with me. Paula Dahl, Nina Mackert and Irene Martschukat even worked their way through the entire manuscript; Maria Matthes and Viviann Wilmot assisted me with the research and the final editing, and Alex Skinner created an elegant translation. Without your help this project would have gotten nowhere.

Last but not least, my special thanks to Alex, Andy, Bille, Dirk, Flo, Harry, Jörg, Matthias, Paddy, Reemt, Sebastian, Silke and all the other boys and girls from Team Altona for their company across thousands of kilometers in and around Hamburg and throughout Europe.

INTRODUCTION:
THE AGE OF FITNESS

We live in the age of fitness. Tens of thousands of people run marathons and compete in all-comers cycle races, while millions go for an evening jog in the park or work out in gyms, where they lift weights and use machines of various kinds or practice yoga; active vacations of all kinds are more popular than ever. In 1970, this was barely conceivable. Hiking vacations were for retirees and windsurfing had just been invented. The Berlin Marathon still lay in the future. Few adults had a bicycle, while gyms were few and far between. Since then, however, fitness has boomed. Let's consider the scale of the fitness market. In Germany alone, active people (and those who want to appear active, or at least aspire to be active) spent over 50 billion euros on fitness-related items in 2015: running shoes and sportswear, weights and carbon fiber bicycles, energy drinks and diet foods. Equally popular are fitness classes and activity vacations, fitness magazines and books, apps and gadgets. Fitness stars such as Kayla Itsines – to mention one of many examples – have millions of followers on Instagram; images of toned bodies are hugely popular on social media.[1]

What those engaged in "getting fit" generally have in common is that they are active, but rarely organize themselves in clubs or associations. They do not participate in a specific league, and they are almost never out to win a competition. Yet they all want to improve themselves somehow. They do not engage in the kind of organized competitive sport that spread from the United Kingdom to other modernizing societies from the mid-nineteenth century.[2] Those who undertake fitness training are not looking to win a medal. Instead, what this practice aims to achieve is a fit body. This body, in turn, stands for an array of partially overlapping forces, abilities and ideals, which point far beyond the doing of sport. These encompass one's health and performance in everyday life and at work, productivity and the ability to cope with challenging situations, potency, a slim figure and a pleasing appearance according to the prevalent standards of beauty. Also important in this context is "doing the right thing," "doing something good" for oneself, and getting the "best" out of oneself, as well as gaining recognition for it. At times, the sheer joy of movement and activity also comes into play. These various driving forces are not mutually exclusive.

The pursuit of fitness[3] is part of a culture and society that concurrently laments increasingly fat bodies. In the twenty-first century, fatness is even referred to as an epidemic, and health problems such as type 2 diabetes and cardiovascular disease are a perennial topic of concern. Particularly in Western societies, but now also worldwide, the consistent message is that the lack of physical activity has assumed "frightening proportions."[4] A so-called sedentary lifestyle and an unhealthy, high-calorie diet are viewed as the main causes of increasing fatness. On the one hand, then, there is a culture of fitness, while on the other there is anxiety over the lack of exercise and burgeoning fatness. What may seem contradictory at first sight turns out to be part of a single social formation, centered on the self-responsible, committed and productive individual. Both sides of this coin (the culture of fitness and the fear of fat) revolve around the successful self, which proves its success by mastering its own body. In (post)modern societies, lack of fitness amounts to a flashing red light.

To gain a deep understanding of our age of fitness, this book delves into history. To illuminate the present through the past means comprehending history as a space "in which the present has been formed."[5] We have to draw on history if we aspire to grasp our own present, identify its problems and paradigms, and engage critically in its most contentious debates.

This entails linking the topic of fitness with the project of the free, self-responsible individual and their history. As this book reveals, historicizing fitness demonstrates that lived self-responsibility and its consolidation as an ideal have constituted a project for more than two centuries. Writing a history of fitness also means exploring the genealogy of competition and performance, and assessing their importance to modern societies, to their organization and to the societal participation of different types of person. Another key question concerns body shape and health and the relationship between the two. Above all, though, a history of fitness is a history of the body as social history: a history of values and norms, epistemic and discursive orders, representations and figurations, technologies and bodily practices. A history of the body of this kind shows how people are placed in a particular relationship to society through their bodies and how they participate in their own emplacement.[6]

My observations focus on recent history, since the 1970s. The last half-century may be considered the age of fitness, and it is no accident that this coincides with the age of neoliberalism. Rather than a generalizing call to arms, here neoliberalism denotes an epoch that has modeled itself on the market, interprets every situation as a competitive struggle and enjoins people to make productive use of their freedom. Neoliberalism thus describes a certain way of thinking about society and subjects, understanding their behavior and classifying it as appropriate or inappropriate. The individual is supposed to work on themselves, have life under control, get fit, ensure their own productive capacity and embody these things in the truest sense of the word. This requirement has achieved unprecedented importance under neoliberalism.[7] Fitness is everywhere. Fitness, as philosopher Michel Foucault might have put it, is a "*dispositif*" or apparatus – an era-defining network of discourses and practices, institutions and things, buildings and infrastructure, administrative measures, political programs, and much more besides.[8]

But I also reach further back into history in order to understand our age of fitness. At times the tracks we need to follow extend back to the eighteenth century, for example when it comes to the idea of liberty and self-determination, or the disciplining of the soldierly body. Yet it was not just the soldier but also the new republican citizen that was required to be disciplined and upright, rather than glutted, degenerate, and physically torpid like the nobility, or stooped and battered like the third estate.[9] In a history of fitness, the middle of the nineteenth century also demands our attention. This is the period when Darwinism, the "survival of the fittest," and the conception of inevitable, natural competition took the stage. And it was in the decades around 1900 that modern societies first experienced a fitness hype. At the same time, they were plagued by a crisis that was experienced, in part, as a crisis of the body. When it comes to the history of fitness over the last few decades, in many ways the late nineteenth and early twentieth centuries presaged future trends more than the cult of the body in fascism and Nazism. Historians have often highlighted the 1950s and 1960s in this regard as well. After years of crisis and war, many people on both sides of the Atlantic once again indulged in the pleasures of consumption. Yet this immediately led to anxieties about its harmful effects on the body, health and performance.

The history of fitness related in this book is a critical one. This means that it pays attention to the ambivalences of fitness. It brings out how societies are governed through fitness – understood as the freedom to work on the body and the successful self. This means doing more than just admiring fitness and more than praising freedom as a fundamental human right and opportunity. In fact, freedom is bound up with the demand, made of all of us, to use our freedom productively and in the best possible way; and fitness perfectly embodies this facet of freedom. People's success or failure in this respect establishes differences, engenders exclusion and legitimizes privileges.[10] The coexistence of, and simultaneous antagonism between, fitness and fatness, their meanings and associations, reveal the manifold tensions inherent in governing through freedom and fitness. Fitness and fatness – often perceived as non-fitness – have a significant impact on whether a person is recognized as a productive member of society, on who may be considered a subject and who may not.[11]

In the course of this book, I will routinely locate fitness in "modernity," describing fitness as its hallmark and regulatory ideal. Modern societies have declared perpetual optimization and renewal one of their core precepts and achievements, and fitness posits the constant optimization of body and self. In line with this, as they have developed over time, modernity and fitness have been closely interlinked. The origins of both lie in the late eighteenth century and both experienced a boom in the decades around 1900. Toward the end of the twentieth century, meanwhile, both modernity and fitness began to change or come to a head in key respects. This applies, for example, to the paradigm of the body's malleability. In postmodernity, working on one's body has even gained in importance and, as sociologist Paula-Irene Villa writes, "Bodywork is always and inevitably work on the social self."[12]

Similar may be said of my references to the "West" as the main setting for the following history of fitness. What I have in mind here is a critical perspective on a community of values, norms, and principles, which include the productive use of freedom, the optimization of the self, and constant progress.[13] Hence, the following chapters focus on the US and Europe, especially Germany, and on the similarities and differences that typify the relationship between freedom, bodies, and social order on each side of the Atlantic. The US is in fact the society most dedicated to the idea of freedom as norm and practice.

Fitness, then, operates via the body, but it is by no means limited to it. So, this book is about much more than "just" the training of the body. The first chapter foregrounds our present and recent past, bringing out the significance of the body and body shape. My focus is on those practices and policies that are directly related to the body and that are obsessively pursued in our contemporary societies. The key terms here are exercise and eating right. Chapter 2 sketches the history of the fitness concept, from the eighteenth century to the 1970s. It shows how the idea of dynamism and the notion that we can achieve anything we aspire to have increasingly permeated modern societies, and it reveals how the notion of fitness, as we know it today, emerged. Chapters 3, 4 and 5 go even further beyond fitness as bodily practice. They scrutinize three fields of tremendous importance to the individual's recognition as a productive member of society and as a subject. Chapter 3 deals with the relationship between fitness and work, and thus revolves around the importance of bodies and productivity. Turning to the relationship between fitness and sex, chapter 4 considers reproductivity and potency. The fifth chapter discusses the relationship between fitness and the ready ability to deal with challenges and achieve our goals through sustained effort, probing how fitness and heroic visions intermesh. For a long time, these visions were of a martial cast. For some time, however, and increasingly, they have been taking inspiration from the struggles of everyday life.

Each chapter in this book forms a coherent whole and may be read individually. But only reading the entire book will convey how deeply fitness is inscribed in modern societies, and how critical fitness is to success or failure, recognition or exclusion, in a society that sets such great store by self-responsibility, performance, market, and competition.

1

"FIT OR FAT"?
FITNESS IN RECENT HISTORY
AND THE PRESENT DAY

Cycling and self-tracking

Anyone who practices cycling – whether the average Joe on their Sunday morning bike ride or a pro ascending the Alpe d'Huez – almost certainly has a little computer on their handlebars. This measures speed, distance traveled and altitude attained, but also, depending on the device, one's pulse rate, cadence, and power output in watts. The number of calories (supposedly) burned is also shown. The goal is obvious: the bike computer is an aid to self-observation. It is intended to provide information about the cyclist's performance level and help optimize their activity, perfect their body, and enhance their potential. The symbiosis of body and technology, fundamental to cycling in any case, has reached a new level.[1]

As far as the targeted improvement of one's performance is concerned, however, such a device has a shortcoming. It registers very precisely what is happening on the bike (only the physical performance, of course, not the joy of movement, let alone the pleasure derived from the landscape). But it records nothing of one's life outside exercise. The device is unaware of how much exercise I get overall, how much beer I drink, whether I eat a lot of fatty meat and potato chips, and whether I get enough quality sleep. To observe and evaluate these things requires

a different technology. If a smartphone is equipped with a corresponding app and supplemented by some gadgets, then one's behavior can
be tracked, measured, and evaluated 24 hours a day. This is known as
fitness tracking or self-tracking. One can also use a smartwatch or a
fitness wristband to do this. Measuring and recording one's actions thus
permeates everyday life, even when one is fast asleep – and all in the
name of performance.

In Germany, about a third of the population is said to record data on
movement, eating, sleeping, and bodily trends in one way or another. In
the United States the figure is claimed to be almost 70 percent, though
the numbers vary widely, depending on who one asks and what, exactly,
one is talking about.[2] In 2007, the Quantified Self (QS) movement
was launched in the San Francisco Bay Area, and it has now spread
throughout the Western world. Its adherents not only measure their
bodily, behavioral, and environmental parameters. They also submit to
psychological tests, genome sequencing and much more besides. The
goal, as stated on the website of the German QS-Community, is to
"reflect upon ourselves and understand what allows us to make better,
more informed decisions."[3] Many self-trackers share their knowledge
and data on the Internet with a community of like-minded people who
are both their associates and competitors. Health insurance providers
on both sides of the Atlantic are now offering discounts to those willing to practice self-tracking and fitness tracking or to submit the data
generated. They have developed relevant apps or provide the necessary technology. According to the insurance companies, this makes it
possible to identify the risk of illness earlier and more effectively.[4]

This raises sensitive social and political issues concerning electronic
patient records and "big data" in the healthcare system. But my concern here is with a quite different matter, namely self-tracking as a
paradigmatic practice of a culture and society that revolves around
free individuals, competition, market, and performance as its essential
principles. The QS movement itself underscores that its activities are
oriented toward "every sphere of life." Hence, its concept of fitness
goes far beyond sports and physical workouts as such. Certainly, in
the first instance self-trackers are out to determine their relationship
with their own bodies. Yet at the same time, their actions and the data
generated make it possible to establish relationships between the body,

the individual, their society, and the environment in which they live. In a society based on its members' autonomy and efficiency, self-tracking can even be considered a practice of engaged citizenship. Citizenship, then, is more than a legal concept. It encompasses the question of who is recognized as a productive member of society, why, and who may make certain claims on this basis. If working on your own fitness is a key criterion for this recognition, then the cyclist of the late twentieth and early twenty-first centuries is the prototype of the good citizen.[5]

Health, fitness, and fatness in neoliberal times

Fitness, then, is more than just the prerequisite for success in sport. In the twenty-first century, a broad consensus exists on this point, regardless of whether we ask health authorities, sociologist Zygmunt Bauman, philosopher Peter Sloterdijk, or kinesiologist Karen Volkwein.[6] Volkwein, for example, defines fitness as "health stabilized through training."[7] At first sight, this definition may appear clear and simple. Upon closer inspection, however, it reveals the tremendous scope and complexity as well as the multiple implications of fitness. First, and quite obviously, fitness is closely bound up with health, and in the recent history of Western societies health means more than the absence of infirmity or disease. Health, as the World Health Organization (WHO) already stated upon its establishment in 1948, is a state of physical, mental, and social wellbeing. This implies that the healthy individual has the means and capacity to meet challenges and live a good, productive life. It also makes health a symbol of success and a precondition for recognition. Second, Volkwein's definition of fitness indicates that health may be stabilized through training or neglected and thrown out of kilter by its absence. This makes health and quality of life – not entirely but to a considerable extent – the individual's own responsibility. They must actively manage themself and their life, taking the appropriate preventive measures. Practices of prevention, in fact, amount to a "crucial cultural technology of modernity." Since the 1950s, "prevention" has become a key principle in medicine and society, one that, according to sociologist Ulrich Bröckling, requires the individual to act "as an autonomous and competent agent vis-à-vis their own life."[8] Third, while health may be stabilized through training, it can never be entirely stable. So, health can never be achieved, at least not definitively. Health is a point that can never be reached, and the older one gets, the further one moves away from it. Those who stop exercising and working on their own fitness are neglecting their health. Health is fleeting. It requires permanent work on oneself and signifies constant action. The logic of fitness is very powerful, even though we all know that illnesses can occur despite constant self-care.[9]

Hence, health is a highly normative concept, one that molds our notions of a good and a bad lifestyle.[10] This is even more true of fitness, as it functions explicitly as a hinge between lifestyle and health. Companies like Jawbone and Microsoft enjoin potential buyers of their fitness bracelets to "Know Yourself. Live Better," and even to "be a better human" (see figure 1). These promptings also come across as promises.[11] Fitness is a regulatory and normative ideal of liberal, modern societies. It not only describes how you are, but what you ought to be – and how you can become what you ought to be.[12]

What we have to do, then, is interrogate how fitness operates, while laying bare the processes of inclusion and exclusion it facilitates.[13] Who is considered fit, and who is not? What happens when some

"This device can know me better than I know myself, and can help me be a better human."

Figure 1   Advertisement for the Microsoft Smartwatch, 2014

are considered fit and others are not? People are governed by fitness, and this is especially true of liberal societies, which are particularly vociferous in demanding citizens' voluntary engagement.[14] For the autonomous and self-responsible individual is central to liberal societies. And self-responsibility means ensuring one's commitment and efficiency in every sphere of life. Those who manage themselves demonstrate their ability to take responsibility for society. Anyone wishing to be viewed as a successful individual and good member of society must be productive, reproductive, and ready to tackle challenges. One has to be hardworking, attractive, and strong. Here fitness plays a regulatory and normative role, though not necessarily through external enforcement in the form of prescription and punishment. Fitness creates zones of marginality and exclusion. This is its regulatory and normative effect. Those who fail to conform to the ideal at play here, who are considered ill or physically impaired, or who are, apparently, neglecting to work on themselves enough to become and stay fit, are marginalized or excluded. The power of fitness, the nature of its requirements, and the emphasis placed on them, have varied over the course of history.[15]

Few things more clearly bring out the power of fitness, its linkage with physicality, and the political dimension of this entire complex than the collective fear of body fat. In recent decades, the fear of fat has taken hold of Western societies more than ever before. At first glance, fitness and fatness seem to be polar opposites, yet they are mutually constitutive. Together, they bring order to a culture and society that privileges the efficient, self-directed individual. For the members of such a society, it is obviously unsettling to hear and read every week, from one source or another, that, for example, "Germany is getting fat," that Germans are less and less active and are becoming "fatter and fatter."[16] There is always a handy scientific study to quote from when the press or the political sphere declares that around half of all Germans are overweight and about one-fifth obese. More than two-thirds of Americans are said to be overweight and almost 40 percent obese, especially in rural areas. Depending on state and demographic group, the obesity rate rises to 55 percent, the key elements being social status, level of poverty and, interwoven with these factors, race and gender. In other words, poor black women in Mississippi are among the fattest of the fat. The particularly fat are considered to have failed to meet the demands of a liberal society. Moreover, fatness is viewed as pathological. It is therefore referred to, using medical terminology, as obesity. Since the late twentieth century, fatness has even been called an epidemic. It is not spread by a virus, but has infected large numbers of people due to certain living conditions and circumstances. The US government officially adopted this medical terminology in 2001 and literally declared war on obesity the same year. The WHO, meanwhile, has for some time been referring to "globesity" to highlight the increasingly global scale of this phenomenon.[17]

I do not intend (and am not qualified) to evaluate the health effects of too much or too little body fat here. The various statements made on this topic are, in any case, highly controversial, while for years the seemingly straightforward relationship between body fat and health has become increasingly contested. For example, the Body Mass Index (BMI) has ceased to be a widely recognized indicator of body fat. Many commentators doubt that the BMI is an effective predictor of disorders and mortality rates. Recent studies have in fact shown that at least a certain amount of body fat is beneficial to one's health. What is more, some research findings are more likely to be published and receive more attention than others, and those who do not subscribe to the prevalent fatphobia seem to experience a certain publication bias.[18] The social demonization of fatness continues virtually unabated. Here the deceptive power of the visible seems to be at work. People feel they can see with their own eyes that fat cannot possibly be a good thing, but makes one sluggish and immobile.[19]

My concern here is not with what is truly healthy or unhealthy, but with the power and persistence of the discourse on fatness and fitness and its social effects. The discourse on fatness is deeply political in many ways. First there is the classic political level. In 2007, the German government adopted the "Fit Not Fat Action Plan," and launched a campaign known as "IN FORM. Germany's Initiative for Healthy Eating and More Exercise" in 2008. Initiatives of this kind have been instigated since the 1970s. Fit Not Fat and IN FORM are intended to embed the "healthy lifestyle as a social value" by 2020, improve Germans' eating habits and increase their physical activity. But it is not laws or punishment that are to pave the way for these changes. Instead, the goal is to appropriately shape the overall framework within which people make decisions and take action, providing them with all sorts of incentives. Government agencies and representatives should be good role models, provide knowledge and information, and motivate people to eat better and exercise more. Germans can continue to decide freely whether to eat fries or salad, whether to stay at home and be couch potatoes or go for a bike ride. But the decision-making architecture should be arranged in such a way as to facilitate a healthy choice. This kind of politics is called "nudging," a form of governance that seeks to prod or steer citizens to make voluntary decisions that are viewed as "better" and "healthier." Certainly, from this perspective, free individuals in free societies should make their decisions freely. But at the same time, they should make decisions that are conducive to their own productivity and, therefore, to that of the community. "Prevention," as the first sentence of the Fit Not Fat action plan emphasizes, "is an investment in the future."[20]

Michelle Obama received a great deal of public attention as First Lady of the United States, and it reached its apogee through her campaign against fat. Her "Let's Move" program was aimed primarily at African American children, the goal being to motivate them to exercise more and eat better. Obama privileged information, incentives, the cooperation of school cafeterias and industry, and her own status as role model. She grew vegetables in the White House garden, cooked with children, skipped, danced, lifted weights, and did push-ups as she made her way through the American media landscape. Of course, the First Lady was aware that a program like "Let's Move" cannot succeed by issuing directives and that fitness cannot be enforced politically. New York mayor Michael Bloomberg failed spectacularly when he tried to ban the sale of soft drinks by "food service establishments" in cups of more than 16 ounces in 2014 (a similar fate befell the German Greens in 2013 with their "Veggieday"). The New York Court of Appeals, the state's highest court, ruled against Bloomberg's "Soda Ban" because the New York City Board of Health lacked the authority to issue such a prohibition. The public and political battle, however, focused not on the powers of institutions, but on civil liberties. The opponents of the Soda Ban assailed the "nanny state" and its alleged fantasies of omnipotence. Michelle Obama, meanwhile, was aware of the tremendous importance of freedom of choice and decision as a political principle, a precept that has shaped the United States since its birth, attaining unprecedented heights since the 1970s. Obama thus eschewed a ban-oriented approach. Instead, she sought to mold the architecture of decision making in such a way as "to make the healthy choice the easy choice," as she herself put it. Nonetheless, Republicans accused her of state interventionism, highlighting the dogged nature of American battles over freedom of choice and decision.[21]

But the political dimension of the discourse on fitness and fatness goes far beyond the classic sphere of politics. It is about more than the actions of lawmakers and members of government, action plans, controversial statutory prohibitions, or sugar and fat taxes.[22] A culture and society that draws its strength and success from the productive capacity of individuals and the population as a whole may be described, with Michel Foucault, as biopolitical.[23] The "birth of biopolitics" took place in the nineteenth century, a process I describe in more detail in the next chapter. Here I give the reader advance notice that a biopolitical order has its sights set on the population and its potential, and it defines and positions people and groups through their bodies and bodily form. Such an order regulates their access to resources and social participation and thus influences the recognition they may experience as productive members of society. Body shape becomes a sign of the ability to make responsible decisions, to function in a free, competitive society and to aid its development. Hence, body shape decides who gets to be a *homo politicus*. Fatness is believed to reveal a lack of these abilities. Just as self-trackers are the prototypical embodiment of the biopolitical fitness society, and supposedly even demonstrate the desire to be and the attempt "to become a better human" (as producers of smartwatches want to make us believe), fatness seems to stand for a dearth of decision-making ability, productive capacity, and motivation.[24]

The crisis scenarios ramifying out from the alleged epidemic of obesity, then, bear witness to more than an individual problem. En masse, as the cover of the May 2010 issue of *The Atlantic* shows so clearly, fat bodies seem to signal a crisis of liberal society, its functioning and principles (see figure 2). The corpulent Statue of Liberty carries an unambiguous message. The survival of the social order, which is based on freedom and builds on the pursuit of happiness, on autonomous action and motivation, is at risk from body fat. In fact, this social order

Figure 2   Cover of *The Atlantic*, May 2010

appears to be facing imminent collapse. Slimness, agility, fitness: in an age of neoliberalism and flexible capitalism, these terms are used more than ever to describe ideal individuals and their bodies. Such terms also serve to characterize the performance of society, economy, and state. Lean bodies for a lean state, fit (typically freelance) employees for fit companies and their "lean production."[25]

"Neoliberalism" denotes a form of society and government that is always and everywhere aligned with the model of the market. This sociopolitical system construes people, in every situation, as market actors subject to competitive conditions. Moreover, neoliberalism, as political scientist Wendy Brown writes, is "a distinctive mode of reason, of the production of subjects, a 'conduct of conduct' [Foucault], and a scheme of valuation." The actions of subjects must be geared toward investing in themselves in order – always and everywhere – to increase their own "portfolio value." The goal is for these investments and one's work on oneself to yield visible results. Such evident success enables individuals to be recognized as productive members of society. Consequently, in neoliberalism the relationship between individual and society is measured in a new way. Recognition as a citizen is not just a matter of rights. Nor is it linked solely with the individual's concern for the public good. Such recognition arises from the individual's success as an investor in themself and from the maximization of their human capital. It is thus the most effective investor that best meets the requirements of a good member of society: only a *homo oeconomicus* can attain the status of *homo politicus*.[26]

The political heft of fitness in neoliberalism is neatly captured by the concept of "biological citizenship." Sociologist Nikolas Rose emphasizes just how much, in liberal societies, concern for one's body and health, the maximization of one's vitality and potential, has become a kind of universal duty.[27] Rose is particularly interested in the social and political implications of genetic engineering and stem cell research. According to Rose, it has become a requirement for good citizens to track suspected health issues down to the basic programming of the body, examine options for correction, and adapt their lifestyle accordingly.[28]

The concept of "biological citizenship" sharpens our awareness of the relationship between bodies, freedom, fitness, civic duties, and recognition. Liberal societies have in fact never done without biologically construed distinctions.[29] For example, upon its founding, the American Republic declared liberty for all its core political principle, yet at the same time it long tied the degree of individual liberty and social recognition to "race," "gender," and "sexuality," that is, to categories conceived in biological terms. And it was long asserted that only white men have the fundamental capacity to get fit and make meaningful decisions about their own bodies and lives. Feminists have fought against this idea since the nineteenth century (by composing an ode to cycling as a personal and political practice, for example).[30] But it was only from the 1960s onward that the various civil rights movements prompted American society to shift away from the idea of fixed, biological categories. Although these categories persist in some measure to this day, they have certainly been shaken to their foundations. Belief in the malleability of societies, people, and bodies, meanwhile, has grown.[31]

This development, however, has changed what we might understand by "biological citizenship." The shaping and optimization of one's body, its capabilities and potential, that is, investment in one's fitness, is now crucially important. Hence, distinctions made through the body are no longer necessarily distinctions between black and white or between male and female (though they still exist and are still very powerful). A culture and society in which fitness is a regulatory ideal distinguishes between "fit" and "unfit" bodies. In other words, there are people who can credibly show that they invest in themselves, work on themselves, and know how to tap their own potential. And then there are the others, who cannot demonstrate these attributes.[32] The determination and ability to optimize the self are of great importance to the degree of one's social and civil recognition, and the fundamental capacity for success or failure in this endeavor appears to show in the body and its form. Fat bodies have become the constitutive, contrasting counterpart to the fit, "capable" body and to the successful person in general. Fat is considered a sign of laziness, ineptitude, ignorance, and lack of discipline, of "wrong," unhealthy behavior. The fat Statue of Liberty, then, stands for the failure of individuals, as well as the crisis of the nation and the liberal-democratic system.[33]

The roots of our age of fitness lie in the eighteenth and nineteenth centuries, when the ideas of liberalism, competition, and Darwinism were gaining traction. These concepts staked out a field that was the prerequisite for the emergence of fitness as principle and practice, and thus a sphere in which fatness could be grasped as a problem.[34] I will explain this in more detail in the next chapter. For now, though, I will stay with the recent past, because a closer look at history since the 1970s helps us better comprehend the vehemence of the discourse of fitness in our immediate present.

Eating "right" since the Me Decade

In the age of fitness, eating right is one of society's obsessions. The issue of what the "right" food might be leads us directly to the tensions between consumer society and the achievement-oriented society (*Leistungsgesellschaft*). Soon after World War II, during its "economic miracle" phase, Germany succumbed to a feeding frenzy. After years of deprivation, Germans could finally afford to splash out a little. Food was once again available in greater abundance, even if the average German family was still on a tight budget. In postwar America, consumption became the core activity of good citizens. Food was not the only element in the consumer republic of the 1950s, but it was a highly important one. It was increasingly manufactured industrially and – especially in the United States – consumed in a "progressive" and "modern" way, for example as a defrosted and heated-up TV dinner, or on the go at the first McDonald's branches. The 1950s were the golden age of the food industry. It grew massively and its actions went largely unquestioned. Americans praised themselves as the best-fed people the world had ever seen. Soon, experts were talking about the end of hunger in America. Yet this applied chiefly to the growing white middle class. Critical press and TV reports, meanwhile, showed the emaciated bodies of African American children in the South, particularly Mississippi. Half the population was evidently starving in the country's poorest and blackest state. In 1967, a TV documentary called *Hunger in America* (CBS) shocked the nation.[35]

In reality, then, the good news that Americans were the "best-fed people in world history" applied only to part of the population. In addition, since the 1950s, doubts had been raised as to whether these allegedly well-nourished people were also the fittest. Some questioned whether consumption, and if so, how much consumption, makes one sick and thus impedes one's performance. The consequences of too much fatty and sweet food, too much alcohol, too many cigarettes, and too little exercise were subject to medical research and public debate. The main focus was on the heart attack, and soon experts had identified a correlation between weight or body fat and mortality. By the early 1950s, the press was already asserting that obesity was probably the greatest threat to human life in America. In a photo essay, *LIFE* magazine described excess weight as a plague.

Slowly but surely, corpulence was interpreted as dangerous, and ever less as a sign of success and wellbeing. The endangerment of middle-aged, white, middle-class men emerged as the dominant trope: men who worked too much, neglected themselves and, as it was expressed at the time, put their health and their lives on the line as they strove to provide for their families and contribute to society.[36]

Given the fear of body fat, it seemed plausible to blame fat as a substance. Although a distinction was soon being made between bad animal and good vegetable fats, American cuisine, like its Central European counterpart, was full of the bad variety. In contrast, Mediterranean cuisine, dominated by olive oil, was soon being praised on both sides of the Atlantic as the great role model. In any event, to continue eating in the same old way was compared to suicide and mass murder.[37] Public discourse made it abundantly clear that fat was the chief culprit, not least due to massive lobbying by the sugar industry. Yet sugar too was subject to similarly dramatic rhetoric and compared with heroin. In America, from the mid-1950s and the days of Dwight D. Eisenhower onward, the White House has been concerned with the fitness of Americans. Eventually, in 1969, the White House Conference on Food, Nutrition and Health urged Americans to consume less fat, cholesterol, sugar, and salt. A trend known in 1970s Germany as the "health wave" now kicked off on both sides of the Atlantic.[38]

For Western consumer societies, the 1970s were a time of both consolidation and change, and the tensions between the achievement-oriented society and consumer society continued to grow. Nutrition and food played a central role here, and they carried an array of economic, social, and political meanings: from so-called countercuisine, which emerged along with alternative lifestyles in the 1960s and articulated an ecological and economic critique, to mass-produced industrial goods on an unprecedented scale. Chicken nuggets, to take one example, have nothing to do with chicken. From a somewhat longer-term perspective, the ensuing years and decades have shown that countercuisine and mass production are not necessarily antagonistic. Alternative health food stores, which sprang up in both West Germany and the United States in the early 1970s, developed into supermarket chains. The success of organic food as a mass-produced commodity demonstrates capitalism's ability to co-opt critical forces.[39]

To better understand the changes that occurred in the 1970s, we first need to scrutinize the economic and social crisis of that era. The United States was struggling with the high social, political, and financial costs of the Vietnam War, the oil crisis, a massive trade deficit and spiraling inflation, leading to stagnant and even falling real wages from 1973 onward. For many Americans, declining incomes were to persist over the following decades. The initial political and economic response was "less": less government, less regulation, less welfare, fewer unions, less pay, less collective thinking, less redistribution. Conversely, there was an emphasis on more individual responsibility, more individual debt, and more individual profit. In the United States and in the capitalist world more generally, the 1970s marked the end of the long New Deal era, with a shift away from the welfare state and Fordism. This is the decade that ushered in the neoliberal restructuring of economy and society. Historian Bryant Simon describes this new era as the "age of cheap." From now on, everything had to be cheap: production, wages, goods, food. European countries in general also entered the "post-boom" era, though changes occurred at a slower pace than in the United States. But the West German social market economy could not hold out against neoliberal pressures for ever, and finally succumbed in the 1990s.[40]

Soya, and above all corn, emerged as crucial food products in the "age of cheap." Particularly in the United States, the area under cultivation and the agricultural corporations (it would be wrong to speak of farms here) grew massively, productivity rose, and prices fell. Most of the harvest went to the meat industry as feed, while the remainder – often in the form of "high fructose corn syrup" – was used in all kinds of food products or was exported. Michael Pollan, one of the most vociferous and prolific critics of the food industry in the United States, refers to a "dilemma" facing the average American eater. Although consumers can choose from an abundance of different foods, almost all industrially processed products are based on corn in one way or another. Corn (like soy) is subsidized by the state, and is mechanically cultivated and harvested on huge industrialized "farms." Other agricultural products such as peaches, strawberries, and lettuce still require a great deal of manual labor, though their production has also been industrialized and rationalized. At the same time, the food industry and the food trade have been among the leading sectors responsible for wage dumping since the 1970s. They have made a significant contribution to the overall decline in real wages, thus creating demand for their own low-cost products. Pollan even surmises that only cheap food has averted an even greater systemic crisis, namely widespread hunger, and thus a mass uprising.[41] In the United States, however, most writers and activists no longer refer to hunger but to "food insecurity." Around a fifth of households are now affected by or at risk of this condition. Food insecurity means that while one may feel a sense of satiety, one lacks access to food that satisfies the body's nutritional needs. In much of the country, such food is simply not available to the poorer sections of the population. In contrast to hunger, food insecurity is not, or is only negligibly, associated with an emaciated body. Today, in other words, being fat is often seen as a sign of poverty and food insecurity, that is, an inadequate food supply.[42]

One might ask why all of this matters to a history of fitness. Social geographer Julie Guthman is one of the most astute analysts of the relationship between capitalism, consumption, and bodies in recent history and the present day. She characterizes the neoliberal political economy as "bulimic." On the one hand, Guthman contends, this system calls for slim, seemingly high-performance bodies, while on the other it steers us toward maximum consumption of industrially produced, highly calorific foods. Their production has become so absurdly cheap, she goes on, that within the capitalist logic of retail and consumption it makes perfect sense to offer, or consume, larger packs and portions at an only slightly higher price. Hence, according to this analysis, the seller ensures customer loyalty (at almost the same labor costs, given that even a "supersize meal" only has to be passed across the counter once), and the buyer gets more for their money. In capitalism, maximum consumption at minimum prices is a very rational behavior. In addition, many consumers are desperate to save money due to falling wages and increasing job insecurity. And those compelled to do several jobs at once to make ends meet are more likely to opt for the fast (and cheap) consumption of snacks and ready meals than for the slow food option. Many poorer neighborhoods are so-called "food deserts," in which it is simply impossible or very difficult to find healthy food. In such a scenario, the much-vaunted freedom of choice and decision – so highly valued as the core of liberalism, and in the United States more than anywhere else – boils down to income, price, and living conditions. Guthman underscores that the correlation between body shape and class, fatness and poverty is fueled by this dynamic blend of neoliberal politics, a growing wealth gap, and cheap, industrially produced food.[43]

The 1970s brought a shift toward less state regulation. Citizens were expected to take greater responsibility for themselves, including their bodies, fitness, and performance. In lockstep with the "age of cheap," a discourse gained momentum that demanded, with increasing urgency, that people "eat right" and achieve a "balanced diet," that they take good care of their bodies and themselves. All of this became the hallmark of the good citizen in a liberal society. By 1976, writer Tom Wolfe was referring to the "Me Decade," deploying capital letters to make his point. "Me and my hemorrhoids" was the acerbic heading of the first section of his famous article. He pointed out that people's concern for their bodies had reached unprecedented levels, prompting them to attach a new and tremendous importance to their dietary habits and physical activity. Many consumption addicts converted to asceticism. "I was in such bad shape," to quote one typical "confession" of the kind that now appeared in print so often; "I weighed 247 pounds and my heart would beat like a drum when I got up from my chair to go to the refrigerator."[44]

The concern for self and body in an alienated mass and industrial society was also fueled by the counterculture of the 1960s and 1970s. That the cultures of emerging neoliberalism and the counterculture shared concerns and goals may seem contradictory. However, both were and are characterized by a predilection for individuality and self-determination, as well as a fundamental distrust of the political authorities. As far as nutrition was concerned, the counterculture called on people to eat a "more natural" diet and to eat more consciously from both a health and political perspective. Exponents of "countercuisine," meanwhile, began to rail against the allegedly corrosive effects on body and society of industrially produced food. The imperative here was to cook for oneself and change how one shopped, that is, to patronize the cooperatives and health food stores established from the late 1960s onward. The first Whole Foods store opened in Austin, Texas, in 1980, embodying the then-new business idea of combining elements of a health food store with those of a conventional supermarket.[45] Whole Foods is now a global corporation, with several hundred stores in and beyond the United States, and has been part of Amazon since 2017. In Germany too, organic supermarkets in trendy neighborhoods are seen as markers of advancing gentrification.[46] People who record their body data are among those who shop in these stores. Meanwhile, organic farming has grown into a huge industry, one that has had a major impact on large areas of, for example, California and southern Spain, with working conditions that are often anything but fair or decent. At the beginning of the twenty-first century, the organic sector is still chalking up growth rates of around 5 percent. Not everything sold in organic markets, however, can be straightforwardly described as healthy.[47]

Ultimately, it is not surprising that countercuisine and the pursuit of a healthier and more "alternative" diet were caught up in the wake of the Me Decade and an ever more widely recognized responsibility for one's own wellbeing. The counterculture shared many of the goals and techniques of a health- and fitness-oriented society, one that valorizes individuality and self-reliance. Alternative dietary trends thus also succumbed to commercialization and the power of capitalism; that is, they became options for broader swathes of society. A healthy diet holds out the promise of "better" body data. In 1985, its discourse pervaded by notions of self-cultivation, self-discipline, and performance, the *Handelsblatt* business newspaper proclaimed that "greater enhancement" of the body would generate "more added value."[48] Of course, the food industry too knows how to benefit from widespread anxieties about health. It never ceases to provide new products, with fewer carbohydrates, that are fat- and sugar-free and go easy on their consumers' cholesterol levels. Rather than merely responding, the industry is proactive, launching research programs to conjure up the dangers and problems its products promise to remedy. The diet industry, with a turnover of approximately $150 billion worldwide in 2014 and projected sales of nearly $250 billion by 2022, would be worth a chapter in its own right.[49]

To sum up, in recent history eating in a way conducive to one's fitness has become an obsession and a powerful normative precept. By no means does this signify that people have lost their passion for candy, snacks, and fast food. On the contrary, the two phenomena depend on and reinforce each other. They typify a culture and a society that distinguish between "good" and "bad" eating habits and "good" and "bad" bodies, and that make them part of the political order. The individual who eats well seems to demonstrate an ability to take responsibility for themself, their family, and the collective, and for the latter's health and performance. They seem to know what is important and right, and to be able to invest successfully in themselves while enjoying the process. Making the effort to cook, writer Barbara Kingsolver contends, is a practice of "good citizenship." Since the 1970s, the interest in healthy food and a matching lifestyle has increasingly emerged as an engine of distinction, between those who are considered thoughtful and aware of their health and performance, and those who cannot claim these attributes. Their ignorance can seemingly be read off their bodies. In the United States, attention is focused not only on poorer and less educated demographics, but often on African Americans. Thus – yet again and despite the successes of the civil rights movement – African Americans are portrayed as incapable of living their lives autonomously. In this context, fast food is depicted as the nadir of thoughtless consumption, as detrimental to one's potential and abilities; according to Paul Nolte with reference to Germany, fast food is the "counterpart of trash TV." Whether this is believed to be the result of the wrong priorities and decisions (an HD television rather than good food, Burger King instead of carrots and potatoes), or lack of financial resources, usually depends on the commentator's political position. Either way, the distinction between healthy and unhealthy, fit and unfit has become a class distinction. This is supposed to signal people's capacity for sensible decision making and their sense of responsibility, for their family, society, and the environment, indeed the entire planet.[50]

The "right amount" of exercise since the Me Decade

In the pursuit of fitness, the right amount of exercise goes hand in hand with eating right. Again, the 1970s were a decade of crucial acceleration in North America and Western Europe in this regard. In West Germany, the German Sport Association's (Deutscher Sportbund or DSB) "Get Fit" (*Trimm-Dich*) campaign was launched in the spring of 1970, its declared goal being "sport for all" (see figure 3). Rather than competitive sport, the campaign promoted the very practices established in the following years in Germany under the English-language label of "fitness." Previously, the term had barely been used in the German-speaking countries. The goal was for increased exercise to enable a greater number of people to achieve a fitter body and enjoy life more. In Germany, mass or popular sports (*Breitensport*) was the name given to this concept. In Austria, the term *Fitsport* was coined to refer to bodily practices directed solely at one's own body and its performance (rather than scoring a goal or winning a race). Austrians also

Figure 3   Poster, DSB "Endurance" advertising campaign, 1975–1978

took part in fitness marches (*Fitmärschen*) and fitness runs (*Fitläufen*) inspired by the "Fit – Be in It!" (*Fit-mach-mit*) campaign, while keep-fit trails were established in German and Swiss forests and parks.[51] In German TV commercials from the middle of the decade onward, what viewers generally saw were average, middle-aged men exercising. The chubby "Karl Gustav" cycles happily through the countryside, while the voiceover explains that "The constant pedaling / keeps heart and circulation young for many years, / because to keep moving, / makes one fit and superior to others." So, while fitness was not about improving one's chances of winning sporting competitions, it was an attempt to outdo others in life as a whole, a life that was, more than ever, conceptualized in terms of competition and rivalry. "Mr. Oskar K." demonstrates one facet of this superiority in another ad. Evidently, jogging is a boon not only to his health and zest for life, but also to his sex appeal. The body language of a statue of a naked woman next to the jogging track, who gazes after him and gives a thumbs-up, along with the mischievous voiceover, leaves us in no doubt about that. The fit body was now considered a beautiful, attractive body.[52]

Sustained by the enthusiasm for sport that gripped West Germany after the 1972 Munich Olympics, millions of people followed the tips they received from Trimmy, the figurehead of the DSB's "Get Fit" campaign. After just a few years, virtually every West German knew who he was, and after about a decade three-quarters of West Germans affirmed, at least in theory, that "you have to do sports to stay healthy."[53] The Federal Center for Health Education (Bundeszentrale für gesundheitliche Aufklärung) also helped spread this message. "Eat well and get fit – you need both" ("Essen und Trimmen – beides muß stimmen") was the name of another campaign launched soon after.[54]

A similar tone was struck in the United States. "America Shapes Up," announced *TIME Magazine*'s cover story in early November 1981. Over the preceding decade, the article contended, America had been gripped by fitness mania. The photo on the cover showed five women and men brimming with strength and joy, evidently having just finished exercising. They are holding up photos to the camera that show them playing tennis, lifting weights, cycling, doing aerobics, or jogging. Another striking aspect of the picture is how *white* fitness was in the early 1980s.[55]

TIME Magazine characterized the belief in one's own youthfulness and magnificence as the true American dream. The near-heroic work on one's fitness, the desire to be slim and toned, the "One! Two!" of the exercise routine, the grunting and sweating in the gym – together they symbolized the attempt to make this dream come true. Other observers in the early 1980s shared *TIME*'s assessment, sweepingly asserting that virtually everyone in America attached great importance to their body in everyday life, with respect to their job and as an expression of their personality. It is hard not to think of Tom Wolfe and the Me Decade.[56]

One of the drivers of the body and fitness mania that overtook the United States in the 1970s was running. Previously, hardly anyone thought of going for a run after work as a beneficial practice, a way of getting or staying fit. Even running marathons was the preserve of a few fanatics. At the time, the United States lacked even the infrastructure that might have facilitated a marathon as a mass event. In 1970, 126 men and one woman set off on the New York Marathon (43 percent were to be finishers), while in Boston – long the most important of all marathons in the United States – women were officially allowed to compete only in 1972. The Berlin Marathon, now one of the largest running events in the world, has only existed since 1974, when 244 people took part, including 10 women. In 1986, the number of runners in Berlin surpassed the 10,000 mark for the first time, a figure already reached in New York in 1979 (11,533, including 11 percent women, with 91 percent of participants crossing the finish line). Every year since 2013 more than 50,000 people have competed in the New York event, with almost equal numbers of men and women and nearly everyone finishing (99 percent in 2013).[57]

While running as a mass sport was still in its infancy in the early 1970s, by the end of the decade about 30 million Americans were claiming to run. Performance- and competition-oriented "runners" strove to distinguish themselves from "joggers." However, if we peruse *Runner's World*, the American running magazine par excellence,[58] the readers' letters and the column penned by health consultant Dr George Sheehan (naturally a passionate runner as well as a doctor) reveal how fluid the distinction between "runner" and "jogger" could be. Although *Runner's World* described itself as a magazine for real runners, many letters, enquiries, and comments were sent in by middle-aged men struggling more or less desperately with increasing body fat and declining performance, men who were, at best, in the process of becoming joggers. When one has a job and finds oneself growing older, as one reader wrote to Dr Sheehan in March 1975, "a glacier of lard" gradually and inexorably spreads over the body. "Fat starts taking over," this reader complained, "then and only then do we lose control of our bodies." More control over one's body and one's life, in a society increasingly geared toward the productive use of freedom, was just what fitness promised and demanded. At the same time, fitness was directly linked with the desire, and obligation, to stay young.[59]

The discussions in *Runner's World* reinforce the point that fitness meant more than the ability to go for a run after work without collapsing or the setting of personal bests over various distances. Some runners certainly ran for the sport, and debates, for example about proper nutrition (during the training phase, immediately before or even during a race), filled many pages of *Runner's World*.[60] But at least as many if not more runners ran to lose weight, recover from work and enhance their ability to cope with it, gain respite from the stress of everyday life, and to find company, increase their sex appeal, and find themselves. It was the latter imperative that inspired German foreign minister Joschka Fischer in the late 1990s. With his passion for running, he concurrently signaled that he could do anything, even lose 65 pounds and run a marathon. But whatever one's ultimate reason for running, it was a practice that ought to be more than just a hobby. Running magazines and dozens of books on running published around the time proclaimed that running would change one's entire life, reorienting it toward health and wellbeing, performance, and success. As a representative example, we might consider an ordinary jogger named Dave Mullens, who hit the sidewalk almost every morning before work with his running group, called "Dawn Patrol," in and around Palo Alto, California. With the fervor of the religious convert, Mullens emphasized that running had transformed his entire existence. Similarly, Joschka Fischer referred to his "new life as a jogger."[61] Often, runners reported something akin to a religious awakening, one that put them on the right path. It was a path they had to stick to from then on, because fitness requires permanent work on oneself if one is to avoid losing it again. The crucial thing is "staying the course," Fischer stressed. "Fitness can't be stored," as *Runner's World* stated in the same vein, "it must be earned over and over, indefinitely."[62]

When *Runner's World* writes about running, it reflects the many different and sometimes contradictory forces that shaped the 1970s as a whole.[63] On the one hand, the running movement was energized by the counterculture, and running was part of the "alternative" push to find oneself that was so typical of the time. Many runners saw themselves as anti-capitalist activists in search of a better way of life beyond mass and consumer society. On the other hand, running simultaneously propelled a growing market in sports-related products, centered on running clothes and running shoes, Nike and Asics, the Berlin and New York marathons, Gatorade, Body Punch, Power Bars, and much more besides. Perhaps more ambivalent even than the coexistence of the counterculture and the consumption of branded goods is the status of the endurance athlete as the ideal type of the neoliberal self. They are part of a culture and a movement, but feel independent and self-determined. They are focused on their own body as they strive to make themself a better person overall. They constantly invest in themself and strive for health, self-optimization and performance.[64] Last but not least, the fervor with which many practiced running, and talked about their conversion to a new way of life, linked the pursuit of fitness with religious revival and the search for moral leadership, the latter two trends being particularly evident in the United States during this period. Fitness, it might be said, was the ethos of a new era.[65]

This new ethos was preached in television ads such as those of the West German "Get Fit" campaign, specialist magazines such as *Runner's World*, and more general publications such as *TIME Magazine* or *Der Spiegel*, as well as exercise guides of the kind penned by military doctor Kenneth Cooper on aerobics. This ethos gained new ambassadors in the shape of the many people who now formed running groups, participated in city runs, charity races and marathons, or exercised, in accordance with Cooper's manual, with a controlled escalation of workouts and a points system, a form of self-monitoring that was not a million miles away from today's self-tracking.[66]

When it came to running, women certainly appeared in magazines and books from time to time, for example in photo spreads, as the subject of an article, and sometimes as authors. Ultimately, however, the discourse of running and the early practice of running were primarily masculine in character. Men were the main actors and the main target group, and the questions, problems, and strategies around which running revolved were male-oriented as well. Even the heart problems that endurance sports were supposed to prevent had masculine connotations. In particular, middle-aged men were exhorted to live like endurance athletes so they could make the most of their potential for many years to come and, as it was often expressed, achieve "true fitness." They had to keep moving, eat a balanced diet, forgo cigarettes and alcohol, and get enough sleep. The idea was that this would enable them to maintain their health, live longer, and achieve a greater and lasting productive capacity.[67]

If one looks back over the history of modern societies, it is apparent that this gendering of physical activity has never been entirely watertight. But it seemed to come undone more than ever in the 1970s. Crucial here is the feminist movement, which made the female body one of its key issues. When it came to the right to one's body and its health, Second Wave Feminism fused the personal and political.[68] Three aspects formed a highly productive mélange here. First, control over body and health was a core concern of women in their struggle for full recognition as political subjects. Second, such recognition is intertwined with the importance of fitness as the hallmark of a productive existence in a liberal society. For feminists to demand a right to fitness, then, was an obvious step. By the late nineteenth and early twentieth centuries, the pioneers of the first women's movement were already doing so.[69] Third, according to political scientist Nancy Fraser, feminism has embarked on a "liaison" with neoliberalism. Fraser points out that feminists have built not only on sisterhood and female solidarity, but also on autonomy and self-responsibility. Elements that are still important and productive in the fight against male privileges and an encrusted gender and social order, Fraser contends, have simultaneously promoted neoliberal values and patterns of sociopolitical order that were already gaining traction in the 1970s and 1980s. And concern for one's body is intimately bound up with these patterns.[70]

Thus, knowledge of the formability of the body, generated not least by the academic study of gender, may mutate from a source of liberation into a demand. Such knowledge not only opens up the possibility of altering bodies and thus undoing the traditionally static categories of sexuality, gender, and "race." In a liberal, competitive order, it also introduces a kind of obligation to make the best possible use of the potential to shape the body. The boom in cosmetic surgery, for example, may be described as the neoliberal offspring of the feminist ideal of the right of disposal over one's body. This is a disposability that demands investment if one wants to achieve success in an environment of now omnipresent competition. Since the 1980s, more and more men have also begun to make great efforts to shape their own appearance, once again confirming how flexible gender boundaries, norms, and practices are.[71]

These tensions, contradictions, and reciprocal effects of feminism and fitness converge in the history of aerobics. The roots of this practice lie in the 1960s, when military doctor Kenneth Cooper developed aerobics as a special form of endurance training for astronauts. Cooper's approach to exercise first achieved broader popularity in the shape of Jacki Sorensen's "aerobic dancing" and Judi Sheppard Missett's "jazzercise," both of them winning women over to fitness training by combining endurance training with elements of dance.

It was Jane Fonda who then rose to become the queen of aerobics in the early 1980s. She had already become famous as an actress and political activist. Now, more than anyone else, she triggered a craze that swept across both the United States and Europe, attracting vast numbers of women. Through aerobics, *all* women (and not just competitive sportswomen) were supposed to learn to control their bodies, get them fit, and act with self-confidence toward them. Hence, aerobics was an important force in the feminist project, the latter being propelled in part by the pleasure and joy of movement. Yet at the same time aerobics was anything but feminist, in that it created and presented sexualized and standardized female bodies that fit a new ideal of beauty. The ideal female body of the 1980s was muscular and slim, toned and sexy. This dual movement – on the one hand self-empowerment, on the other adaptation to certain systems of norms and values – is fundamental to subject formation in liberal societies in general and thus to the recognition we can receive as their productive members. In American English, many of the new fitness practices ended in "-cize" – aerobicize, jazzercize, dancercize, powercize, and even nutricize. This is another sign that bodies and subjects were now assumed to be in a process of constant becoming. Fonda was an important ambassador for the fit female subject and for female fitness as a new ethos.[72]

Like no one else, Fonda also helped boost demand for special aerobics outfits. In the 1980s, aerobics – at least as much as running – was part of a new cult of fitness and consumer market. In the United States alone, about 25 million people practiced aerobics during this era, while around 70 million, half the adult population, worked on their fitness in one way or another. Many of them bore the "fit look" and were part of a new everyday culture of fitness. No matter if they were working out or not, they wore sneakers, legwarmers, leggings, leotards, and sweatbands. Spandex was the material that best emphasized shapely bodies, while laying bare the merest hint of a midriff bulge. The new Fitness Barbie, meanwhile, wore a close-fitting leotard, in addition to legwarmers and a headband, when working out in her Barbie Fitness Center. And, of course, in the burgeoning genre of the music video, fitness and toned-up, conventionally beautiful bodies were extremely popular and constantly repeated motifs.[73]

Workout videos were also part of the new fitness market, and Jane Fonda may be considered the inventor of this genre. At the time, the VCR was a new technology. Although manufacturers had developed various devices in the 1970s, it was not until around 1980 that the VCR began to appear in American and European households, after which it spread like wildfire. In 1982, Fonda launched her first workout video, at just the right time. *Original Workout* – with a beginner's and advanced aerobics program – sold 17 million copies and is one of the bestselling video cassettes of all time. Many more tapes, later CDs, and most recently online videos followed, produced and modeled by Fonda herself, but also by many others who followed in her wake. Styling became more and more important as time went by, and the market seemed limitless. In significant part, the attractiveness of workout videos lay in the sweating, mostly female bodies that romped about in them; scantily clad in tight-fitting garments, they performed sometimes lascivious movements, while emitting moaning sounds.[74] In addition, Jane Fonda supplemented the images of exercising, "beautiful" women (and a few men in the back rows) with medical- and sports science-style digressions on cardiovascular health. Another important reason for the success of such videotapes was that the video recorder opened up new fitness training options. It enabled people to exercise at home whenever time allowed, and there was no requirement to look good while doing so. They could watch the exercise guide while working on themselves, skip certain exercises by hitting the fast-forward button, and repeat or go over them again by rewinding. They could also stop the tape to slake their thirst – all on their own terms, in their own living rooms.[75]

Those who did not exercise at home went to a gym. Gyms had existed since the nineteenth century, and even in the early days they were meeting places whose importance went beyond physical exercise.[76] So-called health clubs had also become increasingly popular since the 1950s, though exercising the body was not necessarily their patrons' primary focus. It was not until the 1980s that gyms proliferated. In West Germany too, musty "muscle factories" in cellars, backyard shacks, or old industrial buildings – where shady types dedicated themselves to swaggering displays of strength on homemade devices – morphed into key settings for a new urban lifestyle. There were still only a few hundred gyms in West Germany in the early 1980s (compared with 8,700 in 2016, with over 10 million members). But these had begun to transform into the oases of workouts and wellness we know today, featuring an array of exercise machines, endurance, heart, and circulatory exercises, health advice, aerobics and other classes, as well as a sauna, pool, and bar. By the early 1980s, contemporaries were already referring to the new gyms as "secular cathedrals for the worship of the body." In much the same way as running and cycling, gyms gave people the opportunity to work out beyond schools and universities, leagues, clubs, and associations – even in Germany, where the latter two institutions were deeply entrenched in the traditional sports system. The gym, moreover, was about much more than rattling through an exercise program. People met their friends there instead of at a restaurant or movie theater. As places where patrons showed a lot of body while wearing scant and tight-fitting clothes, where they sweated and moaned together, gyms created an atmosphere of intimacy that could be conducive to one's success when flirting at the bar later on.[77]

Working out at a gym had long entailed an emphasis on bodybuilding, but in the course of the 1980s, this increasingly took a back seat.

Like few other bodily practices, bodybuilding illustrates the designability of the body, but – despite fluid boundaries – it is not part of the realm of fitness. The bodies of bodybuilders are about transgressing limits; they are dysfunctional pieces of art, serving only to embody a certain aesthetic, which does not equate with fitness in the sense of everyday performance. On the contrary, in everyday life the bodybuilder's bulky frame tends to get in their way. Bodybuilders, according to art theorist Jörg Scheller, are artists. As early as 1977, Arnold Schwarzenegger claimed this very status, as he revealed in an interview in the documentary *Pumping Iron*. He is doing the work of a sculptor, Schwarzenegger rhapsodizes, though one who must chisel thousands of tons of iron to create his masterpiece.[78]

"Fit or fat?"

Many of the threads of this chapter on fitness in recent history are woven together in a slim volume from 1977 by Covert Bailey, a soldier, nutritionist, author, television presenter, and apostle of fitness. *Fit or Fat?* is its both simple and suggestive title, a leading question that captures the ethos of neoliberal subjectivity. Bailey's guide to bodies and exercise is full of observations on the body-as-machine, weight measurements and body fat percentages, exercise intervals and recovery periods, exercise intensity and pulse rates, "good" nutrition, protein, sugar, and fat. At the end of the book there is a log for a 12-month exercise program. Here the reader finds pre-printed forms designed to help keep them on track and, as the Quantified Self community would put it today, to make "more informed decisions" about their fitness and life, and even to become "a better human." "Join those of us who are proud," Bailey's book concludes by exhorting readers, "to be getting the most out of the bodies we are given. Start now!"[79]

Bailey's book articulates the performance and body fetish that took hold of the Western world in the 1970s and 1980s and continues to this day – in an accelerated form, in fact. Fitness enthusiasts were not only keen to produce a toned and powerful body, but also wanted to present it in the best possible way. They now wore figure-hugging, sleeveless T-shirts or skin-tight leotards that left little to the imagination, not only while working out but also outside the gym. The mania for fitness and the body was focused entirely on oneself, one's success, on having control over one's life and happiness. Contemporary critics such as historian Benjamin Rader were already referring to a "new strenuosity" and the "strenuous life," that is, an industrious and relentless lifestyle, one that Americans were once again being exhorted to embrace and that was subject to a new round of evangelization.[80] Here Rader was alluding to one of the most famous speeches in US history, one that dates back more than a century. In 1899, New York governor and future president Theodore Roosevelt had called on Americans to embrace such a "strenuous life": an indefatigable, industrious, physically active way of life that would equip them to survive in a globally competitive environment and the Darwinian struggle for existence. In Europe as well, achievement through physical training and healthy eating are not inventions of the 1970s, even if it was then that they entered a boom phase and ushered in the age of fitness. The history of fitness dates to the nineteenth century, and in fact we can trace it still further back.[81]

2

FITNESS: TRAJECTORIES OF A CONCEPT SINCE THE EIGHTEENTH CENTURY

"The eternal fitness of things"?

Hence, in the twenty-first century, fitness is not something one has, but something one has to work for and maintain if one is to count as a productive member of a liberal society. Modern fitness is dynamic, signifies endless activity and builds on people's efforts to ensure their health, performance, and quality of life, to enhance and optimize them.

This was not always the case. When the discourse of liberty, individual rights, and human happiness gained currency in Europe and the United States in the eighteenth century, fitness was not a byword for self-responsibility or individuals' scope to shape their lives. On the contrary, fitness stood for an insistence on preexisting principles and conditions. Fitness, a term used exclusively in English at the time, had nothing to do with altering and improving one's fate, but meant fitting into a rigid order that was claimed to be beyond the influence of the individual.

A paradigmatic depiction of this static form of fitness, which was to be cited again and again until the late nineteenth century, can be found in Henry Fielding's novel about the foundling *Tom Jones* (1749). The novel is a commentary on eighteenth-century English society, its rules, organizing principles, and morality. The stubborn philosopher and teacher Mr. Square blusters about fitness whenever he assails the changing times and advocates the traditional notions of virtue, morality, and social order. To place these on an unshakable basis, he invokes "the unalterable rule of right and the eternal fitness of things."[1] Square, swimming with the intellectual currents of the eighteenth century, bases his thinking here on natural laws. His fellow teacher Reverend Thwackum, meanwhile, brings the divine will into play in order to assign everything under the sun a fixed place in the world and social structure. This static meaning of fitness, unusual from today's perspective, is even more evident if we look at German translations of the novel. In the first German edition of 1750, the quoted passage is translated as "the unalterable rule of right, and the eternal coherence of things" (*die unveränderliche Regel des Rechts, und der ewige Zusammenhang der Dinge*); an edition of 1771 refers to the "eternal propriety [*Schicklichkeit*] of things." The translation of 1841, meanwhile, emphasizes the "unalterable *Zweckmäßigkeit* [aptness] of things." As late as the middle of the nineteenth century, terms such as *Tüchtigkeit* (implying ability, proficiency, and efficiency), *Leistungsfähigkeit* (performance) and optimizability were not used to convey the English term "fitness."[2]

Those who spoke of fitness in Fielding's day invoked a world and a society featuring principles and a social order that ought to be taken for granted and regarded as unshakable; things were good and right just as they were. To work steadily on oneself in order to enhance one's potential, gain new skills, and advance in life would have run counter to these conceptions of fitness and their relationship to the order of the world.[3]

From the late eighteenth century onward, however, the Atlantic world changed fundamentally. The Enlightenment postulates of freedom and self-determination challenged existing ideas of a static social order. Human life and human society became more dynamic. "Man" was now considered a rational and empathetic being who was free, held his fate in his own hands, always had a choice, and could provide himself with rules, laws, and a government.

During the British colonial era of the seventeenth and eighteenth centuries, North America had already offered people opportunities to get ahead in life, as well as for political and social participation, of a sort unthinkable in Europe at the time.[4] Upon its foundation, the young United States was widely regarded as a place where the promises of the Enlightenment were now being made good on. The Declaration of Independence on July 4, 1776, cut all ties with the British Crown and Parliament and affirmed the right of every human being to life, liberty, and the pursuit of happiness. It is significant to the history of modern fitness that the Declaration of Independence declared not happiness itself, but the active pursuit of happiness – of self-fulfillment, security, prosperity, and property – a basic condition of being human. And yet, this "pursuit of happiness" was not just a right, but also a kind of duty, one that was part and parcel of person-hood in a free society.[5] What is more, if God had previously assigned human beings a particular place in the world, it was now regarded as God's will that people actively strive to make their lives good, to be successful, and to progress. Hence, as the principle of social organization, and of the world as a whole, the "unalterable rule of right and the eternal fitness of things" of the eighteenth century was superseded by the right and duty to take personal responsibility, to work on oneself and one's wellbeing, to strive actively and autonomously for happiness and quality of life. Henceforth, the global and social order as well as human existence were conceived in dynamic terms and geared toward the improvement of one's lot. However, as the eighteenth century drew to a close, a physical readiness and ability to perform were not yet regarded as prerequisites for achieving this. This changed only in the second half of the nineteenth century, when the static concept of fitness was gradually replaced by a dynamic one, and the body moved to the center of the social order.[6]

Whenever reference is made to liberty, equality, and self-determination in the history of liberal societies, it must be remembered that people were in reality less equal than postulated in the Declaration of Independence, even in the United States. The country's paean to these three values went hand in hand with a political reality of bondage, inequality, heteronomy, and the persistence of slavery. Ultimately, the potential to work productively with one's freedoms and thus to be regarded as a sustaining force in a free society was largely restricted to white men.[7]

Yet with regard to white men as well, many skeptics warned of the risks and difficulties involved in the American experiment. One urgent question facing the young American republic was whether one could truly build a society on the readiness and ability to embrace achievement and self-responsibility. In addition to women and slaves, did too many white men require control and guidance, especially those of a lower social rank? Their bad habits were also feared in Europe, but in the liberal United States the question of what their consequences might be took on a special urgency. Early political debates already revolved around the question of how strong the political leadership of a republic should be in relation to the liberties of the individual. On the one hand, crucial liberal principles gained traction in these debates, namely limited government, a lean state, and the market as an essential means of interaction. These were principles that were to mold the social order of the United States henceforth.[8] On the other hand, from the beginning the liberal credo of a lean state and individual autonomy was accompanied by the doubts and anxieties of the middle classes. Were the lower orders truly ready to govern themselves and successfully pursue happiness, rather than indulging in alcohol and other vices? The propertied class doubted that all Americans were "fit" enough for a liberal republic with its rights and obligations, even if "fit" was not the term used in the early nineteenth century.[9]

Soon members of the middle classes began to form the first social movements seeking to teach people how to work on themselves, manage themselves, and strive for success, as well as to resist alcohol and loose morals. Another approach to putting liberal societies on a more stable footing was to be novel educational, reformatory, and penal institutions, which now emerged on both sides of the Atlantic, with the young United States setting the pace. This development was underpinned by a changed concept of punishment, with its goals, practices, and meaning being redefined. Punishment was no longer to mean inflicting shame or pain on those who violated norms. Instead, the goal was to "correct" and "reform" those concerned, making them "fit" for a free society. Encouraging individuals' capacity for self-reflection and ability to participate in society was now the declared goal of punishment. The concept of optimizing and improving people began to take shape, to inscribe itself into the social and political order and to mold its instruments, though the real-world effects of this concept were often limited.[10] The new penal and educational institutions also operated via the body, either forcing it to work or locking it up and immobilizing it. They thus started with the body, but the stated goal was neither to torment the body nor to improve its performance. This was not about achieving fitness in the modern sense. Rather, the body functioned primarily as an instrument for improving character.

Nonetheless, in the first half of the nineteenth century – in both Europe and the United States – an array of systems was already at large concerned with the care of the body in everyday life, its health and its potential. One might think, for example, of various forms of gymnastics, which was intended to teach the new bourgeois individual an upright posture, or the vigorous *Turnen*, which arrived in the United States with German migrants from the 1820s onward. Yet it was the nation rather than the individual and their success that lay at the heart of *Turnen*.[11] It was not until the middle of the nineteenth century that a growing number of key actors called for greater attention to be paid to the body *qua* body and its individual performance. Thus, in 1855, the *North American Review* sharply criticized various experts in the optimization of the self, namely "physicians, educationists, and religionists," for woefully neglecting the importance of the body to individual and social progress. Similarly, a few years later the *Atlantic Monthly* contended that "physical culture is [now] on top of the wave."[12] This was a matter of work on the body, which had less to do with molding a human being's character or nature. Instead, the focus was on the body as body, which now became the target of optimization and a sign of a successful way of life. The Protestant ethic now set its sights on the body itself.[13] As modernity continued to unfold, henceforth the body and its potential received a new level of attention, reinforced by the dynamism of capitalism and the burgeoning machine age. Physiology, which sought to understand the body, its potential and performance, rose to become a leading international discipline in the second half of the nineteenth century.[14]

The extent to which the middle of the nineteenth century ushered in an era of major shifts in the history of the body is evident if one looks at the concept of fitness itself. Only now did it begin to become more dynamic. Previously, the meaning of the concept of fitness had barely changed. It had long referred to a specific "fitness for purpose" of certain people and things, their aptness for a particular function or position; this was not about their self-achieved physical performance. The static meaning of the concept of fitness, then, had long persisted, even in the United States, which had of course committed itself to breaking with tradition and with all rigid structures.[15] As late as the 1860s, in the *Atlantic Monthly* for example, fitness primarily served to describe aesthetic aptness or to categorize specific abilities, such as those possessed by a specific person with respect to a particular role, be it a railroad entrepreneur, editor, curator, or artist. It was certainly believed that practice and an ability to learn were conducive to accomplishing a certain feat. When fitness was invoked, however, the focus was still on whether a person had a particular aptitude and was fit or apt for a particular position, rather than on whether they could attain such attributes.[16] The notion of fitness was applied to a wide range of phenomena. It was related to such mundane issues as the correct temperature of a plate for a given dish, on other occasions to matters that could scarcely have been more politically explosive. Were southern slaves, freed in 1865, "fit" – that is, cut out to vote? Commentators still regularly spoke of "natural fitness" and also of the "eternal fitness of things," drawing on Fielding's eighteenth-century formulation.[17] Only in the second half of the nineteenth century did this begin to change, slowly but surely.

Fitness, Darwin, and the invention of inescapable competition

A key event in the history of the fitness concept was the appearance of Charles Darwin's *On the Origin of Species*. First published in London in 1859, the book was released the following year in New York, as well as in German and Dutch translations, and soon numerous other languages. Since then, a notion of fitness as a prerequisite for success, even survival, in a world of supposedly all-pervasive competition has been closely associated with Darwin and his thinking. Yet Darwin did not invent the idea of competition as an instrument of social organization. For many decades, in fields such as population theory and political economy, scholars had been thinking in terms of competition for scarce resources. But it was Darwin who now anchored competition in natural history, helping ensure an increasingly close coupling of the social and biological sciences in the following years and decades. The connecting link was the idea of competition as an inescapable ordering principle.[18]

When it comes to a concept of fitness entangled with notions of (literally) existential competition, an idea that emerged over the next few decades, once again Darwin's authorship was partial at most. Although he used the term fitness in 1859 in the first edition of his book, it was to be several years before he referred to the "survival of the fittest." The social philosopher Herbert Spencer coined this phrase in his *Principles of Biology* of 1864 (five years after the first publication of *On the Origin of Species*), from which it migrated to the emerging social sciences. Darwin himself picked up on Spencer's formulation in a new edition of his book in 1869, praising it as a very fitting expression for the process he had in mind.[19] This was the endless play of variation, selection, and adaptation, which determined the outcome of the relentless competition, indeed struggle, for access to favorable living conditions and scarce resources. Nevertheless, for Darwin fitness was not something that individual creatures actively brought about. It was not a being's work on its performance that resulted in victory or defeat, survival or death. Rather, according to Darwin, it was contingency that determined which living creatures best fit a specific environment and therefore survived. A look at early German editions of Darwin's book underlines this reading, which predominated in the German-speaking countries as well. Borrowing from Spencer's *Principles of Biology*, these texts consistently conveyed the "survival of the fittest" by the phrase *Überleben des Passendsten* (implying aptness).[20] In Darwin's work as elsewhere, fitness was still static, and the fittest was the most apt. His writings were not initially built on the notion of dynamic fitness as the effect of work on oneself and the targeted optimization of one's potential.

However, the concept of fitness as something one can and must work on in order to increase one's chances of success and survival was no more than a small step away. Who could fail to come up with the idea of working purposefully to gain advantages and a better point of departure amid this mélange of competition, struggle, and the freedom to pursue self-care? Who would not seek to use their liberties to their own advantage in a context of inescapable competition? For the members of a society increasingly geared toward performance and competition, fitness acquired in this way would make survival more likely and thus help optimize – within and across generations – a collective that was conceptualized in both biological and social terms. Failing to work on oneself and indulging in bad habits, meanwhile, risked the degeneration and, at worst, extinction of a species. The fact that the differing scientific positions of Charles Darwin, French biologist Jean-Baptiste Lamarck, and others frequently intermingled in this discourse did nothing to stem its momentum. On the contrary, the Lamarckian reading of Darwinism in particular fueled the progressivist ideology of modernity, because the belief that acquired characteristics and abilities could not only increase one's own chances of survival and success, but would also be passed on down the generations, makes work on the self seem even more significant. This concept of transgenerational transmission has recently regained its momentum in epigenetics.[21]

Let us recall here once again how important freedom and individual responsibility had become as political principles at this point in time, particularly in North America, and to a lesser extent in Europe as well. The concepts of the freedom of the human individual and of personal responsibility are central to the impact fitness was subsequently to have. Especially in the United States, they led to the formation of a new liberal political and social order, with all its distortions, including the persistence of slavery. But even in Germany, liberalism and the idea of freedom were conveyed by terms such as "responsibility" (*Mündigkeit*), "independence" (*Selbständigkeit*), "independent thinking" (*Selbstdenken*) and "autonomous action" (*Selbsthandeln*). Nonetheless, liberal thought was never as central to the European nations' political self-understanding and political practice as in the United States.[22]

Yet many intellectual pioneers of liberalism came from the Old World. I will mention just the Scot Adam Smith here. In 1776, the year of the American Declaration of Independence, he introduced the free market and competition to economic and political thought with his book *The Wealth of Nations*.[23] For the nineteenth century, meanwhile, John Stuart Mill is regarded as the key European theorist of liberalism, and in his writings on political economy he fused the market economy, individual freedom, and limited state power. Mill's *On Liberty* first appeared in 1859 (and thus the same year as Charles Darwin's *On the Origin of Species*); there he writes that the true source and foundation of freedom and social development is the individual's drive to improve their own skills and opportunities. This sounds very much like fitness. The term itself does not appear in Mill, but his text is pervaded by notions of fitness. And Mill's blueprints for society, individual agency, and the human potential for optimization are based on a dynamic self, of a kind absent from the work of the naturalist Darwin.[24]

Liberalism (with liberty and self-responsibility as the central principles of human existence) and Darwinism (with competition and struggle as the essential principles of all existence) formed highly productive synergies in the mid-nineteenth century. Their coexistence modulated the old, static concept of fitness over the decades that followed, further fueling belief in individual responsibility for the progress and success of both individuals and the collective, while bringing the body more clearly into play. Of course, this dynamic understanding of fitness did not replace the static version in one fell swoop. In reality it supplemented, expanded, and modified it over the years and decades. At times, "natural and acquired fitness" were discussed in the same breath.[25] Performance and success in competition were now interpreted as a synthesis of relevant physical conditions (such as well-proportioned limbs and strong lungs) and a strong will. The latter was the first prerequisite for wringing out every last drop of one's potential and even expanding it.[26] Individuals were now exhorted, ever more explicitly, to proactively make themselves and their bodies fit. This fitness was in turn regarded as a sign of a high overall level of commitment and performance, and these were necessary if one was to exist and survive in a world of competition for resources and social participation. Consequently, fitness was poised to become a central concept in liberal societies, one that pointed far beyond sport. In fact, it stood for the fundamental ability, which was considered a virtue, to work on oneself and to take responsibility for one's performance.[27]

This historical shift helped dissolve the belief that human beings were subject to certain rigid, natural limits of a political, social, and physical kind. The magical key to stretching and overcoming these limits was "exercise," and a variety of authors now argued vociferously that one's body and health could and should be strengthened systematically and enduringly through exercise. As the Scot John S. Blackie wrote in a book widely read on both sides of the Atlantic, nothing in this universe works without exercise and effort. Through the body, the typically modern belief that everything is feasible and moldable now encompassed people's lifestyles. Only those who voluntarily and joyfully looked after themselves and their bodies, who acted in a self-reliant and self-controlled manner, would be successful and progress. This included close observation of oneself, gathering and evaluating information about oneself and one's body (about eating and movement, weight, excretions, etc.) and of course exercising, all without overdoing it. Striking the right balance was crucial. The new fitness concept and the associated new culture of exercise formed part of a burgeoning "self-culture," which was translated into German as *Selbsterziehung* or "self-education." Yet successful "self-education" required one to follow the advice of those with more experience (such as parents, teachers, and foremen) or of the many experts who began to shape the debates on the body, performance, and their improvement around this time. It was claimed that the new fitness experts, working in fields such as physiology or training theory, were best placed to recognize how to improve the health and performance of a body. Relevant manuals now appeared in large numbers. A book by Danish athlete and gymnastics teacher Johann Peder Müller from 1904, *Mein System. 15 Minuten tägliche Arbeit für die Gesundheit* ("My System. 15 Minutes of Daily Work for Health"), became a European bestseller.[28]

The increasing momentum of the concept of fitness was part of a comprehensive melange of development, progress, and competition that penetrated virtually every sphere of life. Fueled by a burgeoning social Darwinism, exhibitions of physical performance were held in a vast number of locations, at the local, regional, or even global level. In 1887, Dudley Allen Sargent, professor of physical training at Harvard University, emphasized that the time had come for the United States to truly understand the importance of physical education to the development of the individual, and thus to American society and the "Anglo-Saxon race" as a whole. A year later, the *North American Review* went so far as to claim that "the history of civilization would seem to be the history of an improving physique." In this context, the physical and civilizational gold standard was the white, bourgeois male.[29]

The individual and collective pursuit of fitness were supposed to form an interlocking pair, and were conceptualized as part of a global "struggle for existence" in all areas, including sports, the armed forces, the economy, technology, and science. This idea was widespread on both sides of the Atlantic, even if a number of European skeptics distanced themselves from the mania for progress in the United States, with some even expressing outright antipathy. The idea of fitness also fueled the rampant colonialist frenzy that enveloped not only the European powers but also the United States as the nineteenth century advanced.[30] In concentrated form, this thinking was present in Theodore Roosevelt's 1899 speech on the "strenuous life." The New York governor and later president of the United States, a self-confessed outdoorsman and veteran, called on every American to lead a "strenuous life" characterized by indefatigability, ambition, activity, and constant progress. This, he contended, was the way to advance America and the Americans amid the permanent competition between nations. Roosevelt addressed his remarks explicitly to white, Anglo-Saxon, Protestant, and male Americans. For him, only they could cope with freedom and self-responsibility and make productive use of both. For Roosevelt, it was the willingness and ability of each individual that underpinned the progress and strength of the collective. And while Roosevelt does not use terms such as fit, unfit, or fitness in a systematic or analytical way, his speech captures the various facets of the *dispositif* of fitness around 1900: the synergies of liberalism and Darwinism, and of freedom and competition; the coexistence of individual self-management and collective progress, and of body and nation; the fostering of the self and the exclusion of the other.[31]

Fitness, difference, and political participation

Just how thoroughly a dynamic notion of fitness penetrated modern societies in the final third of the nineteenth century can be grasped with the help of Michel Foucault's concept of biopolitics, which outlines how the body, along with the organization and cultivation of life, became central to modernity and its policies. Around 1900, individuals and collectives (society, the nation, the "people") were urged to become more efficient, productive, and resilient – in a word, fitter. The idea that bodies have to be constantly worked on and activated in order to improve their abilities had increasingly taken hold as a norm. It was simply considered "normal" to work on oneself. But fitness not only demanded work on the self. It also established differences, namely between those who could gain recognition as efficiently working on themselves, and those who failed to do so. In a modern society, the former were regarded as successful subjects, while the latter were not, or if they were, then to a much lesser degree. Fitness had become an ideal that organized society and regulated who could participate in it, in what ways and to what extent.[32]

From about 1900, then, some were only partially granted the ability to achieve fitness, and thus full social recognition and participation, if they were not fundamentally denied these attributes. The inclusion of some in and the exclusion of others from full social and civic participation was not new at all. To discriminate and exclude is well-nigh constitutive of societies that have committed themselves to liberty, the ideal of self-improvement, and the model of the autonomous subject. These societies claim to valorize the human being above all else, but nevertheless distinguish between those acknowledged as capable of using their freedom successfully and productively, and "others," who are not.[33] Hence, diverse "caesuras," aligned with categories such as "race" and ethnicity, gender and class, sexuality and age, permeate society. These biologically and physically conceived caesuras regulate the extent and type of social participation. In fact, the biopolitical logic of inclusion and exclusion implies that the "death of the other" will make one's life "healthier and purer."[34] Death is not necessarily meant literally here, but as a metaphor for various forms of social exclusion.[35]

In the final third of the nineteenth century, the idea of dynamic fitness became ever more deeply embedded in social and political thought and action. Thus, the question of who was cut out to be a citizen was increasingly negotiated under the heading of "fitness." Ultimately, fitness was seen as an expression of the ability to perform as well as the ability to govern oneself, to cope with a competitive environment and thus to be a productive member of society. Yet by claiming to ensure performance- or achievement-based justice, liberal societies have concealed inequalities and mechanisms of exclusion.[36] When reference was made to fitness and citizenship, this was not a matter of citizens endowed with vested rights or holding particular passports. It was about being able to make claims, and these were derived from the supposed capacity for self-improvement and constructive participation in liberal societies.[37] Those who ensured the strength and health of their own bodies documented their awareness of the importance of their own performance and thus of their labor power, their ability to fight, and their capacity for procreation, an awareness that was in turn considered fundamental to both individual and societal success. In other words, those who attended to their fitness showed that they wanted to make a contribution and thus expressed claims to participation and recognition. This argument was often made at the time, and not just in the United States. In European countries such as Germany or the United Kingdom as well, the body had become the instrument whose activation could ensure one's political and social participation and membership, as well as providing recognition and privileges.[38]

By now fitness was conceived in highly dynamic fashion, yet was crisscrossed by static axes. On the basis of "race" or ethnicity, gender and other categories, it was thought possible to judge which people were "naturally" equipped with the potential to be free citizens and which were not. In the United States, on the cusp of the twentieth century, a controversial debate revolved around whether certain groups did in fact have a "natural" sense of duty, an "instinctive" sense of purpose, and an "inherent" love of work, qualities that would enable them to become citizens of a liberal society. The main groups at issue here were former African American slaves after emancipation, indigenous peoples after military subjugation, women fighting for the right to vote, uneducated peasant immigrants from Southeastern Europe and Filipinos after colonization.[39] It was even asserted that the fitness of different people and groups for self-government, political participation and citizenship was one of the most pressing questions that liberal societies had to face henceforth.[40]

The decades around 1900 are regarded as a time of tremendous social change and as the first modern age of the body, which found expression in the discourse of fitness in a range of ways. Everything revolved around the body, its performance, its readiness to perform, and the improvement of both. In addition, it was the body, with its supposedly varying potentials, from which differences were derived in a society of purported equality. The tremendous social dynamism of this era was an irritant, and the body, particularly the supposed natural superiority of the white male body, seemed to promise stability. The body operated as a kind of anchor of social order in times of fundamental change.[41] However, this seemingly natural superiority of the white male body had to be repeatedly asserted, staged, and actively produced in order to ensure its widespread acceptance. The fitness of the white male body, and thus the display of its supposedly natural superiority, required permanent activity.[42]

At the same time, it was claimed that the bodies of the modern, and increasingly urban, world faced a number of problems that placed a question mark over their alleged status as bastion of stability. First, many commentators believed they could observe an increasing lack of physical challenges in modern societies. In the case of the United States, this was associated with the loss of a previously defining historical factor, namely the idea that (white, male) American bodies were forged at the frontier in the West, where they supposedly turned wilderness into civilization. At the end of the nineteenth century, however, the continent was regarded as settled and the era of the frontier as over. This was experienced as a great loss, and it was believed that the lack of physical challenges would lead to the sustained weakening of American men. A variety of actors now demanded compensatory action. Concurrently, and this was a second problem, modern cities were regarded as places of sensory overstimulation, which was blamed for physical and mental states of exhaustion of truly epidemic proportions. Fears abounded of a novel disease, especially rampant in the white middle class, called neurasthenia. This condition was symptomatic at the *fin de siècle*, and thus played a role similar to that of coronary heart disease or burnout in the late twentieth and early twenty-first centuries.[43]

Commentators now referred to an outright crisis of American society. This sense of crisis was partly fueled by dynamic migratory movements: first, of Chinese workers to the American West, then people of Catholic and Jewish faith from Southern and Eastern Europe who migrated to the American East and Midwest, and African Americans leaving the South. These migratory flows unnerved white, Anglo-Saxon, Protestant America, which feared the loss of its social and political hegemony. Contributing to the diffuse and unsettling sense of living in a time of rapid change was the first women's movement, its demands and successes inspiring profound fears among white men.[44]

With respect to all these challenges, the activation of the body, and especially the white male body, seemed to be, if not the only response, then certainly a fitting and important one that stood to reason in an era of social Darwinism. Given the prevailing culture of competition and the "survival of the fittest," physical weakness inevitably appeared particularly threatening and physical exercise seemed like an especially promising antidote. Increased physical activity, especially for white men, was thus considered the best form of therapy and prevention in the age of neurasthenia. Exercise in the fresh air and healthy eating were the best ways to produce and perform the alleged naturalness of white male superiority. A "bacillus athleticus" went around, and "exercise, exercise, and exercise" was claimed to be the best way to counteract physical degeneration. A novel enthusiasm for gymnastics, cycling, swimming, and other activities geared toward the training of the body penetrated everyday life in modern societies around 1900.[45] At the same time, "good" nutrition became a veritable obsession. To eat "right," to choose a "healthy" diet, and practice occasional fasting were signs that one was dealing carefully with oneself and one's body as society now demanded. Nutritionally sound eating habits, precise self-observation and, often, a decent amount of meat, were believed to help maintain and improve one's performance.[46] Soft, fat bodies were less and less indicative of prosperity and success in life; increasingly, they signified failure, weakness, lack of self-management, and unfitness in the age of biopolitics.[47]

The new hype surrounding the body was particularly prevalent among white bourgeois men, and it was one means of restabilizing the societal balance of power. With thoroughly fit bodies, white men would spell out their extraordinary level of performance, while also preparing themselves for economic success in the context of capitalist competition, thus reaffirming and legitimizing their privileged social position. Characters such as fitness guru Bernarr Macfadden and Königsberg bodybuilder Friedrich Wilhelm Müller, who became a global icon from North America to New Zealand under the pseudonym of Eugen Sandow, countered all the talk of crisis by showcasing what a white male body was capable of. Their bodies confirmed and fortified fitness as an ideal and practice that would bring out the best in people, especially white males.[48] New sports and fitness magazines displayed the bodies of Sandow, Macfadden (who published some of the magazines himself), and others on countless occasions. They thus shaped the belief in physical education as one of the guiding principles of a free and competitive society in which white men were out in front by virtue of their supposedly superior abilities. Magazines such as *Physical Culture*, part of Bernarr Macfadden's media empire, or the sports magazine *Outing*, left no one in any doubt that fitness through training was the foundation of a healthy body and thus of success of any kind, be it in the world of work, as a businessman, politician, or soldier.[49] "Weakness is a crime," to quote Macfadden's motto, "Don't be a criminal!"

Although the focus of the body cult was on white, bourgeois men, other social groups also sought to attain greater social and political participation through their bodies and fitness. Bernarr Macfadden's physical culture explicitly addressed women as well as men. In an era of competition and physicality, fitness was very well suited to female empowerment, perhaps because it was so closely linked to masculinity and whiteness, and thus to the main insignia of social hegemony and political power. Thus, on the one hand, fitness marginalized certain social groups and individuals, but on the other it opened up spaces in which they could lay claim to greater social participation. As philosopher Judith Butler might put it, fitness denoted a field of both limiting and enabling forces.[50]

Members of the African American community sought empowerment via the body. By the turn of the century, black sports stars such as the boxer Jack Johnson and the cyclist Major Taylor had already demonstrated what was possible and feasible against all odds and social limitations. With regard to the broad African American population as well, black intellectuals and politicians, such as W.E.B. DuBois and Emmett J. Scott, underlined the importance of good, healthy, and productive forms of physical exercise to success in the struggle for political rights and social recognition. African Americans, they asserted, needed sports facilities, swimming pools, and tennis courts if they were to succeed as citizens of the United States.[51] A similar picture emerges with respect to Jewish body politics on both sides of the Atlantic. Sport and physical training were supposed to counteract contemporary notions of feeble Jewish male bodies. "Muscle Jews" (*Muskeljuden*) were meant to symbolize a modern, self-confident Jewry, one that demanded political and social participation.[52] Another example is Czech migrants in the United States who practiced *sokol*, a form of group gymnastics, in order to get fit and demonstrate that they were well suited to becoming Americans, while remaining connected to their home country.[53] Last but not least, feminist Frances Willard and her love of cycling provide us with another case in point (see figure 4). For Willard, cycling

Figure 4 Frances Willard learns to ride a bike
Source: From Frances E. Willard's *A Wheel within a Wheel: How I Learned to Ride the Bicycle, with some Reflections by the Way*. Woman's Temperance Publishing Association, *c*.1895

embodied the entire liberal-democratic philosophy of life. Cycling, that is, meant hard work on oneself in parallel with moderate pleasure. Those who rode a bike, as Willard waxed lyrical, nurtured their physical strength and strength of character, acquired new skills, opened up new spaces, and advanced in life. They learned to rely on themselves, without rejecting the advice of those who had already attained advanced cycling skills and had a better command of both technology and body.[54]

Ultimately, by the early twentieth century, the changed concept of fitness – as high performance achieved through active physical exercise – had become inscribed in the minds and bodies of modern people. It was to be a long time, namely the 1960s, before the English word "fitness" appeared in German-language texts. Nevertheless, by 1900, ideas about corporeality were more dynamic, in Germany too, than they had been a few decades earlier, and they were linked with individual motivation and performance. This is evident if we take another look at German editions of Charles Darwin's *On the Origin of Species*, but this time translations produced around the turn of the century. These increasingly ceased to translate "survival of the fittest" as *Überleben des Passendsten*, implying aptness, instead referring to the *Überleben des Tüchtigsten*, which suggests proficiency and industriousness. From the late eighteenth century, *tüchtig* was increasingly used to describe diligence-based, above-average performance. *Tüchtigkeit* was to be the German equivalent of the English "fitness" henceforth.[55]

In the United States, "fitness" and "fit" were firmly anchored in everyday language by the early twentieth century. In 1915, the sports magazine *Outing* stated that the expression "keep fit" was now in wide use and very familiar to all Americans. The "pursuit of happiness" extolled in the American Declaration of Independence had taken on concrete form as the "pursuit of fitness" – through work on the self, which meant, above all, exercising regularly and eating a balanced diet. But how one ought to exercise and eat and how much, how appropriate the exercise and diet were, and what effect they had, supposedly depended on one's gender and skin color. The *dispositif* of fitness operated through the coexistence of a dynamically conceived self-optimization and static boundaries, which were drawn along the lines of "race," gender, and other categories.

The idea that work on the self had to be aligned with scientific standards now gained ever more traction. The pursuit of fitness should adhere to the most recent guidelines produced by training theory and nutritional science. Exercise sessions, food, and the success or failure of one's actions had to be precisely measured, recorded, and coordinated. By and large, it was claimed, the same rules of life applied to "the average American" as to an athlete.[56] The maxim here was that everyone should constantly exercise in order to achieve the best possible results in a competitive society.

Science, meanwhile, had spawned a new field that was also dedicated to human betterment: eugenics. It succinctly demonstrates the at once inclusive and exclusionary power of fitness. Eugenics sought to make distinctions between fit and unfit, to select, to foster the survival of the fittest, and thus to create a highly productive "national body," defined by notions of "race." Behavior-oriented management and intervention also played a role here, not just one's genetic make-up. Like fitness, eugenics was a transnational, modern phenomenon that nonetheless took different forms in different places. Both scientifically and politically, eugenics was a recognized and well-established field. In 1907, renowned US sociologist D. Collin Wells proclaimed in the prestigious *American Journal of Sociology* that eugenic thinking must become the new religion of modern societies and trigger appropriate political action. That same year, the state of Indiana passed the first eugenics law, in other words considerably earlier than Germany and other European countries.[57]

Fitness in an era of crisis and war

The meanings and functions of fitness and the body shifted once again in the 1930s. Nazi Germany saw the growth of an unprecedented fanaticism surrounding the body and performance, which found expression in the worship of sporting and soldierly bodies as well as laboring and reproductive bodies. In fascism, however, physical training was less of a liberal technique of the self; the central social leitmotif was not the successful individual. Instead, fascists celebrated training, competition, and the performance of the body in the service of a nationally and racially imagined community of the people or *Volksgemeinschaft*.[58] This certainly entailed connotations of the kind of "life reform" (*Lebensreform*) that had become familiar, chiefly in Germany, from the turn of the century, that is, the idea of counteracting the distortions of modernity with the liberated, well-maintained and well-trained body. Another significant force in the Nazi cult of the body was the German *Turner*. From the beginning of the nineteenth century onward, they devoted themselves to the training of the body, but worked with commands and their execution as a means of advancing the nation and the *Volk*, rather than valorizing the individual and self-regulated fitness so central to the liberal *dispositif*.[59] In Nazism, high-performance bodies were those that served a collective fantasy of performance and purity that was oriented toward the aesthetic and political ideal of the "Aryan racial body." To be sure, the *Volksgemeinschaft* (community of the people) did not operate solely through the coercive integration and subordination of the individual, but also through voluntary and at times even enthusiastic participation.[60]

On the other side of the Atlantic as well, in the 1930s the meanings of bodies and their performance shifted, as did the relationship between the two. With the economic crisis, which attained unprecedented proportions, from 1929 onward the United States' hitherto more or less limitless confidence in the forces of liberalism and competition waned. Critics dismissed the market, competition, and individualism as the essential if not sole elements guiding US society, and collectivist and welfarist ideas now gained currency. Historian Jeff Cowie describes the era of the New Deal, the war years, and the first postwar decades as the "great exception" in terms of the political, economic, and social traditions and maxims of US market liberalism. Of course, this ideology never disappeared completely between the 1930s and 1970s, but it became less dominant as a result of the economic crisis and the associated social traumas. Franklin D. Roosevelt's New Deal and, with certain qualifications, its successor programs, from Harry Truman's Fair Deal to Lyndon B. Johnson's Great Society in the 1960s, Cowie contends, stimulated the rise of a cross-class and cross-group collective spirit in the United States. This mitigated the power of the social Darwinist precept of the "survival of the fittest."[61]

The economic crisis and the New Deal ushered in a shift in the preconditions for fitness as a regulatory ideal. The relationship between body, work on the body, and citizenship changed. Now the primary task was to nurse bodies emaciated by crisis back to health through a collective effort. People were to be satiated and made strong and thus turned back into high-performing citizens. Given the unprecedented economic crisis, it had become impossible to credibly claim that those without a job did not want to work. Rather than unwillingness or inability, external conditions were now identified as crucial factors in human failure. Hence, numerous New Deal programs were intended to shape the conditions of human existence and, within these external parameters, help people to help themselves. Work programs were meant to provide a solid framework for autonomous self-management. For example, in the Civilian Conservation Corps, by general consensus the most successful government job creation measure of the era, work on nature was at the same time work on the male body and work on the nation. Work programs taught ideas and practices of good citizenship that were focused less on individual success and more on collectives such as the family and the nation.[62] This also applies to the art of the New Deal. Commissioned by the state, this now appeared in the form of murals in countless public buildings. Such art proclaimed that strong working bodies were both a part and a result of national effort.[63] The proximity to fascist and state socialist body imagery is unmistakable.

Corporeality, then, lost none of its political and social significance in the 1930s. But the objective of high performance and the practices intended to achieve it were now less part of a self-culture than of a collective project. Fitness – in the sense of self-practices in a liberal society geared toward performance, competition, and individuality – lost its prominence.

In World War II, muscular, strong, and vigorous bodies continued to constitute a national project in the United States. Together, these bodies were supposed to form a collective body that would resist the fascist enemy with all its might. In principle, the same applies to the United States as historian Charlotte Macdonald has shown for the British Commonwealth. Bodies were brought into play collectively as a means of defending a liberal social order against dictatorial threats – across genders. The female icon of the American home front was a worker in the armaments industry, "Rosie the Riveter." Rosie flexed her muscles. Her strong arms, which she showed off on numerous posters, would boost war production and help defend America.[64]

Fitness and consumer culture

World War II was barely over when the biopolitical concern for health and performance began to refocus on the individual and their self-management. One of the backgrounds to this was the postwar economic boom in the West. West Germany, for example, became the land of the economic miracle, gripped by a so-called feeding frenzy. The era of ration cards was over and richer food was back on the table. With budgets still tight, many meals remained simple, but West Germans could consume again and even put on weight. Things were evidently on the up.[65]

For the United States, after two decades of crisis and war, the 1950s meant being able to resume and even surpass the consumerism of the early twentieth century. More than ever, the consumer and buyer became the ideal type of the free citizen in a market society. Those who consumed a lot were acting in the national interest. First, after difficult times, they were helping strengthen economy and society, and second, the Cold War demanded that consumption become a political practice in opposition to an enemy that had embraced a planned economy. The so-called kitchen debate between US Vice President Richard Nixon and Soviet Premier Nikita Khrushchev at the American National Exhibition in Moscow in 1959 has become legendary. There Nixon praised the fully equipped kitchen of the American home as an indication of the superiority of consumer capitalism over communism and a planned economy.[66]

At the same time, initially in the United States, a debate kicked off over the way in which consumption might endanger the performance and competitiveness of society and its members. The once again rich food and the growing number of everyday amenities such as TVs, cars, and escalators were not just regarded as an expression of capitalist strength. Soon they were also being identified as causes of the increasing weakness, softness, and corrosion of capitalist bodies. By 1950 commentators were, for the first time, describing obesity as the country's top health problem. Most identified the cause as the availability of a greater amount of more substantial food, but also mentioned the lack of exercise. The fact that many African Americans were still suffering from hunger in the 1950s and thereafter was barely mentioned in these debates.[67]

In the wake of this incipient fear of fat, issues of fitness again received more attention. International comparative studies in the early 1950s made a significant contribution here, showing that American children and adolescents aged six to nineteen were less physically fit than their counterparts in Austria and Italy. The high-consumption American lifestyle was identified as the cause, and the President's Council on Youth and Fitness (PCYF) was charged with doing something about it. As an alliance of private individuals and prominent figures, non-profit organizations and various corporations, the PCYF was supposed to activate American youth, expressly seeking to achieve not only physical but "total" fitness. This comprehensive fitness was conceptualized in physical, emotional, mental, and social terms, similar to the WHO's concept of health, which became established during this period and, to this day, defines health as physical, mental, and social wellbeing. In the liberal, democratic United States, however, work on the body and on health, even if it was initiated by the White House, could not look state-controlled, let alone totalitarian. It must in no way bring to mind Nazi Germany or the USSR and the high-performing bodies propagated in both states as a means of advancing the national cause. Americans were meant to be active on an autonomous and voluntary basis, because it was healthy, enjoyable, and consistent with their self-image as American citizens. Just what "total fitness" might actually be and how to achieve it, however, remained unclear. This lack of clarity may be interpreted as a shortcoming of fitness as a political project. But we might also view it as confirmation that fitness is grounded in the principle of working on oneself. The pursuit of fitness relies on individuality, self-activation, and the struggle for success; it neither requires concrete measures nor entails specific targets.[68]

The growing political and social concern about fitness during the 1950s was not directed solely at children and adolescents, but also at the adult population. One important background factor here was the fear of coronary heart disease, an anxiety that ran rampant in the consumer society of the postwar decades. Heart disease was the object and driver of a new epidemiology. Although heart disease was not contagious in the true sense of the term, it was believed to be highly determined by environment and behavior. This meant that it spread rapidly in a particular culture and society at a particular time. The new epidemiology relied on large-scale, long-term studies (especially in the town of Framingham, Massachusetts) and operated on the basis of a model that localized risk factors and linked them back to the social environment and lifestyle of individuals and social groups. This perspective fit perfectly with the broad concept of health, in which social factors as well as individual responsibility played an important role. Diet, alcohol and tobacco consumption, stress, work, and level of physical activity were now linked with the prevalence of heart disease. Prevention took on central importance, with experts and commentators invoking the power and importance of self-responsibility. Prevention, of course, requires every person to pay attention to their health and fitness and to ward off illness.[69]

I would like to make two other key points here. First, the main focus was once again on white men from the middle of society: men in their forties who often worked in middle management and were mostly sedentary at work, earned a good salary, and had a decent standard of living, but who were stressed, smoked, drank too much, and exercised too little. The alleged coronary crisis thus revolved around the very men who occupied a hegemonic position in US society, that is, who had the greatest access to social resources. At the same time, in the 1950s these men were once again being described as beset by crisis. They had supposedly been softened by the consumer society and homey *togetherness* – a key term in the self-description of American society in the 1950s. The pressure to accept their subordinate role within large corporations was also said to be detrimental to their energy and their drive, and that was ultimately bad for America too. The heart attack was not only considered a sign of physical weakness, but was also seen as proof of the special dedication of white, middle-class men, who worked themselves to death to ensure the prosperity of society and their families.[70] The "sick man" is a discursive trope that has taken root in analyses of the gender and social order. To this day, it implies the man's sacrifice for the good of family and society.[71] For the 1950s (and even later), this trope is so central that sociologist Barbara Ehrenreich has constructed her social diagnosis of these years, to quote the title of her book, around *The Hearts of Men*.[72]

Second, there was still no consensus in the 1950s as to whether physical exercise did in fact have a preventive effect, and whether it could and should be used to reduce the number of heart attacks. The health effects of sport were contested, and experts even discussed its possible harmfulness. In addition, for average men, a trained body was not yet unreservedly regarded as an aesthetic ideal. Calls to correct one's bodily form were directed above all at women, who ought to embody the female ideal of slimness. Corpulent men were considered stout, strong, and male, and thus normal. Rather than exercise, it was relaxation and, above all, making do with less food or alcohol that were propagated as the best ways of maintaining men's health. Their wives were made chiefly responsible for implementation here.[73] John F. Kennedy may have declared the physical enfeeblement of American men a national security problem and elevated the fight against "softness" to the status of political program. (He also ridiculed Richard Nixon's Cold War "kitchen politics" and raved about big rockets as a symbol of both military and male potency.) Yet at this point in time virtually no one thought about going for a jog in the evenings, let alone recording their body data, in order to keep fit.[74] In 1960, the guidebook *The Art of Keeping Fit* informed middle-aged men about the symptoms of looming illnesses, and about diets, forms of relaxation, and also a little about various casual sports (such as skiing, sailing, and golf). Training theory and training programs, sweat and breathlessness, were absent from this guide.[75]

This was soon to change. Kenneth Cooper's bestselling *Aerobics* was the overture to the 1970s, when the body and fitness were seen as key tools of individual advancement within an increasingly neoliberal social order and an increasingly flexible form of capitalism. One had, in every respect, to be motivated and willing to perform, productive, potent, ready for anything, and capable of the extraordinary – while managing to look good as well.

3

WORKING

"Corporate fitness," or: getting fit for work – Part I

Half-amused, half-admiring, in February 1980 *Der Spiegel* carried a report on a new trend in US companies. Workouts during lunch breaks were becoming increasingly popular. At Boeing, on the west coast, employees jogged through a tunnel system under the factory building, while Prudential Insurance, on the east coast, provided a trendy gymnastics-for-fitness program on the roof of its skyscraper. The era of cozy, unhurried "3-Martini lunches" was apparently over, and getting fit at work was now the order of the day, with *Der Spiegel* referring to "sweat-inducing activities of all kinds."[1]

In the early 1980s, running tracks, swimming pools, and gyms on company premises reflected the self-image and politics of a new generation of American companies. But companies that considered themselves innovative, and that were soon being classed as part of the so-called New Economy, went one step further. Not only did they build fitness centers, they also provided more flexible incentives in an attempt to get their workforce in shape and keep it that way. For technology firm Hewlett-Packard (HP), for example, a fitness center in one particular location made little sense. After all, HP was spread across a number of locations in California's Silicon Valley. It thus seemed more effective to provide funds to enable the workforce to become active on their own initiative and independent of the corporate infrastructure, for instance by establishing a basketball team or running group. Other companies funded weekend outings to all-comers and charity races, or even trips to take part in the New York or Boston marathons. Still others negotiated discounts at one of the then approximately 5,000 professional health clubs in the United States (there are now nearly 40,000).[2] Some companies awarded points and corresponding bonus payments to employees who did sport, based on the scoring system elaborated by Kenneth Cooper in the appendix to his groundbreaking 1968 book *Aerobics*.[3] Lean people in lean companies, flexible bodies for a flexible capitalism, was the maxim at play here.[4]

Corporate fitness, as this new practice was called in the United States, would allegedly benefit everyone, a win-win situation for companies, employees, and the economy. The companies supposedly reaped an excellent return on every dollar invested. First, to quote the assumptions at large at the time,[5] employees who kept themselves in good physical condition had fewer absences due to illness. Second, they were more self-confident, productive, and creative. Managers emphasized that physically active people not only looked better, but also worked better. The sports programs were intended to promote productivity, initiative, and self-management. In addition, employees would allegedly gain practice in working hard and be imbued with team spirit, while also being encouraged to identify with their company. Third, companies with a strong fitness program were claimed to enjoy an advantage when it came to attracting high-performing new employees. In an era of body worship, such a program impressed "employees more than any social security benefit," as one top manager in California boasted, according to *Der Spiegel*.[6] For him, the winning formula was: guided personal initiative and work on the self instead of fringe benefits. This was consonant with the dominant sociopolitical mantra at the turn of the twenty-first century. The new US welfare laws introduced by the Clinton administration in 1996 and, at the beginning of the new millennium, the German Hartz IV reforms, and especially the *Ich AG*, a business start-up grant intended to promote self-employment among the unemployed, marked the end of the welfare state, as previously understood, in the United States and Germany. Through these and similar reforms, governments put their faith in the "enabling welfare state," which makes citizens responsible for themselves as market actors, rather than protecting them from market risks through social safeguards.[7] Fitness – in other words, performance capacity, which each individual is responsible for attaining, and that requires ceaseless cultivation – is the core of this way of thinking and acting.

For employees, it was assumed to be at least doubly advantageous to participate in company fitness projects. First, so the argument went, this gave them the opportunity to work on both their appearance and health. In addition to physical exercise, these programs thus promoted better nutrition and weight loss, while also discouraging the consumption of harmful stimulants. Second, it was claimed, fitness training was beneficial to one's career. Those who regularly exercised and worked on themselves would develop a personality that would enable them to do better in life and in their jobs. Hence, one could sweat one's way to more than just points and bonuses. Going for a run or working on oneself in the gym held out the promise of a more rapid ascent up the career ladder, because one was generally more successful as a person. "At the invisible end of the treadmill a vice presidency may be waiting," wrote *TIME Magazine* in November 1981, as it took stock of the first decade of fitness mania.[8]

Last but not least, there was the economic or national level. From the 1950s onward, a closer connection had been made between individual health behavior and national performance. The impact of the famous and highly influential Framingham Heart Study, for example, continued to be felt scientifically, journalistically, and politically. Since Framingham, coronary heart disease had been considered a new form of socially harmful epidemic, triggered by a fatal mixture of social conditions, living environment and lifestyle, individual neglect, and bad decisions. Heart disease was regarded as an effect of changing worlds of consumption and work, overly fatty food, excessive consumption of alcohol and cigarettes, and a lack of movement in everyday life and at work. It was viewed as the illness of those who did sedentary work in offices and succumbed to the temptations of the consumer society.[9]

Few accounts of corporate fitness failed to mention the economic costs of physical inactivity and heart disease. In the United States, a total of 132 million working days were lost in 1977 due to heart attacks alone, costing nearly \$30 billion.[10] Fitness programs were meant to counteract this and extolled health promotion and disease prevention,[11] both of which had achieved an unprecedented degree of popularity. They promised to boost both individual and national performance and competitiveness (as well as the gross national product). In addition to this, from the 1970s the booming fitness and sporting goods industry was to become one of the strongest growth sectors worldwide, with substantial effects on the global economy. Over \$30 billion a year was being generated by the sale of running shoes and energy drinks, aerobics classes and dietary products, swimming goggles, stopwatches and more in the United States alone, as *TIME Magazine* reported in the early 1980s.[12]

Industrial recreation and company sports in the history of capitalism

But the managers of the late twentieth century were not the first to come up with the idea that physical activity could boost performance. Since the beginning of industrialization, physical activation and recreation have formed part of the comprehensive measures taken by manufacturers. Their goal was to organize their workers' leisure time in such a way as to increase their output. (Though given the 12-hour working days, one can scarcely refer to leisure time as such.) These measures were characteristic of the "organized capitalism" or "welfare capitalism" of the nineteenth and twentieth centuries. Its core strategy is described by the historian Brigitta Bernet as "insourcing," that is, the "productive integration [of wage laborers] into a national community and into the apparatus of a given firm."[13] This insourcing, typical of the "old" capitalism, contrasts with the outsourcing of the new, flexible capitalism so dominant in the recent past and at present. This form of capitalism largely eschews paternalistic programs. Instead, it focuses on lean people, lean companies, and a lean state, while extolling people's personal responsibility for their performance and productivity. The "freedom of self-care" has replaced the "solicitous siege."[14]

The following examination of the period from the beginning of the nineteenth to the end of the twentieth century will identify, within the coexisting realms of work, exercise, and recreation, continuities between the "old," paternalistic and "new," flexible working worlds. The thread running through both is the concern with "reasonably" rested, healthy, fit working bodies, and with boosting their productive capacity.[15] But there are also clear differences, as we will see, especially with regard to the strategy of insourcing in the "old" capitalism and outsourcing in its "new," flexible variant.

As early as the beginning of the nineteenth century, Welsh manufacturer and reformer Robert Owen already wrote that gardening, walks, and even dancing in the fresh air would turn wretched wage slaves into more content and thus more productive workers. In Owen's cotton mills in New Lanark, Scotland, these forms of physically recuperative activity were made possible by a whole package of measures. Daily working hours were reduced and better dwellings built. Owen also took up the fight against alcohol ("the most dangerous agent of destruction of labouring power," as Antonio Gramsci[16] wrote more than a century later) and prohibited its consumption on the premises. Owen wished to show that a caring approach is more humane than oppression, but above all, more efficient and thus conducive to productivity.[17]

What was already emerging here, then, was the welfare capitalism that was to take off in the second half of the nineteenth century. Physical recuperation, both active and passive, but above all in the fresh air, became part of a new overall package of company policies. These were meant to prevent workers from developing bad habits and instead help improve their health, increase their productivity, and strengthen their loyalty to the company. The focus here was on disciplining, that is, the integration of bodies into a controlled system in order to increase their vigor. Another business objective was to alleviate the growing tensions between labor and capital, while weakening the increasingly powerful unions and combating socialism.[18]

The employers, then, were trying to guide their workers' way of life, even when the working day was over and they had left the premises. The goal was to fence in family life and leisure time in such a way as to make them conducive to job performance. Often, employers' engagement had a Christian or Protestant angle, and in the United Kingdom and the United States they collaborated with organizations such as the Young Men's Christian Association, which became more and more influential as the nineteenth century progressed. Less alcohol and gambling, more sport and edification, were the goals shared by both groups. The lower classes (and, in the United States, growing numbers of non-Anglo-Saxon and non-Protestant immigrants from the 1880s) were supposed to learn a "moral way of life." Physical fitness and competitive sports were regarded as the expression of this lifestyle, as well as a promising and cost-effective way to promote it.[19]

Soon, large-scale company facilities were created that aimed at more than just increasing production. They facilitated insourcing, that is, the comprehensive integration of workers into the corporate body. One American flagship project was implemented by the Pullman Palace Car Company, a driver of industrialization during the railroad boom with its sleeper cars. In the early 1880s, the company built an entire workers' town south of Chicago, partly in reaction to the strikes and worker unrest of the 1870s, which mainly affected the railway industry. Pullman, as the town was named, was intended to take the wind out of the sails of the union movement. Similar projects existed in various European countries. Saltaire was established in northern England as early as 1851, and some time later, on the eve of World War I, Siemensstadt was founded in Berlin.[20] To stop the workers from drinking and gambling, and indulging in other popular but unproductive and supposedly immoral forms of recreation, these settlements were to offer a comprehensive range of amenities: libraries, a zoo, gardens, and a park with recreational and sports facilities. Projects such as the new town of Pullman were part of a broad social movement to establish public parks and playgrounds, one that gained traction as a result of the body and sport mania of the late nineteenth century. Over the years, Pullman's sports programs became increasingly important to the company. A specially created Pullman Athletic Association organized mass and competitive sports, as well as company teams under the firm's aegis.[21]

While the so-called Pullman paternalism was struck by crisis in the 1890s and this specific project failed, "industrial recreation" in general now boomed. In Germany, this mainly took the form of company clubs, reflecting the typical German *Verein* structure.[22] On the eve of World War I, more than 230 companies in the United States had programs that encouraged physical activity during lunch breaks or after work. Most of these programs were aimed at the broad mass of workers and focused on bowling and baseball. Local politicians often acted as the companies' partners, and more than 3,000 public sports facilities were established in parks and playgrounds in just under 500 US cities.[23] In Germany, after hesitant beginnings in the German Empire, industrial recreation became more significant in the Weimar Republic, in which "a sound physical culture" was increasingly regarded as the "basis of a rational way of working." The promotion of sport by companies and the public authorities was a matter of "preventive welfare," as Berlin mayor Gustav Böß emphasized in 1921.[24]

Physical exercise and industrial recreation interacted with the development of a new understanding of the body in industrial societies. Since the 1840s, humanity had found itself living in the thermodynamic age, which understood the body as a site of energy conversion and thus as a "human motor."[25] Everything now revolved around strength or power relative to work, and "labor power" became the measure by which one might relate the performance of humans and machines. This almost inevitably led to the key question of how to conserve labor power and prevent fatigue. It was no longer laziness but fatigue that was increasingly considered the main cause of non-work. Manufacturers, as well as physiology and the science of work, which studied the working body, power, and performance, sought ways to counteract fatigue, with these disciplines becoming leading sciences in the second half of the nineteenth century.[26] Before 1860, not a single study had appeared on the fatigue of the human motor, yet by the end of the century this topic – like the productivity of labor – was on everyone's lips. This was especially true of muscle fatigue, but also of mental fatigue and the then ubiquitous exhaustion-induced neurasthenia.[27]

The fear of fatigue in an industrial, work-oriented society, and the modern discovery of body optimization and fitness training (as described in chapter 2) thus went hand in hand. Anxieties over fatigue were also consonant with the idea of competition as a natural necessity, a notion closely linked with Darwin and his reception. Only those who learned to master fatigue would succeed in a world characterized by competition and the survival of the fittest. And here fitness increasingly meant self-improvement rather than aptness.[28] Soon, in addition to exercise, a whole arsenal of knowledge, techniques, and tools became available to minimize fatigue and increase productivity. Research was conducted, for example, on the worker's diet, which was now imagined as the supply of energy to the working body.[29]

Recreation and moderation, regulation and exercise were key strategies for combating fatigue and increasing physical performance, above all work performance. Exercise, it was thought, would optimize the use of energy, because a fit body performed activities more efficiently and needed less energy for the same movement than an unfit one. How widespread and how complex the interest was in understanding individual movement sequences and work processes in detail is also evident in the photographs taken by Eadweard Muybridge and Etienne-Jules Marey. Marey took a keen interest in physical exercises and, among other things, photographed the 1900 Olympic Games in Paris.[30]

Muybridge's picture series from the 1880s break down a sequence of movements, such as the planing performed by a carpenter, into numerous individual moments (see figure 5). The fact that Muybridge – when his models were men – chiefly depicted work processes or sports practices illustrates once again how closely sport and work were

Figure 5   A carpenter planing. Photogravure after Eadweard Muybridge, 1887, Wellcome Collection, London
Source: Wellcome Library no. 27833i

intertwined, with the body as interface. It also shows how gendered sport and work were. Although many women worked in factories, Muybridge's working models are all male. He generally shows women washing themselves and tending to their bodies, or bashfully turning their naked bodies away from the camera.[31]

But the goal was to optimize overall productivity not just through analysis and exercise, but also by ensuring that each worker focused on individual work stages and performed the smallest possible number of movements. The division of labor had been extolled as a means of increasing productivity since Adam Smith and the beginnings of political economy in the late eighteenth century. Some 135 years later, the division of labor was perfected in the system created by American engineer Frederick Winslow Taylor.[32] Through precise observation and analysis of individual movement sequences and work steps, their breakdown into the smallest possible elements with the help of a stop-watch, and their recomposition on the assembly line, the labor power within the factory-as-body was to be optimally utilized. This approach was in fact to become the defining characteristic of an entire era, from the turn of the century to the 1970s. The terms Taylorism and Fordism – named after Henry Ford, who introduced the assembly line at his car factories in Flint, Michigan, and who also perfected mass production and welfare capitalism – not only designate a mode of production, but an entire economic and social order.[33]

Here the close connection between work and sport is crucial, and has two key facets. First, contemporary exercise and work experts explicitly emphasized the close kinship of work and sports practices. "Today the same principles [as with respect to the optimization of work processes] apply to the design of exercises," as a text from 1927 underlined. Taylor himself, as it happens, was an enthusiastic sportsman and characterized his system as the sportification of work.[34] Second, "physical exercises," from exercise breaks in the workplace to sports days organized by company clubs, were intended to counteract the specific form of fatigue induced by repetitive factory work. Sporting official Carl Diem commended sport to companies as a means of reducing sickness and accident costs, delaying disability, increasing production, and strengthening people's "intellectual defenses against sedition and mental defenses against the soullessness of the Taylorized work process."[35]

The new class of white-collar workers

It was not only the perfection of factory work and a specific use of the working body, but also increasing accounting, administrative, financial, and management activities that typified the economic and social order of Fordism. The new class of white-collar workers (as opposed to blue-collar workers) had begun to develop in the second half of the nineteenth century, and in a comparable way in Germany and the United States. White-collar workers formed a class that the theorists of capitalism, from Adam Smith to Karl Marx, had not envisaged.[36] The concept of white-collar work is vague, encompassing all sorts of quite different employees, from female office workers to male top managers.[37] Yet all these employees are united by the fact that they work predominantly in a sitting position and, therefore, do not keep their bodies in good shape through their work. This was already being discussed as a problem around 1900, especially in relation to men. The enfeebled body of the neurasthenic, male white-collar employee became a symbol of the threats and crises besetting modern societies. The latter were, after all, defined by movement, acceleration, and high performance. In the cage-like offices of the modern work world, however, "pen-pushers" risked becoming "physically unresistant cerebral cripples," as German writer and rowing fan Richard Nordhausen hyperbolized. The white-collar employee soon attracted the interest of numerous sociologists and public intellectuals, from Siegfried Kracauer to C. Wright Mills. This category of worker was to become one of the characteristic forms of subject in modernity.[38]

It was not just the shirts and collars that were white. The crisis-stricken bodies of this group of workers were also thought of as white – and male. Thus, the diagnosed lack of physical activity primarily affected those bodies that were believed to have been made to transform nature into culture, in the name of liberty, progress, and civilization. Katherine Blackford – a US expert in personnel management and industrial psychology, who would probably be called a life coach today – was one of numerous voices in this debate. She and many others emphasized that the white male body was not only meant to constantly reach new heights of sporting prowess, but also to clear forests, build roads, raise armies, conquer continents, erect buildings, develop machines of all kinds, build industries, and trade goods across the world.[39]

To be clear: henceforth, sports programs for blue-collar workers as known since the beginnings of organized capitalism continued to exist. But the fitness mania affected white-collar more than blue-collar workers. It was their bodies that were considered beset by crisis and in need of an antidote. In addition, calls to engage in physical activity were directed primarily at men, though women worked in offices too. If, as contemporaries believed, "the history of civilization" was "the history of an improving physique," then they were primarily thinking of the male physique (and thus of a male-dominated civilization). The male body was understood as a body engaged in production, while the female body was primarily geared toward reproduction and desire. The new world of work, with its bookkeepers, administrators, and managers, all of whom did office work without strengthening their bodies, thus represented a pressing societal problem, probably an even greater threat than the repetitive work on factory assembly lines.[40] Bourgeois men now began to exercise their bodies to make and keep them fit. Especially in Germany, white-collar employees often exercised in their own clubs and associations, or at least in their own departments, keeping their distance from the working class and the sport of blue-collar workers.[41]

The economic crisis of the 1930s caused the anxious discourse centered on sedentary employees to die down temporarily.[42] At the same time, the performance, sports, and body fetish attained a new level of intensity in Nazi Germany. Nazism radicalized the modern ethos of bodily performance, informed by the racist idea of a single *Volk*. Industrial recreation was brought into line with Nazi ideology, massively expanded, and geared toward strengthening the biopolitical ideal of the *Volkskörper*, "the people's body," while also constructing the imagined *Volksgemeinschaft*, "the people's community," as powerful and productive. The task of the *Deutsche Arbeitsfront*, the German Labor Front, by far the largest Nazi mass organization, was to provide an institutional home for all "working Germans of brain and brawn." The mass sport fostered by the *Deutsche Arbeitsfront* and its *Kraft durch Freude* ("Strength through Joy") organization was supposed to "eliminate excess fat in our people," as its head Robert Ley put it. It was to "massage away big bellies, restore flexibility," and thus enable "every single person" to achieve peak performance, providing "the greatest benefit to the people's community."[43]

In the United States of the 1930s, the sedentary white-collar worker also became a minor problem. This was because (as we have seen) the great depression was one featuring hungry bodies and a weakened collective body, whose recovery would supposedly depend, above all else, on the strong (blue-collar) worker's body, dedicated to serving the American nation.[44] At the same time, the vast majority of corporations lacked the money to invigorate their blue- and white-collar workers through company sports programs, and in view of the widespread hardship, food aid would probably have made more sense. Yet in the course of World War II, corporate sports programs gained momentum as the US economy rebounded, and then experienced a final renaissance, in this form, in the 1950s. In that decade, more than 900 companies were members of the National Industrial Recreation Association, a body founded in 1941 by 11 corporations to revive American corporate sports; in 1953, a total of 30,000 corporations spent some $800 million on their workers' sports programs.[45]

However, in the consumerist mecca of the United States and, a few years later, the Germany of the economic miracle, public and scholarly attention focused less on sports programs for blue-collar workers and more than ever on sedentary white-collar workers. As early as 1930, Siegfried Kracauer had stated that "hundreds of thousands of salaried employees throng the streets of Berlin daily" as well as the modern working world of the office. In 1951, sociologist C. Wright Mills wrote in his book *White Collar* that the United States had, over the previous half-century, become a nation of white-collar workers, who now made up the majority of the working population. These employees preferred to wear gray flannel suits and at most casual wear, but neither overalls nor fashionable sportswear. They drove or took suburban trains to the office, but never went to work by bike, and they tended to sit in front of the TV cradling a highball after work, rather than heading to the gym with an energy drink (it was not until the 1970s that such drinks entered the market). On both sides of the Atlantic, physicians soon identified middle-aged, sedentary white-collar workers as the prototypes of an affluently overweight consumer society increasingly suffering from heart disease and diminishing performance.[46]

Sociologists and other intellectuals issued dire warnings that the man in the gray suit was more than just a health problem. He stood, they asserted, for the slackening of modern society, and particularly American society, which now lacked the very dynamism and forward momentum that had once made it great. C. Wright Mills with *White Collar*, David Riesman with *The Lonely Crowd* from 1950, and William Whyte with *Organization Man* from 1956 lent profile to the sociology of the white-collar worker and thus to an international field of research that we can trace back to the aforementioned Siegfried Kracauer. A broad public discussed its exponents' hypotheses with growing agitation. In the figure of the conformist white-collar worker, with a weak heart and no thirst for action, fears of the dwindling productivity of the capitalist individual fused with concerns about the loss of social dynamism and strength. It was not the "hearts of men" as a whole, but above all the hearts of white-collar workers, that stood center-stage in this diagnosis of societal crisis.[47]

Male passivity was identified as one of the greatest problems of post-war white-collar society, symbolizing the aforementioned lack of drive. Letting things happen instead of making them happen, being acted upon rather than taking action – in the open-plan offices of the twentieth century, the white-collar worker was described by C. Wright Mills as a mere cog in the great wheel of administration. The routine processes involved, he contended, amounted to Taylorism without a factory.[48] The Cold War made the conformist clones of white-collar society even more menacing: the United States was, after all, seen as a haven of liberal individualism in the struggle against a communist dictatorship that stymied all individuality and initiative. (The other side, meanwhile, imagined itself as a working society, celebrating "heroes of work" and "socialist womanhood," whose avatars were renowned for their capacity to knuckle down.)[49] Seen from the perspective of Western middle-class gender patterns, a passivity of female white-collar workers seemed unproblematic, because it was believed that women were naturally passive. Male passivity, on the other hand, undermined the gendered self-image of modern society, the nation's productivity, and its ready ability to cope with challenges. Coupled with constant work-related anxiety, subservience in the office was also finding expression in lethargy in the bedroom, as contemporary observers warned.[50]

Hence, being a white-collar worker was the opposite of fitness: members of this group were passive rather than active, conformist and ailing rather than autonomous and powerful. Yet fitness training as a remedy was a strange and at best amusing idea for most men in the 1950s. The idea that it was beneficial to work up a sweat played a negligible part in their concept of life. Initially, the occasional source of inspiration here and there did little to change this picture. In the United States, TV star Jack LaLanne had been demonstrating various exercises on the small screen since 1953, showing his mostly female audience what to do (and what they should get their partners to do) in order to "feel better, look better, so you can live longer."[51] Competitive sport was not of interest to middle-aged men at all, except as spectators. It offered them a projection screen, displaying the thirst for action, heroism, and career opportunities that were usually mere illusions in real life, as in the case of football for Arthur Miller's traveling salesman Willy Loman and his son Biff.[52]

At the same time, the problem of clogged coronary arteries migrated from medical publications into an ever wider public consciousness.[53] Only temporarily were they discussed as an exclusive, elite phenomenon afflicting stress-stricken executives, and more in Germany than in the United States, despite the fact that German observers were keen to highlight the supposedly American roots of the problem and of the diagnosis of "manager's disease."[54] In the United States, it was essentially assumed that while pressing deadlines and too many responsibilities were certainly stressful, it was above all overconsumption and lack of exercise that were behind the heart failure of white-collar society.[55]

In 1959, men's magazine *Esquire*, already a critic of the alleged waning of America and its men, published a guide to the art of keeping fit. This volume shows quite clearly what working on one's fitness was taken to mean in the late 1950s. In a solicitous tone, the book informs readers about various health issues, first and foremost the heart, insomnia, fatness, and sex in middle age (a topic that tended to come up, with a nudge and a wink, when it came to men's health). *Esquire* also offered strategies aimed at resolving these problems, chiefly the right diet and the right amount of rest and relaxation. Readers were given less encouragement to exert themselves physically, however, and were certainly not urged to engage in systematic workouts. After all, cardiologists at the time warned of the potentially detrimental effects of fitness training and "exercisitis."[56]

"Corporate fitness," or: Getting fit for work – Part II

Soon, however, health and fitness brochures for male office workers appeared more frequently and recommended a different, more intense approach to physical exercise.[57] The fitness hype that then kicked off in the 1970s in liberal, competitive societies was not limited to humans and their bodies. Becoming and remaining lean, flexible, and fit was the maxim at play here, and numerous companies also began to adhere to it. This approach promised to help companies get ahead amid the increasingly fierce competition typical of what were often "new markets."[58] "Watch that waistline!" urged *Forbes Magazine* in 1970, with the cover picture showing a pot-bellied, middle-aged manager on the weighing scales. Many companies had grown fat rather than building muscle, the text claimed. The 1970s, it went on, would be the decade of slimming down.[59]

The following history of the 1970s economic crisis and sociopolitical changes has been told many times. My goal here is to recapitulate it, relate it to the history of fitness, and show how, in the late twentieth century, "breathlessness [became] the normal state of affairs."[60]

The 1970s spelled the end of the postwar boom and economic miracle, as the oil crises of 1973 and 1979/80 brought sharply rising energy costs and calls for belt-tightening even in the United States. The years of plenty were over for now. Severe inflation, coupled with declining and even negative growth rates, went hand in hand with a production crisis and rising unemployment, a phenomenon that had been largely forgotten since the Great Depression of the 1930s. The crisis of the 1970s and its consequences have been described as a "structural break" in the modernity of industrial society. Perhaps structural change would be a more appropriate term, but in any event the 1970s ushered in the end of Fordism, and thus of an entire era.[61]

The political and economic response was: more market, more competition, and less redistribution. Gradually, liberal societies abandoned the vision of a Great Society or welfare state, and instead paid homage to the lean state, keen to rid itself of excess weight. For companies as

well, the priority was to slim down and become as fit and flexible as a
yoga-trained body, in order to survive in an environment of accelerat-
ing competition. Lean production was the new mantra. This started
once again in the car industry, but unlike the assembly line, it was not
Ford in Michigan that led the way. The pioneer this time was Toyota
in Japan, where, as observed in the United States of the early 1970s,
companies had been exhorting their employees to participate in fitness
training for some time. Other Japanese strategies were just-in-time
production, a shift away from warehousing, and the streamlining of
the overall production process and apparatus. Outsourcing rather than
insourcing was the formula underpinning this renewal of capitalism.
These changes were integrated into increasingly global economic,
investment, and trade structures.[62]

These changes affected the world of work in several ways. First, many
observers marveled at the Japanese work ethic, and at Japanese workers'
identification with job and company, which sometimes extended to
karōshi, death by overwork. Second, the Toyota-style manufacturing
process reduced the importance of the assembly line to production.
More important now was working in teams, with flatter hierarchies,
shared responsibility, and a higher degree of personal responsibility
for the success of the group. This was in keeping with the new boom
in project work, which was soon to be transformed from a critical
experiment pursued by the left-wing alternative scene into the core
working format of flexible capitalism. As we have seen, flat hierarchies
and shared responsibility are very well suited to inducing people to
voluntarily work overtime, even to the point of self-exploitation. It
should be borne in mind, however, that even in flexible capitalism, class
differences and coercive relationships are omnipresent, especially in the
low-wage sector.[63] At the same time, thirdly, especially in the low-paid
sector, the production of labor-intensive goods has increasingly been
relocated to sites where wages are lower, unions are weak, and workers
have few rights. This may be Bangladesh, but it may also be Romania or
North Carolina.[64] In the industrialized countries of the global North,
this meant fewer and fewer jobs in the manufacturing sector (for example in the American "Manufacturing Belt" or Germany's Ruhr region),
the end of "standard employment conditions" for many male employees, and the emergence of temporary work (especially in the low-wage

sector). The proportion of those working in the service sector also grew, with ever fewer of them enjoying the traditional status of fully employed white-collar workers under labor and insurance laws.

It is not the white-collar worker that embodies the key subject type in flexible capitalism, but rather the "enterprising self." This does not mean that all of us have become entrepreneurs in the classical sense, but rather that the enterprising self rose to become the leitmotif within the wide-ranging "economization of the social."[65] The *homo oeconomicus* became a formative social figure, because the challenge posed to individuals was to optimize their chances of success and prove themselves on the market. It was no longer the "blue-collar" or "white-collar" worker, but rather the "worker-as-entrepreneur"[66] that represented the new ideal type of the labor market, epitomized in Germany by the Ich-AG – the individual as company, a concept supported by the German government, for which the ground was laid discursively and politically from the 1980s onward, and which was then introduced in 2003. The Ich-AG condenses the requirements of autonomization, responsibilization, and flexibilization, which now faced companies and individuals alike. The externally controlled blue- and white-collar worker of Fordism became the enterprising self of flexible capitalism. Its sphere of action extends far beyond the field of work, to encompass human existence in its entirety. As "life entrepreneurs,"[67] we are called upon to constantly see ourselves, and prove ourselves, as subjects capable of effective action. Here the importance of fitness is evident. The fit body, after all, advertises itself as the best evidence of entrepreneurial agency and competence within a human life. Actively and self-responsibly, the human being is supposed to take their life into their own hands and work on themself to maximize their self-esteem, health, and performance.[68]

In case of doubt, one should allow oneself to be assisted in this endeavor by those whose knowledge is based chiefly on their greater experience. The coach has thus become a key figure in the age of fitness. Almost two centuries ago, a coach was someone who helped students at elite universities navigate their way through their exams. In the late nineteenth century, he migrated into the world of sport, before finally becoming deeply embedded in the working world and beyond at the end of the twentieth century. The coach, then, is another piece of the puzzle, one that illustrates the close entanglement of body and capitalism. In addition, from this point on, trainers in gyms became more than sports coaches. They not only helped train the body, but acted as "confessors, entertainers, whip-wielders and salesmen, psychologists and idols." This is how *Der Spiegel* described the functions of the coach when he appeared in Germany at the end of the 1990s.[69]

The modern debate on fitness and work had been going on in Germany for over a quarter of a century at the time. In the early 1970s, it had started haltingly, and was mostly still firmly focused on the United States and what was happening there.[70] In these early years, the West German version of corporate fitness did not yet truly reflect the idea of the enterprising self or the new economy; this was not the neoliberal fast lane. It was more like a mixture of George Orwell and the notorious German administrative state. To be sure, incentives for self-management and rewards already played a role. For example, those who completed one hundred exercises found in a brochure entitled "Get Fit in the Office" received a pin and a certificate from the German Sport Association (DSB): push-ups on the edge of one's desk, standing up and sitting down quickly, or rotating a telephone book around one's hips. However, if a company wanted to improve its employees' fitness through a major campaign, it would have to get not only the DSB on board, but also the unions, the employers' association and, if at all possible, the legislature. Even then, according to *Der Spiegel*, it was still vital to combat resistance from "left-wing sport-haters," who denounced corporate fitness as a perfidious strategy pursued by capital to achieve the maximum exploitation of the working class. West German companies, meanwhile, were still extolling gymnastics broadcasts on television screens in open-plan offices, quasi-mandatory fitness stations en route to the cafeteria, and mass gymnastics breaks, familiar from Japan, as innovative ideas. At the same time, however, West German observers underlined the need to come up with more individualistic approaches, given the country's past and its conflict with the mass societies of socialism.[71]

About a decade later, around 1980, the tone and emphasis began to change when it came to the topic of fitness, work, and success. We should understand these shifts as part and parcel of the global flexibilization of capitalism. Their form, intensity, and pace varied in different countries, partly depending on how persistent the structures of the welfare state were. In the 1980s, fitness debates revolved, for example, around the renaissance of the bicycle, which returned as a means of transportation in everyday life, while also serving managers, in its ultralight and ultramodern variants, in their free-time pursuit of fitness. Trendy sports such as triathlon were now a hot topic as well, providing a new challenge for the better-paid "pen-pushers" in particular. At the time, US magazines were packed with articles about the cyclical rise and fall of recreational fitness trends focused on the experience and performance of the body. Being fit and looking fit were now a matter of common sense, representing health and performance as beneficial to one's career. Being fat, on the other hand, was considered the "kiss of death" in the competitive job market. Fat people were often regarded as "second-class citizens," and were pushed out of the working world, as *Der Spiegel* wrote in a 1978 report on the fledgling Fat Rights Movement in the United States. A few years later, in Germany too it had become a matter of course that "those who look 'good' are more likely to get good and lucrative jobs." Some observers captured this in the striking diagnosis of a "new lifestyle racism," which recognized the humanity only of those who were healthy or looked the way healthy people were imagined to look.[72] Everyone else, they asserted, was being pushed to the margins of society. The kinship of racism and fat phobia, as invoked by the term "lifestyle racism," consists not only in their discriminatory practices and policies, but also in the fact that both operate via the deceptive self-evidence of the visible.

In the 1990s, the foci of corporate fitness shifted again. A new field of action was activity outings, such as company cycle rides or rafting. In addition to physical exercise (and of course fitness was, at least to a degree, a prerequisite for activity trips), teambuilding rose to prominence. Sweating, overcoming obstacles, and mastering challenges together was thought to strengthen team spirit. Company activity trips of this kind could now be based in hotels that laid on a bespoke program. There, in addition to exercise, the emphasis was on self-realization courses and the consumption of wholefoods (which were new at that time). Fitness, according to *Der Spiegel*, had now become a "catch-all term," under which everything that "has even the slightest connection with physical exercise" was subsumed.[73]

At the end of the twentieth century, so-called corporate health management had joined the now rather antiquated practice of company sport. Corporate efforts to promote health through self-responsibility and preventative self-care, then, had largely supplanted welfare and disciplining.[74] Collective sports outings were just one of many possible measures and strategies that companies formulated to strengthen their employees' personal resources and thus help their human capital self-optimize. From bowls of fruit in the office through working groups to health advisors and counselors: the goal was to provide everything that might increase wellbeing and motivation, and thus enhance performance. This could take the form of a voucher for the local gym. For some time, gyms in the United States had been presenting themselves as new temples of postmodernity, sites where the body has become the object of worship. Gyms also transformed into oases of wellness, where fitness was understood as a service. By cooperating not only with health insurance companies but also with gyms, companies hoped to set their final gymnastics-free zone in motion. Absences due to illness continued to decline (partly because many people could no longer afford to be off sick), and for large companies it even made financial sense to install their own gyms. Most companies, however, took a more flexible approach, negotiating special rates at a nearby or chain gym.[75]

Breathlessness as par for the course

The desire to enable the working body to perform better through the use of exercise and sport is not unique to flexible capitalism. This is evident in the organized or welfare capitalism of the nineteenth and twentieth centuries, company sports programs and industrial recreation, and the relationship between sport and work under the Nazi regime. It is also reflected in the reception of the risk factor model in East Germany, a construct that became inscribed in health policies on both sides of the Iron Curtain from the 1960s onward. It may have been the greater centralization of state socialist societies that initially made it even easier to implement the risk factor model within health policy in East than in West Germany.[76]

One key difference between the organized capitalism of the nineteenth century and the flexible capitalism of the late twentieth and early twenty-first centuries is the main target group of measures and strategies, with a shift away from the blue- to the white-collar worker, though ever fewer of the latter enjoy the benefits traditionally associated with that status. As we have seen, the measures and strategies involved have also shifted away from insourcing toward outsourcing.[77] At most, the paternalistic programs of welfare capitalism are present today in remnant form, and have diminished more in the United States than in most other Western countries. It is more common to nudge the "workers-as-entrepreneurs" of the present to pursue voluntary self-care, and in the United States conservative liberals assail even this as state interventionism and a restriction of personal liberties.[78]

In the age of fitness as self-care, resistance has become even more difficult. At the end of the day, we all know that our body – our health and fitness – is our greatest asset. Hence, we feel the need to cultivate, nurture, and hone this physical capital, so it can serve convincingly as both precondition for, and expression of, the capacity for autonomy and performance, in the job market and in life in general. Thus, the right to one's body has turned into a responsibility and even a duty. Being fat is seen as a sign of failure to uphold this responsibility, as a failure to carry out this duty. Body fat thus contributes to the production of social inequalities in a new and different way and is becoming entangled with the established categories of gender, skin color, and class (and more besides). These are less static than they used to be, but they are not necessarily any less powerful. In other words, those who are fat have poorer prospects on the job market, and this is even more true of those who are fat, poorly educated, and lower-class (with these criteria often being interdependent). Quite obviously, today being fat is no longer a sign of prosperity, but chiefly a marker of poverty.[79]

In neoliberal times, preventive self-care is the task of each and every one of us. Fitness practices, and even relaxation methods originating in South and East Asia, serve to bolster resilience, and it is surely no coincidence that this concept, derived from materials science, has boomed within the body politics of the early twenty-first century. It has become imperative to make oneself and one's body more flexible, resilient, resistant, and elastic, and to guard against exhaustion, by training the body and finding the right ratio of stimulation to relaxation.[80] The principle of elasticity permeates everyday life, extending into the spandex clothing of the fitness movement.[81] Spandex lays everything bare: strength and weakness, muscles and midriff bulges. This makes it the material par excellence for flexible bodies in flexible capitalism, in which breathlessness has become par for the course (even if the motto of the German get-fit movement of the 1970s was "run without wheezing"). The efforts made here are not primarily meant to serve the nation or religion, let alone a racially imagined "national community," but are chiefly intended to advance one's own progress.

4

HAVING SEX

"Performance plus" through the "phallus pill"

On May 18, 1998, *Der Spiegel* diagnosed the onset of a "new sexual revolution." A few days before, Viagra had been approved for sale in the United States, and from September men would have access to "erections on prescription" in Europe as well. The new "wonder pill" was tremendously successful. Shortly after it appeared on the market as a medicinal drug, physicians in the United States were issuing around 40,000 prescriptions every day,[1] with a black market flourishing on both sides of the Atlantic. Within a very short time, Viagra had made Pfizer the second-largest pharmaceutical company in the world, with expected stock returns already doubling the year before Viagra gained approval. The reason was simple: Viagra promised nothing less than an end to male impotence, whose epidemic proportions had been lamented by experts and the media for 25 years. US studies stated that 50 percent of men over 40 were affected by "erectile dysfunction," to quote the medical term that had been in circulation since the 1970s and that became firmly established with the advent of Viagra. This little pill promised to provide a simple remedy, with no need for a penile prosthesis, vacuum pump, injections in erectile tissue, or lengthy therapy sessions with a psychologist. An on-demand pill was more effective than all previously

known remedies added together, at least if the goal was to achieve an
erect penis apt for acts of penetration. "Yes, VIAGRA works!", cheered
the cover of *TIME Magazine* in May 1998, while German urologist
Hartmut Porst declared in *Der Spiegel* that this "pill improves sexual
performance decisively." Self-tests had confirmed it: "The erection is
harder, kicks in faster, and lasts longer. Almost every man who would
like to be sexually active will want to try this pill."[2]

Viagra stands for sex in the age of fitness. Harder, faster, and longer-
lasting are the criteria identified by the aforementioned urologist in
an interview with respect to the successful "sexual performance" of a
pepped-up male body. In 1998 – the year of its approval as a medicine –
sex researcher Leonore Tiefer was already writing critically that Viagra
was not only meant to help unwell men, but above all represented
notions of energy, success, strength, and straightforward problem solv-
ing. And, of course, the hardening of the body.[3] In Germany, too,
opinion was divided as to the sexual and social implications of this pill.
Der Spiegel was impressed with the sexual fitness that Viagra promised,
but feared that "performance sex" would supplant tenderness. In the
same article, Viagra was praised as a medicinal remedy for the suffering sick and criticized as "penile doping" that was designed solely to
enhance male performance.

Yet these two interpretations of Viagra, as medical therapy and
performance-enhancer, are less far apart than they may seem at first
glance. This is because health and performance merge in the concept
of fitness. Fitness, after all, is viewed as health achieved through one's
own efforts, and thus as a prerequisite for success and recognition
in an achievement-oriented society. Both success and recognition can
also be achieved or squandered through sex. And yet, sex and an erect
penis have long ceased to symbolize solely the male ability to conceive
offspring. "In an era in which the individual proves themself chiefly
through performance," wrote *Der Spiegel* editor Susanne Weingarten
of Viagra as the latest therapy for boosting masculinity in a phallus-
oriented fitness society, "a limp dick in bed is every bit as harmful to
one's self-esteem as flab, stuttering, or unsportsmanlike behavior."[4]
In line with this, Viagra was just one of many medicines that began to
flood the market as so-called lifestyle drugs. And these were in turn part
of a whole arsenal of products and measures geared toward so-called

body enhancement. At the dawn of the new millennium, *New York Magazine* stated that "using prescription drugs to work a little harder, sleep a little better, relax a little faster, has become a given in the city's mainstream." More and more pharmaceutical products were intended not to combat disease, but to make life a little better and render the individual somewhat more successful in their pursuit of happiness. The body is part of the "upgrade culture."[5]

Many of these remedies aim to optimize the body, and are geared toward norms that individuals struggle to uphold, often due to advancing age. Age-related changes are often considered to be impairments to wellbeing and health handicaps, which the successful person in the age of fitness has a duty to combat. Thus, increasing body fat and, among men, thinning hair and a limper penis, are the objects of a *dispositif* of fitness and health. At the same time, they have become the target of self-responsible action and medical intervention. The terminology used brings out the medicalization of everyday life and aging. A product such as Xenical is intended to combat "obesity" rather than fatness, Regaine is for "androgenetic alopecia" rather than hair loss, and Viagra is a remedy for "erectile dysfunction." The latter pill is intended to help men achieve erections and penetration as the best indicator of ageless, healthy masculinity.[6]

Viagra points up several facets of fitness in neoliberalism. First, it draws attention to the meanings of sex in a society that is body-oriented, one that requires motivation and performance, and their constant demonstration. Viagra leads us into the manifold entanglements of fitness, body and sex, gender and age, but also skin color and sexual preference. When Viagra hit the market in 1998, it helped to bring male sexuality and physicality more clearly back to the center of societal attention, and it made a rather white and heteronormative impression. The shock of the AIDS epidemic had, after all, endowed gay sex with a renewed stigma.[7] Viagra, then, is much more than "just" a pharmaceutical product. It is deeply woven into social patterns and power relations, their alteration and consolidation.

Second, Viagra directs our attention toward bodies' relationship with things and substances, and thus toward everyday doping in the competitive society. As a pill for body optimization, Viagra shows how much success or failure is not only down to a supposedly autonomous individual, but also to factors that are, in the first instance, located outside of individuals and their bodies. After all, the wonder pill must first be invented, produced, procured, and swallowed, that is, supplied to the body from outside. At the same time, it is clear that individuals and bodies cannot exist outside of a network of forces that make certain decisions, practices, and enhancements possible in the first place. This is particularly striking in the field of sex, since sexual performance can only be partially improved through training.[8] Third, if we look back as far as the nineteenth century, we find that the optimization of the body with respect to sex is no invention of recent history (despite all the historical differences). Viagra, in other words, has a backstory dating back to well before 1998, while also making its own, novel impact. It has stirred up new expectations and ideas and become inscribed in the body-oriented, achievement-oriented, and competitive society of the late twentieth and early twenty-first centuries.

Hard at any age

Viagra's first figurehead was the then 74-year-old Bob Dole. Dole had been a senator for Kansas for many years. But in the United States and beyond he was mainly known as the Republican candidate for president in the 1996 election. His opponent was the then 50-year-old, still boyish incumbent Bill Clinton. Clinton already had a reputation as a notorious adulterer at the point when, in 1998, his lust for young women became the subject of hearings before the House Judiciary Committee. At the time, conversations in the United States frequently revolved around the Lewinsky Affair and the "Oral Office." Sex and presidential potency dominated the US news, even more than in the days of John F. Kennedy. In this sexually charged social and political climate, the aging Bob Dole raved about Viagra on *Larry King Live*, arguably the United States' most famous and successful political talk show. Dole had contracted prostate cancer in 1991, suffered from impotence, had already tested Viagra in its test phase, and then became Pfizer's first major brand ambassador, often with his wife Elizabeth at his side. Generally speaking, in fact, heterosexual couples over the age of 60 who did not want to (and should not have to) do without sex in their later years were at the center of Viagra's first advertising campaign. The "new elderly," as they had been called in Germany for a few years, were highlighted as a target group. The idea here was that people should age positively and "successfully"; they should be well-off and, enjoying excellent health, partake of the pleasures of the consumer and leisure society. Sex was as much a part of this as traveling or attending the theater. Although Viagra's ad campaigns were aimed primarily at middle-class, older, white, heterosexual men, Viagra also promised their wives greater satisfaction through better sex. And the advertising campaigns launched to promote Viagra left no room for doubt that women's sexual satisfaction was achieved through male penetration.[9]

At every opportunity, Pfizer sought to make it clear that Viagra was responding to a serious health problem. In this way, the pharmaceutical company latched on to the discourse on self-responsible, health-promoting behavior and the pursuit of overall wellbeing. At the same time, it tried to distance itself from the long tradition of shady quacks seeking to grow rich by offering remedies for male impotence. Pfizer thus also created a medically justified need for its own product. This, together with the funding of medical research, is a key strategy in the marketing of pharmaceutical products.[10]

For Viagra, an important reference point in scientific research was the Massachusetts Male Aging Study (MMAS). Published in 1994, it found that 52 percent of men between the ages of 40 and 70 suffered from erectile dysfunction of varying intensity, from minimal to complete. In the course of clinical research into Viagra, scientists then developed the International Index of Erectile Function (IIEF), which has been translated into 32 languages and has become the global standard. An erection was not something that men had or did not have: its quality and reliability could now be placed on a scale. And for more than half of men over 40, this scale showed that their "sexual health" could be improved. Age, the Massachusetts study asserted, was the biggest risk factor in erectile dysfunction, ahead of heart disease, high blood pressure, diabetes, depression, smoking, and other factors.

In an era when active and "successful" aging was on everyone's lips, this was information that was bound to receive broad attention. The data suggested by extrapolation that 30 million men in the United States were affected, so erectile dysfunction could be described as a true epidemic. While other studies produced different findings, they received less attention. Pfizer's interests were well served if every instance of evening flaccidity was regarded as erectile dysfunction requiring medical intervention. The men affected, for their part, were mostly relieved if their psyche, personality, and thus they themselves, were not identified as the problem leading to impotence. It was manifestly easier to deal with an organic condition affecting the regulation of blood flow (which is where Viagra came in).[11] Impotence sounds like debasement to the ears of many men, places a question mark over the man as a whole, and requires him to deal with himself. Erectile dysfunction, on the other hand, is a diagnosis concerning a single part of the body, whose functionality could usually be restored simply by taking a pill.[12]

Soon Viagra's target group was no longer just seniors after prostate surgery, but also that societal segment that was in any case at the center of the fitness mania: men of 40 and above, and even younger men, who were feeling the first signs of aging and were sometimes tired in the evening, so that the penis was not as hard as they would like and had possibly been used to.[13] Although Viagra officially addressed itself to elderly and middle-aged men who perhaps worked too hard, in practice those who partied too hard were soon using it as well. Viagra rapidly gained a reputation as a new party drug, one that guaranteed sexual performance no matter how long and wild the late-night revelries had been. Thanks to Viagra, an even greater emphasis was placed on male sexual performance, and as journalist Susan Faludi underlined, Viagra helped ensure that the success of this performance was increasingly judged by pornographic standards.[14]

The "impotence boom"

Since the early 1970s, the discourse of the "impotence boom" had laid the ground for Viagra. "Has it hit you yet?", asked men's magazine *Esquire* in October 1972. The question was rhetorical. As the cover showed, even male sex symbol Burt Reynolds (then only in his mid-thirties) was compelled to look down aghast at what had been his greatest asset. The impotence boom was embedded in a nagging anxiety over masculinity itself, one that burgeoned from the 1970s onward. This was not the first time that Western societies had been struck by a crisis of men and masculinity. On the contrary, since the nineteenth century, modern men have constantly doubted their own sex, and such crises of masculinity have all too often been taken as a sign of an overall crisis of society. However, the sense of crisis that had gripped white, heterosexual men since the 1970s seemed even more nagging than before. After all, their political and social hegemony was being questioned more profoundly than ever before by the civil rights movement, women's movement, and gay and lesbian movement.

Describing these shifts, with an originally medical term, as a crisis, implies a call for intervention. Such a precarious situation must, after all, be stabilized, and the patient cured. Within this logic, physical strengthening is an obvious goal, so the fitness movement as a whole can be understood as a response to what was perceived as a moment of crisis. This applies to the body mania among men, but may also refer to women's fitness work. In both cases, fitness must be interpreted as a sign of the capacity for social and political participation: in the former case entailing a claim to hegemony, in the latter with a view to expanding it.[15]

Sex was an important element in this crisis scenario. In the recent past, feminism, along with the lesbian and gay movement, had clearly demonstrated the importance of sex to the social order and to one's degree of social recognition.[16] Their critique was as sexual as it was sociopolitical. It focused on the phallus and on a penetration-centered, heterosexual imperative, and described lesbianism as a personal and political alternative. Feminism seemed to pose a risk to the man's potency and social hegemony that was, perhaps, even more powerful than age, excess weight, and smoking combined. After all, feminists exposed the vaginal orgasm as a "myth," such that penetration and thus the erection diminished in importance. The idea of the clitoris as a source of female pleasure gained traction, fueled by research such as Alfred Kinsey's 1953 study on female sexuality, and the work of Virginia Johnson and William H. Masters, the leading sex research team of the 1960s. As a feminist organ, the clitoris then surged to political prominence. It ultimately altered notions of what was sexually normal, fundamentally challenging prevalent and socially structuring practices such as coitus, along with ways of life such as heterosexual marriage, and questioning their claim to sole validity.[17]

This was extremely unsettling for many men. Many felt that women were weakening male potency at both the personal and political levels.

It did not matter whether they were independent of sex with men as lesbians or, as heterosexually liberated and now sexually proactive women, overwhelmed men with their ideas and desires. In 1978, Louise Brown was born as the first test tube baby. If the clitoris and contraceptive pill had separated sex from reproduction, in vitro fertilization then separated reproduction from sex. Penetration finally seemed to have become obsolete. Between the nineteenth and late twentieth centuries, sperm had mutated from the fuel that kept the world going into a "raw bio-material," according to sociologist Paula-Irene Villa, that can be "produced, stored, sold, tested, used, and thrown away."[18]

To stem the decline in male hegemony, a whole arsenal of forces had been working toward the "remasculinization of America" since the late 1970s. These forces were articulated in various ways and in a range of fields. They celebrated a new male corporeality in popular culture, vigorously propagated the great importance of the father to family and society, and valorized the private arming of white men as a sign of their strength and sense of responsibility. The common goal of these various forces was to socially recenter the heterosexual and generally white man, and Viagra became inscribed in this culture and politics of the resuscitation of male strength. In the form of a simple pill, it offered an antidote to upheavals both sexual and social. This pill strengthened men and their egos by boosting their sexual fitness and promising to give them back control in the bedroom. Viagra maintained the idea that successful penetration is crucial to the contentment of humankind and thus to the stability of society as well. *Playboy*, unsurprisingly, rejoiced at the "little blue miracle," the end of clitoral tyranny, and the comeback of the penis.[19] Even today, Viagra commercials pop up on the screen if one googles "clitoral orgasm."

"Penis doping"

Viagra is part of the *dispositif* of fitness. To recall: a *dispositif* is a powerful ensemble of discourses, institutions and things, up to and including laws, administrative measures, everyday practices, and much more besides, which imbues society with a certain order. Since the 1970s, the *dispositif* of fitness has more than ever been focused on the body, exhorting individuals (in different ways and with variable objectives depending on age and gender) to demonstrate their determination to be fit.[20] Viagra also highlights the fact that in the fitness society, performance deficits can be combated through other means than just diligent work on oneself. This objective may also be pursued through medication (surgical intervention being another option). *Der Spiegel* referred to "penile doping." Viagra, then, is representative of a variety of means and measures that are deployed when training and prevention have proved incapable of getting body and self fit enough to perform at a high level.

Since the mid-twentieth century, pills have increasingly been the means of choice to cope better with everyday life. Thus, in the United States, the number of medical prescriptions increased eightfold between 1959 and 2009 – at a time, ironically, when the US government declared war on drugs. Since 1997, in the course of a generally comprehensive process of deregulation, the country has also permitted the direct advertising of prescription medicines to consumers, a course naturally pursued assiduously by Pfizer in the case of Viagra. Patients began to forthrightly demand what they want from their physicians. The age of fitness is also the age of the pharmaceutical industry, which has become one of the most profitable industries in the world.[21]

The principle of approaching diminishing performance, which is often associated with aging, as a health problem treatable with pills, has become established since 1950 in the everyday professional, social, and sexual life of Western societies. The notion of "sexual health" has been around since the 1960s, and it has been claimed to be achievable regardless of age. This is consonant with the logic of consumer society, namely that people should be able to buy remedies quickly and easily. The idea here is that wellbeing, success, and social recognition will be enhanced by a purchasable product.[22] In line with the same logic, a species of everyday doping has become established and widespread, including (though not restricted to) the field of sex. Why should the limits of sex not be expanded ever further, as was evidently possible in sport, asked urologist and sex counselor Dudley Danoff in 1993, before Viagra had even moved center-stage in the "consumerist erectile economy."[23] Unlike doping in sport, everyday doping does not necessarily involve supplying bodies with illicit substances, but typically with officially approved, medically prescribed drugs. The boundaries between enhancement and doping, between permitted and unauthorized remedies, are of course blurred, even in sport. Both are united by the goal of increasing performance and improving the individual's position in a competitive system, helping ensure success and thus enhancing what is regarded as quality of life. "If there is a freedom to pursue self-improvement," to quote cultural studies scholar Karin Harrasser, "where and how are we to draw the border" between acceptable and illicit substances?[24]

In sport, rules of fairness are often cited as a reason to prohibit doping. In everyday life, however, performance-enhancing substances are, in principle, accessible to anyone who can afford them. Fairness is not at issue here.[25] But is doping even contrary to the principles of sport? After all, it is sport, with its competitive principle, that encourages doping by exhorting people to maximize their performance. So, while sport and fitness are different things, the former paradigmatically embodies the culture and society of competition and fitness.[26]

Given the historical cycles of fitness, competition, and consumer culture, it seems more than a coincidence that, in both sport and everyday life, doping practices have risen to such prominence since the 1960s and 1970s – and have ultimately been pursued with such a lack of consistency.[27] At the same time, the transitions between competitive sport, fitness, and everyday practice are fluid: the use of performance-enhancing substances – from energy drinks through dietary supplements to painkillers, pills, and sprays – is common in amateur and mass sport as well.[28]

Electric belts, rejuvenating surgery, and the psychologization of sex in the nineteenth and twentieth centuries

Yet neither in the world of sport nor sex are performance-enhancing interventions a recent development. This is apparent, for example, if we trace the relationship between sex and performance back to the late nineteenth century. The "spermatic economy" of the Victorian era was coming to an end at the time. In continuity with the premodern theory of humors, this spermatic economy declared semen the bearer of the highest form of vitality, placing it at the center of the social order. Men should be sparing with their seed: a careless approach would jeopardize their energy and vitality, which only they, as men, possessed, but which they needed to reproduce and cope in a competitive world. In the nineteenth century too, then, vitality was imagined in sexual terms, but it was not necessary, and was indeed inadvisable, to constantly demonstrate and thus frivolously squander this vital force. On the contrary, male moderation was crucial. The evidence of the highest form of male achievement was to father a child and provide for a family. Male potency was chiefly a matter of reproductive capacity.[29]

The sexually moderate and providing father persisted as a male ideal, and as the hub of social order, into the late nineteenth and twentieth centuries.[30] But the "first sexual revolution" around 1900 lent growing social significance to other male characteristics, namely physical strength, youthfulness, and sexual aura. Body fetishists like the American Bernarr Macfadden, and strength athletes such as Friedrich Wilhelm Müller from Königsberg, were only too happy to display their hardened bodies. They were the new idols and the first male pin-ups of their time. Müller was to gain worldwide fame under the stage name of Eugen Sandow. The name Eugen ("the well-born" in Greek) highlights just how much bodily aesthetics was entangled with performance. This entanglement was integrated into a Darwinist system of competition and selection, a system that had been regarded as fundamental to human existence since the late nineteenth century.[31]

Genetics was booming at the time. Nevertheless, henceforth the issue of potency or impotence focused less on procreative ability, and more on sexual performance. The latter was considered an expression of male power and energy. These, however, were considered to be at risk from modern "overcivilization" and neurasthenia in particular. George M. Beard, medical luminary par excellence in this regard, referred to "sexual neurasthenia," which he claimed was sapping modern men's reservoir of sexual energy.[32] It thus seemed merely logical that at the end of the nineteenth century diligent physical exercise, cold baths, and the right diet were just as prominent as numerous remedies, ranging from an array of powders, through the electric belt, to a vaccine against fatigue (which was at the very least an object of investigation).[33] These were intended to strengthen the man and preserve his youth. Fatigue had in any case become the central problem of the modern achievement-oriented society, whether during sex or at work.

But potency aids were just one element in a wide range of measures that promised to realize the dream of eternal youth and preserve
productivity. Surgery was another. The boom it enjoyed from the
late nineteenth century onward was due in part to the invention of
anesthesia and thus to changing medical options. Another key driving
force was the desire to adapt one's body to normative expectations by
every means possible. Plastic surgery gained importance in the form of
beauty-enhancing operations and, after World War I, reconstructive
surgery. More important in our context, however, are rejuvenating
operations.[34]

Male youth in particular was supposed to find expression in a vital
sexuality. One of the pioneers of rejuvenation was Paris-based neurolo-
gist Charles-Edouard Brown-Séquard, whose work still cleaved to the
"spermatic economy" of the Victorian era. Believing in the vital force
contained in sperm, in 1889 the 72-year-old experimented on himself,
injecting an elixir of water, blood, semen, and a paste of crushed canine
and guinea pig testicles into his bloodstream. As a result, he contended,
his physical strength grew noticeably. In the following years and decades, a veritable youth mania and rejuvenation hype broke out on both
sides of the Atlantic, extending from popular culture to the biosciences.
Medical-therapeutic efforts to preserve youth soon proliferated. They
ranged from hormone treatments through the stimulation of one's
gonads to the implantation of others' gonads. Monkey farms on the
French Riviera bred the raw material required to boost male potency.
One of the leading scientists in the field was Viennese physician Eugen
Steinach. Steinach transplanted embryonic tissue and gonads, while
also performing vasectomies in order to rejuvenate his patients. He
believed that sperm and fertility were irrelevant to a man's youthfulness, productive capacity, and masculinity. What seemed important
to him was what he called internal secretion. For Steinach, "mating
ability" was more important than "fertility."[35]

It was above all Steinach who talked in terms of rejuvenation. He
also emphasized that his research was not intended to actually make
men younger, but more active and productive. Both these states were
conceptualized primarily, though not exclusively, in sexual terms.
For women, rejuvenation promised to mitigate the menopause and,
if necessary, to restore their fertility and ability to give birth. In the

1920s, the boundaries between rejuvenation and cosmetic surgery then blurred, especially with respect to women. Female rejuvenation gradually came to be focused on achieving a sexually attractive body rather than facilitating childbearing. The female "consumerist body" was the complement of the male "productivist body," which should prove itself through its performance. As historian Heiko Stoff argues incisively, the rejuvenation project countered "the aged, sexually dubious, pathological, and tired body [with] the fulfillment of a desire – a historical novelty in this form – for youth and beauty, along with physical and sexual performance." This happened in different ways for male and female bodies. Basically, however, it was not procreation, but desire, performance, and consumption that were the key desiderata. At times, the ideals of youth and virility, according to Stoff, were undermined by "the caricature of the randy old lecher," familiar to us today from the debate on Viagra.[36]

Eugen Steinach was nominated for the Nobel Prize for Medicine no less than eight times in the 1920s and 1930s. He and his colleagues were thus by no means outsiders. At the same time, their way of producing sexual fitness was highly controversial. In the decades that followed, the surgical intervention was to take a back seat to another concept from the science of sex, one that had been developing in parallel. This, however, aimed less at the body than the psyche, in an attempt to explain and treat impotence. The godfather of this concept was Sigmund Freud. Although Freud did not completely deny the importance of organic factors to impotence, he considered the psyche and its relationship to sex the main cause. He understood psyche and sex as mutually influencing: for him, mental problems were contingent on sexual problems and vice versa. He focused on the man, his desire, his potency, and his fears. Even the boy fears punishment, according to Freud, because his Oedipal desire is directed at his mother. This supposedly leads to a castration complex that may manifest itself as impotence in the adult male.[37]

Freudian thinking had become widely established after World War I and in the 1920s, be it in Vienna or Washington DC, Berlin or Boston. Freud regarded gender relations as particularly important to men's potency, a notion familiar to us in light of male fears of feminism in the 1970s. Even in the roaring twenties, the more self-confident and sexually proactive women were already claimed to be unsettling large numbers of men. Hence, men blamed either their mothers or their partners for their potency problems – or both. As the twentieth century wore on, Freudian psychoanalysis was to become the leading instrument for interpreting and treating problems afflicting the relationship between the individual, their fellow human beings, and society. After World War II, the United States in particular became a nation in therapy.[38]

Until well into the 1990s, impotence remained a matter for psychologists. Initially, even the studies produced in the 1950s and 1960s by Alfred Kinsey and Masters and Johnson did little to change this. When various authors sought to explain the connection between feminism and the sexual revolution on the one hand and the impotence boom of the 1970s on the other, the psychosexual interpretive scheme was ready to hand. At the same time, however, the new era of corporeality began, and it increasingly shaped perspectives on impotence. More and more urologists began to interpret male sexuality as an organic phenomenon. In specialist circles, it also became less common to refer to impotence; the term "erectile dysfunction" was increasingly used, implying physical rather than psychological causes. What physicians had been propagating for several years became the subject of broad public debate in the late 1980s, namely that the cause of a limp penis was not always to be found in one's head. In at least three-quarters of cases, it was asserted, the body is in fact the cause of erectile problems. Risk factors such as alcohol, smoking, diabetes, or even hard training on the hard seat of a road bike should be avoided, as urologist Irwin Goldstein of Boston University emphasized – and this at a time when the road bike was spreading as a popular recreational tool for successful managers. Although physicians in the 1980s did not propose Steinach's rejuvenation, they did recommend vacuum pumps, implants, and injections as remedies for a lack of hardness. The latter in particular were highly effective, though rather unpleasant to administer. Everyone, according to *TIME Magazine*, was now trying to make medical procedures less invasive. No wonder, then, that there was great excitement when Pfizer discovered, essentially by accident, that the active agent sildenafil was causing erections to get harder. Sildenafil facilitates and improves blood flow into the penis and thus the erection (though the latter still requires sexual arousal). Test subjects for a new heart drug containing this agent had noted this side effect and refused to return their samples. As so often, then, chance helped advance bioscientific research.[39]

Things that make a difference

Fitness symbolizes health and productive capacity, which are maintained or induced by constant work on oneself. The attempts made to foster fitness and sexual performance through external interventions, substances, and pills highlight the fact that the human individual by no means acts independently of external forces. On the contrary, work on the self is influenced by a range of different factors. In addition to Viagra and other remedies, these include the sexual sciences and medicine, the pharmaceutical industry, consumer society, feminism, the politics of male crisis, and much more besides. Together, these factors create a powerful network of different, mutually reinforcing, partly opposing forces and operations. They form what has been dealt with for quite some time under the rubric of "sexual health." This is closely woven into the *dispositif* of fitness and thus forms part of the extensive and polymorphous order that is centered on fitness and held together by it.[40]

In this book on the age of fitness, when I emphasize the power of the *dispositif*, discourses, or even the Viagra pill, I also critically question the paradigms of (neo)liberal politics. For they assume the autonomy of actors, positing them as the self-responsible anchor of the social and political order. Certainly, people make daily decisions and take action. But they are influenced by many other forces and operations that affect them and that make up the conditions for human action. People act in a far from independent fashion; instead, to cite sociologist Bruno Latour, they are "made to act by many others." Latour refers to such "making others act" as "agency," though this no longer necessarily and exclusively involves human actors. What is crucial to this kind of agency, then, is not so much the intention or the autonomy of the actor, but whether an element within a complex network of relationships and operations "make[s] a difference in the course of some other agent's action or not." This "element" may be sexual-scientific discourse, the rationality of consumer society, the sex hormone testosterone, the pharmaceutical industry, or a pill such as Viagra, which in turn absorbs scientific practices, political and commercial interests, individual needs, and much more besides. And just as it makes a difference whether one goes shopping with or without a basket (to take just one of the many examples Latour mentions), it makes a difference whether one has sex with or without Viagra. Of course, Viagra does not determine the action, it does not make the decision to have sex or to refrain from doing so, nor does it engage in sexual intercourse. But it enables, empowers, encourages, changes, and perhaps even prevents, and it does so in different ways for different participants.[41]

What applies to Viagra and sex is also worth considering when it comes to other areas and practices of fitness. Countless forces act upon individuals, bodies, and fitness practices. Is the cyclist's body even conceivable without a bicycle and a bicycle computer? Is the shoe part and parcel of the runner? Both bike computers and shoes make a difference when the goal is to optimize fitness and self. What about running tracks and running clubs? Leotards and sweatbands? Energy drinks, power bars, magnesium tablets, breath sprays, bananas? Training and the life sciences? Statistics and nutrition? To consider their impact is to change our perspective on human bodies whose boundaries are fundamentally blurred and open. To stick with Viagra: this pill regulates sexual functionality, but is itself dependent on countless other factors and does not work without sexual arousal. This illustrates how much body and pill are interconnected, much like stump and prosthesis. In fact, in the debates on its modus operandi, Viagra has been compared to a prosthesis or crutch, which do not work without physical activation, just as the body cannot function without the technological aid.[42] Technology and things "pervade" bodies.[43] Viagra helps create new possibilities and new needs, revive old ones, restore social orders, shape ideas of good and proper sex, and may create large numbers of new sick, dysfunctional men, whose erections and bodies are regarded as optimizable only because Viagra has created this possibility. There is always room for improvement.[44]

How Viagra makes masculinity

Hence, if things change existing situations and thus affect actions,[45] the question arises as to what difference Viagra makes and how men and women describe this difference. Here we can consult surveys of Viagra users, which have been carried out in a number of countries, such as Germany, the United Kingdom, New Zealand, Sweden, and the United States. These studies are usually qualitative rather than quantitative. All in all, it is plainly apparent that, as the respondents perceive it, Viagra makes a major difference, and in a number of areas of life. Yet Viagra alters the perception of erectile dysfunction and how to deal with it before it has even been taken.[46] Of course, perceptions and assessments differ depending on who one asks. Most of those asked are heterosexual men, with smaller numbers of gay men, and relatively few women. When women are surveyed, they are usually asked about their partners' erections, and less often about their own experiences and perceptions.[47]

Many men emphasize that Viagra helps them regain control of body, self, and situation. The pill thus eliminates uncertainties and insecurities. It relieves men of the fear that they will be unable to function and instead provides a sense of taken-for-grantedness and security. Some users compare Viagra with a prosthesis. In fact, they explain, it is even more than that: it not only restores a specific physical functionality, but also creates a sense of completeness as a man. Other impairments, according to one physician respondent, reduce vision or hearing, but not masculinity. The idea of masculinity that shines through here is quite simple and reduced to the erect penis. In interviews, a variety of Viagra users affirm this simple concept of masculinity. As men, they finally feel they are in the ascendant again after decades of critique of phallocentric maleness. Viagra promises an ability to control functionality, and performance, the latter being of key importance to modern ideas of masculinity.[48]

In general, and unsurprisingly, performance is a major reference point when men talk about Viagra and its effects. Here, above all, performance means the ability to achieve erection and penetration, which many men surveyed regard as the core of sexual activity and as the goal of their performance. Viagra reinforces this perspective. Doctors emphasize that Viagra firmly integrates sex into the performance-centered age of fitness and increases the pressure on patients and doctors themselves considerably. The doctor mutates into the agent of wish fulfillment, whom the patient expects to improve his life and enhance his abilities without resistance and by prescribing pills. And since the development of the International Index of Erectile Function, these abilities have even been viewed as measurable. However, at times Viagra increases men's sense of insecurity, because they attribute their sexual performance not to themselves, but to the pill. On the one hand, consuming Viagra is "doing masculinity" par excellence, yet on the other, every pill is an admission that one cannot hold one's own.[49]

Men often associate the "ability to perform" with being young. Here youth is understood as a generic, normal state, which Viagra restores. Only through Viagra, as one older user put it, does the body know what to do, and through it one becomes "oneself" again. This self is a young and potent one. Viagra creates a sense of rejuvenation and holds out the prospect of achieving, if not eternal, then at least longer-lasting, youth, and of meeting the requirement for "successful," that is, sexually fulfilled, aging. Sexual fulfillment is equated with the ability to achieve an erection and coitus – through Viagra as in other ways.[50]

In interviews, many men also stress how much Viagra, or the ability to engage in sexual intercourse, has strengthened their relationship, be it a long-established or new one. At times, they explain, it was their partner who suggested that they use Viagra. Many men regard it as important to their masculine self-image to give their partner pleasure through penetration and to live up to their supposed responsibility for their partner's sexual satisfaction. Viagra, they claim, enables the man to show, through his erect penis, how greatly he desires his partner.[51]

Only rarely, and this is of course due in part to the selection of interlocutors in existing studies, does male–male sex, the expansion of sexual boundaries, wild partying, or the porn scene come up. It is references to Viagra as an aid to norm-adherence that predominate: it helps one demonstrate one's performance capacity, lead a fulfilling life, and maintain a good (heterosexual) partnership, or age successfully. At the same time, Viagra helps shape what it means to be a man, to age successfully or lead a fulfilling life in the first place. Overall, men often try to endow the use of Viagra with an air of normality. Hence, they often place consumption of the potency pill on the same level as bodily care, or back exercises. Apparently, they wish to present Viagra as a means of obtaining and maintaining a functional, healthy body, which is necessary in order to receive recognition from one's partner as well as society.[52]

If they are surveyed at all, women also report that Viagra makes a big difference in their lives and in their relationships. But they usually evaluate this difference differently than men. Often, they complain, their partners as well as doctors barely consider the fact that Viagra is an intervention in a relationship, and affects both of those involved. In marketing campaigns, it is above all ("beautiful") women that one (that is, men) can reacquire thanks to Viagra. In medical consultations, as many women interviewees state, women's role is chiefly to support their partners and help them tackle their erectile dysfunction. They figure less often as actors with their own needs, interests, ideas, and desire. Women interviewees underline the extent to which Viagra intervenes in sexual culture and helps focus this culture, and society as a whole, on the man.[53]

Around half of women stress that they see little benefit in the way Viagra changes the nature of sex, increasing its intensity and frequency. On the contrary, they lament, Viagra helps refocus sex on erections and coitus, making it more monotonous. Increased male desire, moreover, often pressures women to have sex more often and for longer than they would like. This pressure is also fed by medicine, sexology, popular culture, and periodicals, from *Playboy* to the *New Yorker*, which are full of comments about men of all ages who want more sex, and different kinds of sex, than their wives. Ultimately, the capacity to attain an erection, and increased desire, function as signs of "sexual health" and thus as fundamentally desirable. Women (but men too) who try to escape this place themselves outside of what is considered desirable and normal. They are denying their partner what is described as fulfilled, healthy masculinity, and a good life.[54]

Many women state that they have adjusted well to their aging partners' declining desire and potency. Men's dwindling capacity for erection and penetration is often associated with greater sexual diversity, which many women appreciate. Men's crisis, then, may be women's gain. Women often describe age-related changes as "natural," in stark contrast to many men, for whom the hardest possible, youthful erections are an expression of the natural. From a female perspective, successful and "healthy" aging often means being able to cope with these changes and seeing them as an opportunity, rather than viewing the capacity for coitus as the sole indicator of enduring happiness.[55]

Some women explicitly complain about the way in which Viagra centers the sexual and social order around men. They note critically that Viagra intervenes both in their personal relationships and in a highly political field, one that revolves around performance and is structured by gender.[56] Viagra promotes a doing of masculinity that is often incompatible with the doing of femininity. It is true that a phenomenon known as Female Sexual Dysfunction (FSD) has received more attention since the turn of the millennium, with Pfizer and other pharmaceutical companies investing in "pink Viagra" for women. But this reaffirms rather than refutes the idea of a gendered disparity. It is Viagra that sparked efforts to produce the diagnosis of FSD, a diagnosis that implies the medical treatability of every possible form of declining sexual appetite. It is claimed that 40 percent of American women suffer from FSD. However, it is unclear here just what "sexual health" might mean if it cannot be read off an erection scale. The approval of a relevant drug in the United States in 2015 has not settled this question. Female desire, as *Newsweek* wrote of attempts to produce a medication, is highly complex, and (so far) no pill has proved truly successful.[57]

Sex in the age of fitness

Sex unfolds within social orders and their power relations. This is something we have known, at the latest, since Michel Foucault and the emergence of the field of queer studies, the rise of feminism, and the struggles to advance lesbian, gay, bisexual, transgender, and queer (LGBTQ) rights.[58] Sex does much to regulate who may participate in society, and how, and who receives what degree of recognition. For a long time, reproductivity was a key criterion in this respect, and it remains important even today. In the age of fitness, however, sexual performance stands front and center. Viagra shows that successful performance does not necessarily have to be the result of continuous work on oneself, but may also be facilitated by aids of all kinds. Substances that enhance performance are a commonplace in every sphere of life. Ultimately, achievement and successful performance are considered a sign of health and of the ability to maintain it as we grow older. Viagra illustrates once again the gendered character of power relations, both sexual and social. In addition, sexual preferences and race are of central importance to a social history of sex, even though race as a category has received less attention so far in this chapter. More than ever before, after the end of slavery the stereotypes of potent black men and available black women became the nightmare and obsession of white America. Virility was also to become a phantasm haunting the civil rights movement. Civil rights were constructed as men's rights, and from the 1970s onward, black feminists made this one of the mainstays of their critique not only of racism, but also of the sexism of white and black men. Contexts such as these continue to characterize the cultural, social, and political importance attached to an on-demand erection. Of course, race not only means being black, but implies that a whole spectrum of skin colors relates to different characteristics of bodies, minds, and characters. This applies beyond the United States, with European (post-)colonialism featuring a similar range of narratives.[59]

Initially Pfizer evidently tried to avoid potential pitfalls by putting white men and heterosexual couples at the center of its marketing campaigns. Pfizer apparently understood "white" as an unmarked and generic category that somehow meant all human beings, and was thus the most innocuous. Over the years, however, Pfizer explicitly addressed a more heterogeneous target group in its advertising, and non-white men appeared in TV commercials and advertisements. Mixed-race couples, however, were nowhere to be seen. In the US market in particular, the relationship between black men and white women is too historically complicated and still too politically charged. It was left to the imagination of male Viagra consumers to transgress this boundary. In the advancing twenty-first century, women of a great variety of ethnic backgrounds – always conventionally "beautiful" – directly address men in Viagra commercials, seeking to convince them that it is worthwhile facing up to their erectile problems. These women often appear in a tropical, vacation-like setting. In one case a white, blonde model is supposed to radiate a touch of the exotic and erotic as she encourages American men always to take along their Viagra in a British accent. Even in 2018, however, we are yet to see a Viagra commercial featuring gay men.[60]

5

FIGHTING

Fitness heroes I

Within eight weeks I can make a hero of myself, promises Hamburg gym *Urban Heroes*. I can even go "from zero to hero" with the help of private trainers and the intensive "Transformer Challenge" program. "Challenge" and "change" are in fact key terms within the workshops of the "urban fitness heroes." With their uncompromisingly sculpted physiques, tough yet enthusiastic and life-affirming trainers push us to change our lives, make the best of ourselves, show determination, get out of our comfort zone, give our all (literally!), and keep going until we reach, and even exceed, our limits. The tagline *#createyourself* appears on the webpage on which the team introduce themselves: urban heroes, with tribal tattoos, in sleeveless T-shirts emblazoned with RUN YOUR HEART OUT, KICK ASS, and BElieve in YOUrself.[1]

"Yeah, you're gonna sweat!", states the *Urban Heroes* website, and this is both warning and promise. Because hard, sweat-inducing training is the sacrifice that must be made in order to receive an uplifting reward: the experience of "energy" and "awe," "getting a sense of one's own physicality," feeling "muscle tone" and "total body tension," the sense that one is "strong, taut, and sexy." In short: feeling life. On the website's blog, called *#HeroNation,*[2] a variety of fitness heroes talk about their sufferings, joys, and goals, which clearly ought to be ours too. Yet there is more at stake here than sport, or the burning of calories and fat. This is a matter of success as a principle, a convincing performance in every sphere of life: at work, when going out, during sex. Other hashtags guiding us through the world of fitness include *#sweatsexy*, *#fitforlife*, and *#neverstop*. Great things, then, are invoked, namely the incurring of agony and the making of sacrifices in order to test the limits of the possible, to do more than just master life and thereby to impress others; in other words, to be a hero or heroine. In a blog post, sports presenter Johannes B. Kerner even imagines that his workouts at *Urban Heroes*, along with his marathons, have taken him beyond the realm of the human. After all, the heroes of Greek mythology were demigods: "I wanted to challenge myself [with the marathon] and see how far I could go. At the end of the day, an achievement like this is near-impossible for ordinary mortals. [. . .] Here [at Urban Heroes] I can rise to the occasion! I can challenge myself and test my limits. When working out to these beats or with a coach, you achieve things you thought couldn't be done." It almost sounds like the postmodern philosophy of the subject when Kerner refers to the good feeling one can attain through "voluntary submission" to a tough workout program.[3]

Making a fitness hero of oneself comes at a price, not least because the Urban Heroes studio seeks to provide people with the most comfortable experience possible, from shower gel through care and styling products to a hair dryer and a fresh towel. Gym passes are available from €25 for one session to €168 for 12 workouts a month. The full exercise program, however, envisages five weekly workouts, enabling one to work on one's entire body, one area at a time. Twelve sessions a month is scarcely going to cut it, so you'll have to dig deeper into your pocketbook. The website thus appeals to the self-made hero's sense of responsibility above all when it comes to paying: "You only live once – invest in your health now."[4]

Whenever fitness is at stake, heroic metaphors and heroic figures are never far away. We find them in gyms called *Urban Heroes* in Hamburg, *Fitness Hero* in the suburbs of Chicago, and *Heroes Fitness* in Stockport in northern England. We also meet them in the *Heroes' Sphere* fitness camp in Spain, a kind of boot camp where affluent Westerners seek to get back in shape in a vacation atmosphere, at the *Heroes' Race* in

the Hamburg suburb of Blankenese, and among the *Cycling Heroes* of
Stuttgart, hobby cyclists who battle their way through the Black Forest,
even when it is "terribly frosty." The Cycling Heroes will often give
you a cheeky wink as they perform their heroism.[5]

There seems to be something heroic about fitness, as is also evident
from a glance at lifestyle magazines like *Fit for Fun* or *Men's Health*. But
why does the hero exercise such irresistible appeal to fitness aficionados
who romp around in gyms or test their limits as runners and recreational cyclists, when we supposedly live in a "post-heroic society"? For
decades, commentators on both sides of the Atlantic have branded
heroes passé. Our society, it has been claimed, no longer has any need
for heroes, that is to say, combat-ready individuals willing to step up
and make sacrifices in order to stretch their limits, render the impossible possible, and thus to become role models demanding emulation.[6]

But when commentators refer to the end of heroism in our contemporary societies, they do not mean fitness heroes, but primarily war
heroes. (The fact that these types of hero overlap is commonly ignored.)
Martial heroism is the progenitor of heroism in general. From Greek
mythology to the twentieth century, battle was considered the best way
to forge heroes, while the battlefield was the best place to do so. Like
the battle itself, then, heroism was by and large a male privilege. While
this conception of heroic warfare has not been fully exhausted to this
day, it suffered deep ruptures during the twentieth and twenty-first
centuries. Key factors here are the millions of dead and injured in
the trenches of World War I, the racist, nationalistic, and genocidal
excesses of the "heroic" under the Nazi regime, and the changing image
of the American GI, who went from democratic liberator to killer
of women and children in Vietnam. The focus of public attention
shifted from heroes to victims.[7] The male war hero as a leading trope in
Western societies was challenged profoundly by the post-1968 political
movements and the fundamental critique of society and patriarchy they
put forward – albeit with different emphases in North America and
Europe. The mechanization of war in general, and remote-controlled
drone warfare in particular, have also significantly reduced the scope
for heroic martial deeds. Whether the hero has truly had their day is
doubtful, however, given the paramilitary culture in the United States
in particular, the veneration of victims and protagonists in the "war on

terror," and the renaissance of the martial hero in an era of resurgent nationalism on both sides of the Atlantic.[8]

Thus, sweeping references to post-heroic societies conceal at least as much as they reveal. In the age of fitness, heroic visions are very much in vogue, and they resonate with the hero's martial roots. If we wish to understand the heroic and martial aspects of fitness, it is important to consider the relationship between war heroism and the multifaceted everyday forms of heroism. This quotidian heroism is defined not just by the charitable campaigns and rescue operations of civil society, but also by readying oneself to master the struggles of everyday life, through the toughening of one's body and rendering oneself productive and powerful. What is recognized as heroic, as an extraordinary achievement, or as an exemplary response to a specific challenge, and under what circumstances, varies across time and space, as does that which is considered to have had its day, to be non-heroic, or even anti-heroic. In what follows, I use the heroic as a means of probing present-day culture and society and thus better understanding the age of fitness. This raises the question of what traces of martial heroism are still to be found in today's fitness heroes and heroines, that is, how grounded in militarism they are. Therefore, we need to trace the historical changes in the realm of the heroic and tease out the overlap between its various forms.[9]

If at all, it is only at first glance that "fitness heroes" seem to be a simple phenomenon. In reality they defy easy comprehension. This is because they acquire their heroic status not as soldiers, but as sportspeople. Yet they are not classic sports heroes, such as Muhammad Ali, Steffi Graf, or Cristiano Ronaldo, as they do not practice top-level sport but rather everyday fitness training.[10] Nor are they the typical, everyday heroes who fight for greater justice, land a passenger plane on the Hudson River, or save a child about to fall from a balcony (Malian refugee Mamoudou Gassama was granted French citizenship for such a deed in 2018). Nevertheless, fitness aficionados embody (in the truest sense of the term) those values and practices, goals and aspirations of our present-day society that are amenable to expression in the language and categories of the heroic: taking on challenges, a readiness to take action and make sacrifices, and a desire to accomplish things one had thought impossible.[11] In order to approach this historically, it is vital to take a closer look at how the coexistence of heroism and social recognition has developed in recent history, and how the spheres of the martial and of fitness overlap.

Citizen-soldiers and national heroes

With the revolution and the Declaration of Independence of July 4, 1776, those living in the British colonies of North America asserted their transformation from subjects of King George III of the United Kingdom into American citizens. They described their detachment from the British motherland in terms of the shift from boy to man. This metaphor was consonant with contemporary patterns of thinking and acting in that attaining citizenship was a privilege of white male property-owners. However, just what republican citizenship meant, apart from being male and white, having property, and the right to oppose oppressive rule, was rather opaque at first. What was clear, though, was that a citizen had not only rights, but also obligations, and that rights and obligations and their fulfillment conferred certain privileges. These were political participation, and the officially recognized right to help shape society and to be recognized as its productive member, along with all the advantages this afforded. Being a citizen in a republic was, therefore, not a matter of descent or birthplace, but chiefly one of civic practice. Through a variety of repeated actions, people practiced and demonstrated (as they have continued to do up to the present), what it means to be a citizen, who enjoys this status, and to what extent.[12]

One of these actions was fighting, for one's own freedom, as well as for the republic or nation. The modern citizen-soldier capable of defense is an invention originating in the era of the Atlantic revolutions. Although it can ultimately be traced back to European antiquity, this being is intimately linked with the birth of the citizen in the revolutionary United States and of the *citoyen* in revolutionary France. "The citizen in uniform," according to historian Ute Frevert, "is considered a mainstay of democracy and citizenship." In both the American Revolutionary War and the Napoleonic Wars, citizen armies proved motivated and successful, despite all the doubts, for example, of experienced military leaders in the young American states regarding the efficacy of their militias and in spite of all the weaknesses they displayed in the course of the Revolutionary War against the tightly organized and disciplined British troops.[13]

The genesis of the citizen-soldier also entailed what might be described as the democratization of the heroic. Until the late eighteenth century, military heroism had been an aristocratic privilege. But in the American Revolutionary War it was not only prominent figures such as General George Washington who became heroes and incarnations of the new republic. Ordinary American soldiers also received more and more recognition for their services to freedom and independence. What had begun in the War of Independence was to be continued in the following wars – against the United Kingdom in 1812, Mexico in 1846–8, and in the American Civil War of 1861–5. The latter saw the introduction of a Medal of Honor. It had thus taken the United States a considerable time to create such a medal in recognition of ordinary soldiers' military heroism. The aristocratic overtones of such heroic insignia had previously been too off-putting.[14]

In Prussia a quite different picture clearly pertained. The wars of liberation against Napoleonic France in 1813 not only brought compulsory military service. The Iron Cross was also introduced as a "military decoration," and a cenotaph was erected for all soldiers who, regardless of their social status, "had died for the Fatherland while performing an act of heroism," or had distinguished themselves through outstanding "military valor." Patriotic military masculinity is not an invention of that era. In the wake of the democratic revolutions in the Atlantic region and the wars of liberation in Germany, however, this concept of masculinity attained a new scale and significance, coupled with ideas of liberty, equality, and nation. Every citizen had also to be a warrior, and as a warrior every citizen could become a hero.[15]

Thus, a league of subjects was to become an army of citizens, who fought for themselves and their cause, and were ready to die for it. Patriotic combat-readiness promised social participation and recognition as a citizen. As such, it was a male domain, that is, only men had to, and were permitted to, prove their capacity for defense, and only those who proved that they had this capacity were considered truly male and were regarded as able and worthy to be citizens. "No being of the male gender who is incapable of defense can count as a man," emphasized Friedrich Ludwig Jahn, the father of German gymnastics, as early as 1813.[16] The armed forces were also considered a "school of masculinity," and a school of civic "virtues."[17] In the United States, meanwhile, the relationship between masculinity, defensive capability, and citizenship was also intimately linked to skin color. Accordingly, recognized heroism was not just a male, but also a white privilege. African Americans fought in every American war, but never received the public recognition they deserved. In the fight against slavery, black Americans were initially barred from serving as soldiers in the Union Army, because war and heroism were supposed to be the sole preserve of the white man. Only from October 1862, in light of the prolonged Civil War, the many casualties, and emancipation, did African Americans serve in the Union army, a development they perceived as a decisive step toward becoming both men and citizens.[18]

Yet this did nothing to change the fact – in the incipient age of the competitive "Darwinist" struggle of all against all – that the nexus consisting of war-readiness, ideas of honor, and notions of masculinity was intimately tied to racial or nationalist fantasies of superiority. This is evident, not least, in colonial wars such as the Spanish–American–Filipino war of 1898–1913, and the two world wars, with their heroic visions as articulated by the likes of a Teddy Roosevelt or Ernst Jünger.[19] American politician, soldier, and self-proclaimed frontiersman and sportsman, Theodore "Teddy" Roosevelt, and German front-line soldier Ernst Jünger, exemplify the coexistence of martial ideas of heroism with the cult of the body and nation, a cult that had grown over the course of the nineteenth century. On the one hand, it was only by working on the body that military clout could be guaranteed, while on the other, work on the body was characterized by a military undertone of struggle and strength that echoes down to the present day.

The correlation between military clout and work on the body can be traced back as far as antiquity. An important turning point in this history is marked by the eighteenth century, when novel and growing attention was paid to the teachability of the body and its utilization. The soldier was one of the prototypes of the teachable body. Nevertheless, with regard to the training of soldiers in the eighteenth century, we cannot refer to fitness training, as this involves the self-controlled improvement of physical strength or stamina. In the case of the preparing of soldiers, meanwhile, the overriding priority was to access the body down to the most automatic of habits and the smallest of details. The emphasis was on optimizing bodily techniques, such as marching in step or handling a weapon, in order to turn the many different bodies into a well-coordinated and smoothly functioning collective. The soldier's body – alongside the worker – was a privileged object of the emerging "disciplines," those methods, according to Michel Foucault, "which made possible the meticulous control of the operations of the body, which assured the constant subjection of its forces and imposed upon them a relation of docility-utility." Thus, disciplinary power strengthens the body by increasing its (military or economic) utility, and at the same time weakens it by making it docile. One key difference from today's fitness heroes is that this type of submission to discipline is not voluntary or, at most, is far less voluntary.[20]

Prussian troops in the eighteenth century were famed for their discipline and effectiveness. From the interplay of the individual units, to the smallest movements of each soldier, every sequence of actions was ingrained to an unprecedented degree. It was this polish that the American militias initially lacked and that threatened to stymie their efforts in the Revolutionary War. And it was at the Valley Forge camp in Pennsylvania, in the winter of 1777–8, that the troops of the United States were first taught "regulations for order and discipline" by Prussian Baron Friedrich Wilhelm von Steuben, to quote the title of his guidebook. How much von Steuben's involvement actually influenced the course of the war is secondary here. But his manual remained in use for decades and is considered a milestone in the history of the disciplining, instruction, and training of modern civilian armies.[21]

However, it would be quite misleading to suggest that American revolutionaries systematically trained in order to enhance their physical performance and enable them to serve as soldiers, and they certainly did not do so of their own accord – though leaders such as Benjamin Franklin and Thomas Jefferson were already extolling the benefits of exercise for the body. Even in an elite forge such as West Point Military Academy, established in the young United States in 1802, physical training was initially neglected.

In Prussia, on the other hand, gymnastics and the German Turner movement began to spread during the wars of liberation, and it had a martial character from the very beginning. When the first gymnastics ground (*Turnplatz*) opened in Berlin's Hasenheide in 1811, the training of the body and of defensive capacity, as well as ideas of the nation and the heroic, were intertwined. From the 1840s, after the so-called *Turnsperre*, or prohibition on gymnastics, and even more from the 1860s onward, gymnastics came to play an increasingly important role in the education of boys in Prussia and other German states, as well as in the Royal Prussian Army. The training program provided for marching and a wide array of physical exercises, with and without equipment, and the gymnasts aspired to combine prudence, boldness, and steadfastness. The "gymnastics body" stood for the inculcated capacity for self-mastery as well as for the performance of the individual for the benefit of the nation. Gymnastics was considered the "best school" for enhancing "the people's defensive capacity"; it was a national movement and was increasingly linked with racially based notions of the people or nation.[22]

The first Turners had already arrived in the United States in the 1820s. Their gymnastics attracted attention at American universities, and soon English translations of German gymnastic manuals were available. But gymnastics attained a greater presence in the United States only after the immigration of a large number of Turners following the failed German revolution of 1848–9. After the Civil War, through a blend of transfer, adaptation, and transformation, gymnastics penetrated ever deeper into American society, its schools, universities, and the armed forces, alongside (and in combination with) forms of physical training similar to those practiced in various European countries. From then on, those who developed an enthusiasm for gymnastics in the United States often had one eye on Prussia's military strength. As US commentators stressed, it was in part undoubtedly Prussian soldiers' superior physical training that had proved decisive in the Franco–Prussian War of 1870–1. At the end of the nineteenth century – at the time of the first major upsurge in sport and fitness – military training programs too began to determinedly integrate physical exercise, emulated soon after by school curricula.[23]

By 1900, no one doubted that "the efficiency of an army was directly dependent upon the physical fitness of all of its members."[24] "The whole military fabric rests upon the physical character of the individuals composing it," was the message emanating from the US army. Elsewhere it was stated, in the best social Darwinist manner, that those "peoples" of the earth who lacked the willingness to optimize their bodies would eventually vanish. Henceforth, a note of social Darwinism could be heard in discussions of performance, the ability to get things done, and defensive capacity.[25]

As the United States then prepared for World War I, expanded its army and navy, and discussed conscription and the training of soldiers for possible combat, the theme of their physical performance also rose to prominence. Soldiers' health, strength, endurance, and the associated confidence were said to be essential to their survival. According to Leonard Wood, a vocal advocate of military fitness, these characteristics symbolized the quality and potential of a nation and its people, and must be practiced. Wood's career illustrates just how much the enthusiasm for fitness at the time was rooted in military, social Darwinist, and colonial contexts that romanticized the superiority and subduing of a nation, "people," or "race." Wood had earned his first military spurs in the wars of conquest against Native Americans and had been awarded a Medal of Honor for this. In the ensuing colonial wars in Cuba and the Philippines, he rose to become a major general, governor of the Philippine province of Moro, and ultimately chief of staff of the US army. Wood was also a physician and a great sports fan. Similar to Wood, his old wartime comrade and ex-president Theodore Roosevelt emphasized that every soldier must meet the highest standards of physical and moral fitness and that "the unfit should be ruthlessly weeded out."[26] When the United States entered World War I in April 1917 and called up all men liable for military service, it was said that "the greatest function of athletics is to educate the men into better fighters." But even though a body and fitness mania had been underway for years, the experience of the military camps and army physicals was disenchanting. First, the physical proved an insurmountable barrier for many young men. They were not considered fit enough for military service, which was extremely disquieting in an era of social Darwinism. As a reason for these physical deficits, both the American public and the political sphere mainly identified poor working conditions and poor nutrition. The US Food Administration, founded in 1917, was charged with providing aid and education, and with teaching the people to eat more economically and better. Second, recruits who passed the medical examination and made it into the training camps (located near the

US–Mexico border), often preferred to frequent the red-light district of Ciudad Juarez, bars, dance halls, and brothels, rather than to work on their fitness. Complaints about such conduct among soliders were also heard in Prussia and the German Empire. The US agency with responsibility for these matters, the Commission on Training Camp Activities, attempted to counteract this by intensifying recruits' physical training, providing sex education, and offering an entertainment program in the camps that was considered morally beneficial.[27]

The biopolitical mantra of the early twentieth century that "no nation ever will survive, whose people are not physically, mentally, and morally fit for survival," was put to the test in a new way by the economic crisis of the 1930s. In view of pervasive poverty, fatigue, weakness, and despair, it was hard to rave about the fitness of American men as a sign of their productiveness and autonomy. The New Deal was thus intended to strengthen the bodies of (mainly white) American men to the benefit of the nation, to cultivate their potential and boost their work performance, and to praise the latter two elements as heroic. In particular, the Civilian Conservation Corps, widely regarded as the most successful New Deal institution with the greatest degree of contemporary kudos, shows just how closely physical fitness, paramilitary structures, and the heroic were interlinked. At the same time, the CCC boys radiated diligence, potency, and eroticism (see figure 6).[28]

Similarly, US motivational campaigns for World War II presented a now strikingly muscular Uncle Sam. He was supposed to awaken the dormant potential for heroic deeds in the fight against fascism and dictatorship. However, the physicals once again told a different story. "Far too many young people are unable to serve their country because they are not in tip-top physical shape," as US army leaders lamented. Fully 35.8 percent of Americans, that is, 6.5 million men, were mustered out as unfit because they appeared to be too physically or mentally weak, or were suffering from a sexually transmitted disease. Commentators identified the cause chiefly as the long years of economic crisis and the emaciated bodies it had produced, but they also claimed that the increasingly mechanized and disembodied world of work had led to a lack of fitness. A newly established National Committee on Physical Fitness was intended to counteract this, led by John Kelly, Olympic rowing champion of 1920 and 1924, in collaboration with representatives of

Figure 6   Civilian Conservation Corps workers, 1930s
Source: Library of Congress, Prints & Photographs Division, FSA /OWI Collection,
LC-USF33- 000068-M4

the armed forces and the medical profession. "Victory through Fitness" was the slogan coined in this context.[29]

The militarization and heroization of the trained body attained its clearest form in fascism. The vision of the tough, strong-willed, high-performing male body, which was ready to fight any battle and make sacrifices for the nation as a *Volksgemeinschaft* ("people's community"), found its most extreme expression in fascism and Nazism.[30] Physical exercises, it was believed, created the basis for individuals' defensive capabilities. The core of this militarized conception of performance was the high-performing "Aryan" body. Its perfection was to come into play above all in the form of military strength, as well as in sportiness, productivity, and reproductive quality, with the latter in particular being demanded of the woman's body as well. In its racist logic, the perfection of the "people's (or national) body" demanded the exclusion or annihilation of all those who could not be fit into this fantasy of performance, purity, and heroism.[31]

Moments of transition to a post-heroic era?

Nazism and its profoundly racist ideology of the master race were the culmination of a militantly heroic politics of the body. This politics was saturated with visions of optimizing some and excluding others. Yet en route to this belief system, the military-heroic ideal had already been deeply ruptured by World War I.

World War I was initially celebrated as an opportunity to show the "old German heroic spirit," but, in the end, soldierly heroism and fitness could hardly be considered decisive to the war's outcome.[32] How were soldiers who had to endure days and weeks in the mud of the trenches, under endless barrage and shrapnel fire, and then – if they survived at all – lived on as "war cripples," the facially injured, or "shell-shocked," to come across as heroic? In Germany alone, 2.7 million men returned from the war with permanent injuries and illnesses. The many injured were a disquieting presence on both sides of the Atlantic, and shell shock puzzled both physicians and military personnel. Clearly, the overwhelming force of industrialized war had eliminated the prospect of becoming a hero in war as an individual. When the war was over, many of the physically and mentally damaged, their productive capacity and virility much reduced, found it impossible to cope with everyday life. Although it was often claimed that men fit with prostheses were able to work, many of them experienced these artificial additions as an expression of a malfunctioning body infested with machine-like elements, rather than as a sign of the possible and feasible. In an achievement-focused society, such individuals inevitably seemed deficient. The overpowering of the human physical form by war and prosthetics intensified the subjugation and massification of the body experienced in the age of mechanized work at the assembly lines of Fordism. "The tiny, fragile human body," to quote Walter Benjamin, was "exposed to a force field of destructive currents and explosions." How does one become a hero under such circumstances?[33]

Yet neither the devastating consequences of the war nor the demobilization of the German army after Versailles could prevent the large-scale remilitarization of German politics, society, and culture in the interwar period. The veritable crisis of the war hero was countered with praise for the "iron will" that those "crushed by war" had shown on the battlefields of World War I and now showed at home.[34] Associated with this were visions of armored bodies, visions that reached their apogee in the (once again) heroically imagined struggle for the race-based "people's community" of Nazi Germany. Yet National Socialism not only took the heroic to a historical extreme, but also pushed it over the edge. When every soldier and laborer was praised as a hero in the name of the "Aryan people's community," and when the missive informing relatives of the death of their husband, son, or brother, was a mere form letter, and all of this was not part of a heroic victory but of total defeat, the hero concept was taken to a point of absurdity. Fifty million war dead and responsibility for the Shoah, moreover, made military heroism for the nation and Fatherland a more than dubious proposition. However, this insight was only to become a majority view in the young Federal Republic following the social upheavals of 1968 and the associated process of coming to terms with Nazism. Due to the social revolution of the 1960s, military heroism came to be viewed with contempt in the following decades. In addition, after World War II, combat missions by German soldiers were taboo for many decades. Until 1999, and the first foreign mission by the German army in Kosovo, German soldiers had no route to becoming war heroes.[35]

In the United States, military heroism retained its potency longer than in Germany, and the decline of the hero was more erratic and ambiguous. One reason for this was that American soldiers had fought and won the so-called "good war" in World War II. They had made sacrifices for liberty, democracy, and the "American way of life."[36] To be sure, the enthusiasm for the heroic American struggle against dictatorship was mixed with skeptical tones that deplored American GIs' experience of violence and traumatization, and questioned hero worship. But more than two decades were to pass before the war in Vietnam deeply unsettled Americans' view of the military and the heroic. First, Vietnam showed that the United States could lose a war. Second, as the war progressed, few could retain the belief that the American GIs in Southeast Asia were making sacrifices for freedom and democracy. In the eyes of many critics, they were involved in a prolonged colonial war, and had become murderers rather than warriors for a just cause. Third, they represented the pursuit of imperial power by political leaders who were lying to their own people. Hence, in much the same way as had occurred in other countries, criticism of the Vietnam War and the mythos of military heroism was part of a fundamental social, political, and anti-patriarchal critique in the United States.[37]

After 1968, then, heroism initially seemed to belong in the past on both sides of the Atlantic. At the same time, however, at least in the United States, commentators expressed concern over the loss of soldierly, heroic qualities in civic life. In the early 1970s, a variety of actors complained that American society had lost its heroes. What they had in mind were men who fought with dedication for what they believed in. What mattered here was not so much the specific objective being fought for as the readiness to fight for something, the willingness to take risks and accept the need for sacrifices. This is just what the activists involved in social movements exemplified as they strove to achieve a more just world, but they evidently made poor heroes for the majority of Americans.[38]

Instead, many observers deplored the supposedly complacent 1950s, with their cozy and standardized suburbs, consumption frenzy, and business corporations, for allegedly depriving the white American male of his strength and dynamism. He had become a "cheap yes man," as Betsy Rath scathingly asserted of her husband Tom, the main protagonist in the 1955 novel (and subsequent Hollywood movie) *The Man in the Gray Flannel Suit*, the prototype of the over-adjusted and apathetic American suburban male. "The white collar man," declared sociologist and intellectual C. Wright Mills as early as 1951, "is the hero as victim, the small creature who is acted upon but who does not act." But it was not just the demasculinization brought about by standardized family life and the standardized working world that stripped the former paratrooper Tom Rath of any vestige of heroism. Tom had also been traumatized by the horrors of war. He would have liked to forget World War II, while his wife Betsy demanded that her husband show more soldierly heroism in civilian life. He ought to get himself out there and fight for something again. He ought to show motivation and commitment, seize opportunities, break through barriers, and actively pursue happiness.[39]

There were widespread fears of a new softness, which soon seemed to find physical expression in the flabbiness of conformist, inactive men suffering from heart disease. The white American man faced the prospect of "slow death by conformity," rather than making his mark through exceptional achievements, wrote Norman Mailer in the mid-1950s. Similarly, historian and political advisor Arthur M. Schlesinger emphasized that the United States was allowing itself to be buffeted by the tides of history rather than making history itself. John F. Kennedy fueled hopes of a revival of masculine heroism in American politics and society, if only for a short time. Indeed, Norman Mailer saw Kennedy as a superhero battling against effeminacy and promoting male hardness and "total fitness." During the Cold War, this was a battle with direct military implications. Mailer rhapsodized about Kennedy as a superman who had come to the supermarket and was brimming with youth, dynamism, and vigor. Today we know this was more appearance than substance, though this did nothing to diminish JFK's aura. But the athletic and boyish hero, who promised to cure the American nation of its lethargy, of its overreliance on insurance and welfare, was no more than an interlude.[40] In the wake of the Vietnam War, many Americans ceased to believe that the United States would conquer new frontiers, and lost all faith in an increasingly corrupt political leadership. The Watergate scandal of 1972 was the nadir in this regard.

Fitness heroes II

Yet the hero was soon to recover. The idea that we have been living in post-heroic societies since 1968 is, at most, a conditional truth. By the early 1980s, the hero had begun to enjoy a renaissance in the United States, in a familiar yet changed form. This process has continued to gather pace in the twenty-first century, not only in America, but in Germany and other countries as well. The new hero, who is often male but increasingly female as well, is meant to represent individuality and autonomy, and should be ready for battle, powerful, and sexy. He or she embodies the values of flexible capitalism and the fitness society, which have become even more important over the years. But let us begin in the early 1980s.

When Ronald Reagan became president of the United States on January 20, 1981, one of his top objectives was supposedly to make the country self-confident and self-reliant once again. For Reagan, it was time to move on from the humiliation of the post-Vietnam era and reverse the sense – so prevalent as a consequence of the economic, energy, and social crisis of the 1970s – that the American way of life had had its day. The revival of the hero was one of the strategies intended to achieve this. In his inaugural address to an audience of millions, Reagan already contradicted the widespread belief that there were no more heroes in America. If one looked just a little more closely, Reagan averred, one would find heroes in all those citizens who took on the challenges of everyday life, who battled through life with diligence and decency, and survived its ups and downs.[41] The most important criteria for this resuscitated heroism were the willingness and ability to take one's life into one's own hands, while demonstrating stamina, and not relying on others, let alone on the government. Only those who trusted in themselves could determine the course of events rather than being determined by them.[42]

The place where one could become a hero now was the battlefield of everyday life. Ultimately, what the new Reagan administration invoked was self-reliance in everyday life, while calling for Americans to fight for success rather than succumbing to self-satisfaction, and to take action and make sacrifices rather than relying on welfare, or what was left of it from the days of the New Deal and Great Society. The rebirth of the hero in a different guise was accompanied by the end of the "social." Good government, the now dominant political ideology proclaimed, was the people's self-government rather than government by others. Everyone, to cite the prevailing political message in an era of neoliberalism, who makes enough effort and manages to cope with the world, is a hero or heroine. The centerpiece of this novel form of heroism was not so much the nation as the individual person and their own success. The individual's determination, and ability, to take responsibility for themself and their life were viewed as the prerequisites for collective wellbeing.[43]

One of the mainstays of the Reagan restoration, that is, America's reanimation in the name of individualism and revitalized heroism, was a renewed body mania. This was by no means specific to the United States. Consonant with the emphasis placed on individualism, autonomy, and flexibilization, this valorization of the body gripped capitalist societies as a whole, at a somewhat different pace and with varying degrees of intensity in different countries. The body mania was also articulated in a range of ways. One variant was the muscular body, which overlaps partially with the fit body but also differs from it. The extreme form of the muscular body is the physique of the ambitious bodybuilder. Bodybuilders, however, are not fitness-oriented athletes. They see themselves as competitive athletes and, above all, as artists. In the cult movie *Pumping Iron* (1977), which depicted the early bodybuilding scene in the United States, Arnold Schwarzenegger, many-times winner of the *Mr. Universe* and *Mr. Olympia* titles, compares his training to the work of a sculptor. But unlike the sculptor, he explains, the shaping of his body requires him to chisel steel and shed gallons of sweat to achieve the desired aesthetic effect. The need for persistent diligence and hard work on oneself, with the goal of achieving an optimal result, is certainly highly reminiscent of the idea of fitness. Yet here the concrete goal of self-optimization, the type of success involved – namely the cultivation of bulging muscles – corresponds at most in a qualified sense to the core principle of fitness. Notions of bodily aesthetics cannot be separated from fitness (one need only think of the importance of being slim in contrast to being fat, or the many images of "fitness heroes" on Instagram). But in the world of fitness, bodily aesthetics must always have, or at least signal, a specific functionality. The body of the ambitious bodybuilder, however, is vain, dysfunctional, and, as Jörg Scheller writes, "ill-suited to everyday life." It is not really fit for work, impotence is a common side effect of hard training and doping, and the bodybuilder's body does not fit into a uniform.[44]

President Reagan was aware, or at least had some sense, of the ambivalent signals emanating from the body that results from "pumping iron." On the one hand, for Reagan, the visibly muscular body was the best symbol of a new policy of strength and of the ability to take responsibility and fight for one's goals – at all levels of society, and both internationally and nationally. At the same time, however, Reagan preached functional fitness, a well-balanced exercise program and a balanced diet. He rhapsodized about hard work such as chopping wood or riding (the hero as depicted in Westerns fits neatly with this concept) as well as open-water swimming and lifting weights in the gym. In line with this, Reagan called his workout program *Pumping Firewood*.[45]

The boom in gyms from the 1980s, however, illustrates the new appeal of the muscularly defined and powerful-looking body, as strikingly expressed in the pop culture veneration of figures such as John Rambo or Rocky Balboa. Reagan liked to present himself as a Rambo fan, and not without reminding Americans of his own film career. Rambo and Rocky (and perhaps the Terminator, played by Arnold Schwarzenegger) may be considered *the* blockbuster icons of the 1980s. They must also be regarded as emblematic of many other characters who appeared in countless B-movies. Both figures were portrayed by Sylvester Stallone, who united within himself a new type of martial hero (the loner John Rambo, who acts in opposition to the system that betrayed him), and a sporting hero and above all everyday hero (the Italian-American boxer and underdog Rocky Balboa from working-class Philadelphia, a figure who literally fights his way upward). Both Rocky and Rambo showed how, with the help of a hardened, muscular, yet highly functional body, coupled with determination, readiness, and the right attitude, one can make one's mark and become a hero. A Rocky statue has been erected in Philadelphia, a city badly hit by economic crisis and post-industrialization in the late twentieth and early twenty-first centuries, at the bottom of the steps before the Philadelphia Museum of Art, a spot made legendary by his movies. This heroic body of Reagan-era America is quintessentially male, white, and heterosexual, and is thus also part of the backlash against social movements, their demands and achievements in the struggle for recognition and diversity. At the same time, however, despite all the conservative counter-forces, social movements have permanently breached many barriers, enabling a variety of social groups to appropriate the ideal of the muscular body. Hence, the gay community too features a cult of body and muscles, and there are female fitness heroines as well. Jane Fonda propelled the body and fitness mania of the 1980s at least as much as Sylvester Stallone.[46]

Hence, the rebirth of the heroic hard body, which seems to have been tougher than ever before, is an element in historical shifts that put the autonomous individual and their readiness for battle at the center of the social order. This willingness to fight, despite seemingly hopeless odds, is the central characteristic of Rocky and Rambo. But beyond Hollywood and beyond the new armored body, many Americans took the call to make themselves battle-ready very literally. In the following decades, a paramilitary culture emerged on an unprecedented scale. Its members armed themselves and – perhaps more than ever – embraced the cult of weapons. Since the 1970s, the number of weapons in American private households has more than tripled and has increased to well over 300 million today. The National Rifle Association has grown into one of the most influential lobbying groups in the United States, with more than four million members. All of this is embedded in a pronounced paramilitary culture, featuring the autonomous warrior as the ideal of the heroic male, militias, target practice, war games, glossy weapons magazines, YouTube channels, and all the associated paraphernalia.[47]

Forming part of the background to this development, we must also consider the great importance in the United States of the armed forces, which have become even more significant since 9/11. Since the end of World War II, there have been only three years, from October 1976 to November 1979, when the United States was not at war. The Department of Defense absorbs much of the federal budget, and with over 700,000 civilian employees and 1.4 million soldiers (in 2015), it is the country's largest employer. In addition, in the era of outsourcing, many private companies are making a lot of money from American military interventions and employ another large group of workers in fields such as logistics and infrastructure. The importance of the armed forces in US society also derives from the fact that so-called minorities have repeatedly used military service – historically one of the key privileges of white heterosexual men – to advance their struggle for civil equality and recognition. This applies to African Americans, and to gays and lesbians, who were tacitly admitted to military service in 1994 and without restriction since 2011, and to women, who have been deployed in all ground forces and combat units since 2016.[48]

At the intersection of the armed forces and society, paramilitary culture, and the heroic hard body lie the Special Forces. The admiration for these military units stems mainly from the fact that they often operate in a gray area, without vast quantities of military equipment, behind enemy lines. Hence, their success or failure, their life or death, depends primarily on their own efforts and abilities. These abilities are not solely physical, but entail physical elements, acquired through a veritable torture of seemingly endless training sessions of almost inhuman harshness. The fascination with the Special Forces, their training and physicality, which is so prevalent in the media and in popular culture, nourishes their mythical heroism. The recent enthusiasm for high-intensity forms of fitness and competition, such as CrossFit, the Warrior Workout or Tough Mudder, derives not least from their elite military associations and the associated fantasies of performance and heroism they arouse.[49]

But the hard body of the late twentieth and early twenty-first centuries is not just the muscle-bound body of the elite soldier or bodybuilder. The fit body, trained for performance and health, is also hardened, is the result of hard work, and is presented as a sign of willpower and the ability to take on tough challenges. The fitness athlete is the ideal type of self-regulated motivation and thus of the neoliberal self. This fitness athlete too has increasingly taken on an aura of heroism since the 1980s, albeit initially less explicitly, via the values and characteristics that are associated with it and that it literally embodies.[50] This brings us back to sports presenter Johannes B. Kerner, who describes the high-intensity training that goes on at the Urban Heroes gym as heroic, just as he does his marathons (even though there are now hundreds of thousands of so-called finishers every year). For Kerner, the marathon, as well as the training undertaken at Urban Heroes, illustrates a willingness to take on the torment of training and to make sacrifices, to grow beyond one's limits and to achieve something extraordinary. The age of fitness operates, in significant part, by promising that we all have the potential to become heroes or heroines.

Let's take a closer look at the running movement and the history of its self-image, which has increasingly taken on heroic overtones. At first, there was rarely any explicit mention of heroism. In the 1970s, running was still too beholden to the alternative movement, that is, to contexts that criticized the heroic as militaristic and patriarchal. At the same time, however, patterns of discourse soon began to emerge that classified running into categories that overlapped with those of the heroic. Thus, first of all, there was soon talk of running as a (substitute) religious practice, which – like the heroic sphere – operated through ideas of the elect. To take up running meant living a thoroughly different lifestyle, starting with a true conversion experience: a paradigm shift away from lethargy and inactivity to diligence and self-control, away from beer and burgers to energy drinks and granola. The running magazines were full of letters to the editor reflecting this change, whose mostly male authors swore that they had embraced a new lifestyle with every fiber of their being. Furthermore, in true Puritan predestinarian style, this conversion placed one among the "chosen," and here the trained body was the best indication that one was doing something out of the ordinary. "A belief in running, 'the new religion'," stated a dedicated runner in *Runner's World* in 1978, "is a belief in oneself, in one's power, in one's ability to improve, discipline and take charge of one's own life."[51] Some sources were already describing life as a "long marathon" and running as a school of life. This sounds very much like heroism à la Ronald Reagan.

Second, it this very struggle with oneself and one's own performance (rather than with others) that increasingly moved center-stage in the "age of me." This was especially true of the middle-aged man, who got "soft, overweight, and old" in his forties and fifties, but who did not have to let this happen to him if only he was strong-willed enough. Fitness athletes, it was asserted time and again, showed that bodies do not necessarily get fat with age, that performance does not necessarily diminish, and that age-related and bodily limits, which had previously been considered natural, do not exist in this form.[52] This self-image helped lend contour to the everyman as a hero, even if this figure was, initially, rarely designated explicitly as a hero. From time to time, however, reports such as that concerning amateur runner Jay Wendt appeared. Wendt needed more than four hours to complete the New York Marathon. No sports star, his biggest fan club was his own family. Still, he was highly motivated, especially when the beats of the *Rocky* soundtrack were booming from loudspeakers along the route. Jay Wendt showed that in a marathon, it was not just Olympic champions such as Frank Shorter who could become heroes, but everyone who managed to go the distance. In the marathon, everyone can be their own hero.[53]

The tone and core themes had taken hold. To run a marathon is to do something extraordinary, and the applause of the masses, testifying to this heroic act, is a foregone conclusion. What became questionable over time was whether a marathon was really enough of a challenge, given that the masses were not only watching, but also taking part and reaching the finish line. In 1979, the number of those taking part in New York exceeded 10,000 for the first time. The number grew to more than 20,000 in 1986, more than 30,000 in 1994, more than 40,000 in 2009, and more than 50,000 in 2013. At first, vanishingly few women took part, but their numbers grew over the years. Heroism was no longer an exclusively male privilege. In 2000, German foreign minister Joschka Fischer took part in the Big Apple's marathon; it was his third (see figure 7). Fischer, then around 50 years old, was probably the most famous German marathon runner at the time. He shed over 60 pounds by running, and in his book he described with great media impact how running had shown him the "long road to himself," regardless of how many other people took part.[54]

For a fair number of people, however, a marathon was no longer enough. The triathlon, especially the "Ironman," and "ultra-runs" exerted ever more fascination as the twentieth century neared its end. On the one hand, the prevalent motto was "more, longer, and harder." On the other, it was claimed that neither distance nor pace mattered. Instead, the crucial thing was goal-setting itself, and to be passionate about something. The idea was that those who feel, during training, that their goals are actually achievable, develop a new kind

Figure 7 German politician and soon-to-be foreign minister Joschka Fischer (wearing 50), here with German running guru Herbert Steffny (wearing 51) participating in the Hansemarathon, April 19, 1998
Source: Getty Images, Bongarts/Staff

of self-confidence. "I felt more in control of my life," enthused James Fixx, the author of one of the world's most successful running books at the time, as he mused on running as a route to human freedom. There was no longer much doubt that working on one's own fitness taught one the techniques for coping with life, for extending and even going far beyond one's limits. Women gradually appeared more often in this new world of heroes, of marathon runners and triathletes. At the same time, however, many sources still tended to reduce them to menstrual problems, to issues of weight and bodily aesthetics.[55]

In the twenty-first century, the renaissance of the heroic in the age of fitness then gathered pace exponentially. *Runner's World*, for example, the world's biggest running magazine, sold in Germany since 1993, has explicitly embraced the heroic since 2004. The annual *Heroes of Running* award combines recognition for the everyday heroism of all runners with special acknowledgment of exceptional achievements and their power to inspire. One of the first awards for example, went to Kay

Morris from Texas. In her Marathon Kids project, she runs with fat children to show them that they can overcome any obstacle, even if it initially seems hard, if not insurmountable. Then governor of Arkansas, Mike Huckabee, was also honored for shedding more than 100 pounds by running and for launching the Healthy Arkansas fitness project. Yet despite all the appreciation for the particular, the core message of the *Heroes of Running* award is still that every runner deserves recognition for their dedication to fitness and their work on themselves, no matter what they accomplish or their reasons for running. The editorial on running heroes in *Runner's World* thus states:

> Go to any 5-K, marathon, track, or running trail in America, and you'll find them. They are the beginners who cross a finish line for the first time. They are the veterans whose commitment to the sport never wavers, season after season, year after year. They are the phenoms and the underdogs who defy limitations and shatter expectations. Every day at *Runner's World*, we are inspired by these runners. They all reinforce how with a simple act – the motion of moving forward – we can shape each other, our sport, our world.[56]

It is also striking that, in recent times, a readiness to perform feats of physicality in the name of heroic fitness has once again taken on clear martial overtones – in Germany as elsewhere. Magazines such as *Men's Health* celebrate "superhero workouts," while high-intensity forms of training and competition like CrossFit or the Warrior Workout are booming, as are outdoor competitions such as Tough Mudder. Thousands of people compete in these obstacle-cum-mud races, with names like Spartan Beast or Warrior Dash. Here competitors not only run many kilometers along trails and through mud, but also scale artificial walls, crawl under barbed wire, and plunge into pools of icy water (see figure 8). Evidently, the fascination exercised by these contests stems partly from the overcoming of obstacles that symbolize real-life problems, as well as from the conquering of territory, and the fact that even the best lone wolves cannot succeed without the team. The maxim at play here is "face your fears, reach your limits, and know you can go beyond them, even if you think it's impossible. Failure is not an option." What could be more heroic? These races simultaneously form

Figure 8 Tough Mudder competitors in Gilford, NH, June 1, 2013; picture published by the Defense Imagery Management Operations Center of the US Department of Defense with the caption: "Tough Mudder events are 12-mile obstacle courses designed to test all-around strength, stamina, mental grit and camaraderie"
Source: Defence Imagery Database

part of an "event culture" that facilitates the experience of heroism in a vast simulation of the struggle for survival. The military facade seems once again to have become compatible with this objective.[57]

"Our future as a species"

Fitness ticks virtually all the boxes of the heroic in the twenty-first century. In the era of flexible capitalism, we are all enjoined, day in, day out, and in virtually every situation, to take on the struggles of everyday life, challenge boundaries, open up and exploit opportunities, surpass expectations, and never let up. The victory to be won in this way is neither a victory over an external enemy nor is it a victory for the idea of a nation, let alone a "people's community." First and foremost, it is a victory over and for ourselves, and over life as a never-ending test of our determination. And this victory is all the more heroic the harder it was fought for and the more sweat it has cost us.[58]

Yet overall, the message we receive time and again is that the weal and woe of liberal-democratic societies as a whole depends on individuals' dedication, and on their willingness to ceaselessly fight for their own fitness.[59] Even from an evolutionary perspective, the fit person appears as the best of the human species: "We [fitness fans] are the guarantors of our future as a species, but the golf cart, the elevator and the TV set are in our way," to quote the narrative spun in the mid-1980s by a report on the importance of running in human history. These technologies, the text averred, fostered inertia and thus underlay the increasing corpulence of growing numbers of people.[60]

The classification of fatness as epidemic underlines the extent to which fat is perceived as a serious threat to a collective body. The fat body is not only regarded as the prototype of the sluggish and sick body, but also of the non-hero in the age of fitness. The fat person can (essentially) only become a hero if they lose weight. Otherwise, the fat body is believed to indicate a lack of vigor and agency, and thus a failure to meet the requirements of society and the prerequisites for heroism.[61] Fat bodies represent the adversary that must be fought, one that is therefore needed in order to make the heroism of those who defy body fat shine all the brighter. And fat is a dogged opponent that strikes back the moment one shows the slightest sign of weakness.[62]

After 9/11, and in a rapidly militarizing society, the United States in particular discussed the fight against fat in the martial rhetoric of national security. The country declared war on fat around the same time it pledged to wage war on terror. Body fat was claimed to be a bioweapon at least as lethal as anything Saddam Hussein could dream up. Yet fat, this narrative contended, is an even more dangerous enemy because it comes not from outside, but from the heart of American society. Self-discipline, a readiness to act, and a healthy lifestyle are the best strategies in this war, as the Council for a Strong America, which advises the Pentagon, stressed in the fall of 2018. Rampant obesity among young people, its report states, poses a threat to the functioning of US troops, while poor national health is a risk to national security. Many Americans, the report warns, are simply too fat to fight.[63]

As we have seen, fitness and fitness heroism have historically had deeply martial foundations. The echo of this military grounding continues to be heard when it comes to fighting, toughness, and perseverance, and more loudly at present than in the late twentieth century. This is apparent in Warrior Workout and Tough Mudder, and texts such as the book by former racing cyclist Olivier Haralambon, who calls the cobblestones of Paris-Roubaix an "army of soldiers" baring their teeth. The drenched, dirty, and freezing body of the cyclist after racing over this surface reminds him of "coal mines, violence, or war." The cycle race as a kind of battle, in which all who persevere become heroes: this is also the rhetoric frequently deployed by the organizers of all-comers' races, where tens of thousands of participants are not concerned with winning, only with overcoming their own limitations and finishing faster than the year before.[64] The hero is the virtually prototypical form of subject in the fitness society, and the fitness hero is the prototypical form of subject in neoliberalism. After all, the fitness society expects its members to assert themselves and achieve an outstanding performance, expand their room for maneuver and overcome limits, to always strive for something special, and more than satisfy the demands of everyday life. The hero ticks all these boxes. Not only are the metaphors of sport, fitness, and fighting ideal means of expressing this day-to-day struggle for success and distinction. As lived practice too, fitness symbolizes the readiness for permanent struggle with oneself, without which one cannot succeed in circumstances of omnipresent competition. "Outstanding performance," writes media studies scholar Norbert Bolz, "in other words, deviance paired with conformity," is the best way to become a hero in our present-day society. If the fitness aficionado strives for a higher good, as befits a true hero, then this good is their own success, raised to the status of social principle. The sum of individual successes, we are given to understand, then leads to the wellbeing of the collective. Accordingly, the prevalence of non-heroes is described as epidemic and thus as a health risk, which threatens the population and society as a whole through the individual body. This is the biopolitics of the twenty-first century.[65]

6

PRODUCTIVE, POTENT, AND READY TO FIGHT?

In October 2018, Tess Holliday became the first so-called plus-size model to appear on the cover of *Cosmopolitan* magazine (see figure 9). Holliday is a star of the scene. She had already made it onto *People* magazine, and had appeared in advertising for H&M. But *Cosmopolitan* is in a different league. The cover triggered a contentious debate. The usual hate-filled comments on fat bodies appeared on social media, but even beyond that, the tone of the debate was shrill. Agitated commentators criticized the fashion and media world for suddenly discovering fatness and increasingly presenting it as normal, and even desirable. A woman like Holliday, they complained, was being turned into a role model, and the social and health consequences would be disastrous.

Other observers, meanwhile, praised the cover image precisely because it was helping normalize fatness, and thus propelling what they saw as a long overdue development. The cover image, they contended, simply shows a fat woman who clearly feels comfortable in her own skin and is presenting her body with self-confidence rather than hiding it. Holliday herself stated that she was in no way seeking to promote fatness through her appearance on the magazine's cover. Instead, she wanted to help people feel satisfied with themselves and their bodies. She is an icon of the body positivity movement, which is out to achieve this very goal, namely helping people enjoy a more relaxed relationship

Figure 9   Tess Holliday on the cover of *Cosmopolitan* (UK), October 2018
Source: © Ben Watts/Courtesy Hearst Magazines UK

with their bodies and thus creating a greater sense of wellbeing and, ultimately, improving their health.

The Tess Holliday *Cosmopolitan* cover appeared in the fall of 2018, at a time when the social and health science perspective on fatness and its relationship to fitness had increasingly begun to shift. Even medical journals had begun to engage in a provocative and open-ended debate on the precise relationship between fatness, lack of education, and poverty,[1] and whether there is a causal relationship between body fat, health, and disease. Some medical texts warned against normalizing fatness. Others, however, asserted that it is not body fat but the condition of the cardiovascular system that is crucial to life expectancy. They also emphasized that a more relaxed relationship with one's body has been shown to improve one's health, in stark contrast to constant and, often, unsuccessful dieting.[2] In other words, the stigma of fatness as incompatible with fitness has begun to soften (at least a little). At the same time, even though fatness and fitness are no longer necessarily regarded as opposites, the performance-ready and performance-capable individual continues to be the norm, and fitness is viewed as the ideal to be strived for.

The medical debate is also making waves in non-scientific media, such as *Die Zeit* weekly newspaper, the daily *Süddeutsche Zeitung* and the *New York Times*.[3] The concept of body positivity has become ubiquitous – to the chagrin even of some of those committed to combating discrimination against fat people. Writers and bloggers such as Magda Albrecht and Jes Baker are not fundamentally bothered by the fact that lifestyle magazines and the fashion industry have discovered body positivity. But they lament the way in which the pop cultural hype has diminished the critical perspective, and sometimes even thrown it into reverse. The constant preoccupation with the body and the self, a phenomenon reflected and promoted by body positivity as a mass-media phenomenon, fits snugly into our body-focused world in the age of fitness.[4]

Albrecht and Baker are part of the growing group of fat activists who have increasingly been making their voices heard in recent years, on social media, and through their blogs and books (as yet, more in the United States than in Germany). They seek to combat discrimination against fat people and critique a society that interprets everything fat people do or do not do, everything they have or do not have, in light of their body shape. Some see themselves as part of a movement that has made Health At Every Size (HAES) its guiding principle. In German, this has found expression in the somewhat trivializing rhyming slogan *rund und gesund* (round and healthy). HAES contradicts the idea that fat necessarily makes you ill, and refutes the tendency to relate every aspect of fat bodies to their fatness. Its exponents also seek to challenge the notion, as it has gained traction since the 1970s, that health is the responsibility of each individual. Some fat activists fundamentally question the claim that we should gear our entire lifestyle toward health and fitness as values.[5]

The political dimension of this struggle was emphasized by US author Virgie Tovar in her book *Hot & Heavy*: "My fat is political because when I show it off it really seems to piss people off. My fat is political because I'm keeping it. My fat is political because it's fucking hot." Certainly, she states, women in particular live in a time of unprecedented opportunities and freedoms, "and yet my freedom to be fat is heavily contested by my government, my community, my television set." Fat and bodies, Tovar contends elsewhere, regulate "access to meaningful participation in society."[6]

When it comes to putting their promises of liberty and equality into practice, liberal societies operate via the body, and here fitness, coupled with the form and materiality of the body, is central. Fat activists have highlighted this thoroughly political dimension of bodies since the late 1960s. They saw themselves as part of the multifaceted social and political movements that demanded recognition and equal participation in society for all people, regardless of their skin color, gender, sexual preferences – or body shape and bodily materiality. Fat activists founded a group called NAAFA, which stands for the National Association to Advance Fat Acceptance. The name and acronym are inspired by the most important and well-known African American civil rights group, the NAACP, the National Association for the Advancement of Colored People. The name reflects the fat activists' agenda, which has been firmly political from the outset. This also applies to another, more radical group called Fat Underground. In November 1973, Fat Underground published the *Fat Liberation Manifesto*, declaring its solidarity with all other groups suffering discrimination and demanding recognition, full political and social participation, and an end to the pressure to diet and the belief that fat is unhealthy per se, that fat people are unfit, lazy, and second-class citizens. Echoing the "black is beautiful" slogan propagated by the Black Power movement, activists began to proclaim that "fat can be beautiful." The *Fat Liberation Manifesto* concluded by recalling the most famous call to fight oppression in world history: "Fat people of the world, unite! You have nothing to lose. . . ."[7]

Fat activism, then, is a form of social critique and political struggle. It rejects "compulsory able-bodiedness" and the "thin [social] contract." Compulsory able-bodiedness does not mean someone forces us to exercise under direct threat of violence, compelling us to make our bodies lean, flexible, and powerful. It means that certain ideas about the body are highly normative, creating differences and exclusions via the body. Philosopher Abby Wilkerson's critique of the "thin contract" makes similar points. Although the society entering into this contract claims to be a union of all people, it concurrently pushes some people to the margins. This social contract not only guarantees rights and participation, but also sets out expectations of those who seek recognition as full-fledged members of a society, and wish to participate in it fully. Anyone who is not slim and, therefore, does not appear fit enough, is frequently stigmatized as unable or unwilling to fulfill these expectations. Such individuals are denied full recognition as citizens and subjects; to cite philosopher Judith Butler, they are expelled to those "'unlivable' or 'uninhabitable' zones of social life which are nevertheless densely populated by those who do not enjoy the status of the subject."[8]

Liberal societies have regulated participation and recognition largely via the body since the eighteenth century. Right from the beginning, skin color, gender, and sexuality have been of decisive importance, in other words, physically conceived categories. When liberalism and Darwinism became more and more intertwined in the second half of the nineteenth century, the principles of liberal-democratic self-management and competition acquired the character of naturally given imperatives. The active pursuit of fitness pushed its way to the center of social organization and individual existence. Henceforth, the form and materiality of the body were viewed as an expression of the ability to govern oneself, to shape one's life, to perform, and to survive in circumstances of omnipresent competition. Fat increasingly ceased to symbolize success and wealth and instead became emblematic of indolence and lack of willpower, bad decisions, a deficient lifestyle and lack of commitment to the world. Fat was scarcely capable of embodying the capacity for sociopolitical activity and participation – and its connotations were chiefly feminine. Modern society contrasted the softness of fat with the firmness of muscle. Henceforth, the muscle stood for agency, willpower, efficiency, and movement. It thus embodied the qualities that were expected of the citizens of liberal societies and that were long imagined as male. Accordingly, in the first women's movement, the exercising of the body was a means of demanding political equality. In the current age of fitness, fitness and the muscular body are no longer thought of so clearly in masculine terms as they were until the 1970s and the social changes wrought by feminism. At the same time, the muscular body, more than ever, seems to represent the ability to take things into one's own hands, to be high-performing and powerful, to achieve staying power, to be successful and potent, and to achieve one's goals. Of course, the right amount of muscle is decisive. Too much is counterproductive. This is why the bodybuilder's body signals vanity and excess. It is dysfunctional and essentially unfit for everyday life. In the first fitness wave, around 1900, bodybuilders were already described as "hyperplastic monstrosities."[9]

Social and cultural scientists Jennifer Lee and Cat Pausé assert that fat people are stigmatized as failed citizens.[10] When Lee and Pausé refer to citizens, they mean a form of belonging that cannot be derived from place of birth or descent. They seek to interrogate who is regarded as capable of coping successfully with the expectations and responsibilities of civil participation. This is not so much a matter of obeying laws, paying taxes, or voting every few years. Full recognition as a citizen, and unconditional membership of a society of free and equal individuals, requires more than this, namely actively taking responsibility for the prosperity, growth, and defense of society.[11] The body is viewed as an expression of the ability or inability to meet these requirements. In recent years, dis/ability studies in particular has shown that full citizenship and the recognition of a person as fully human are derived from notions of the ideal body.[12] All other bodies are considered to be in need of improvement, treatment, and healing in order to turn people into apt citizens. Crucially, these days bodies and the possibilities and abilities ascribed to them are mostly conceived in dynamic rather than rigid terms. The exhortation to work on ourselves, to change our lives, to improve our existence, and, to this end, to cultivate a proactive relationship with our body and ourselves, has thus become all the louder.

The stigmatization of fat people as failed citizens is always associated with the moralizing accusation of failure, as well as with the injunction to try harder and to work on oneself.

Fat activists' struggles and the debates on compulsory able-bodiedness, the thin contract, and failed citizens underline that fitness is more than just the ability to do sport successfully. In other words, physical training and nutrition are not the only fields in which one can, and must, acquire recognition as a citizen. We might even say that being in motion and eating responsibly are means to an end. They are signals of a willingness to achieve and civil empowerment in other areas as well, which are central to the polity, its existence, and its prosperity.[13] A trained body, according to philosopher Peter Sloterdijk, serves as proof that one is capable of "practicing and working on one's own vital form."[14] This body demonstrates a fundamental willingness to work on oneself and one's potential, and to stay on the ball, and not just when it comes to success in sport. One must be productive and potent, or at least appear to be so, in order to gain social recognition. One must be ready to fight, willing and able to literally give one's all. At all times. Only in this way can one prove oneself as a good member of a free, competitive society that emphasizes self-reliance and participation, and strives to achieve prosperity and growth.[15]

If we look first at the relationship between fitness and work, we find that from the very beginning of the capitalist era, physical training was considered an important tool for maintaining and enhancing work per-formance. Concern over the productivity of the working population is not an invention of our time. But only flexible capitalism expects workers themselves to have a highly anticipatory relationship with their labor power, productivity, and health. Fit and flexible bodies in flexible capital-ism – this phrase captures what is required of all worker-entrepreneurs who put themselves, their bodies, and their performance up for sale in the market. Only in the age of fitness, in an era of prevention and responsibilization, has corpulence become an outright disadvantage as individuals compete for the best job. Because those who are fat, the logic at play here suggests, are incapable of taking responsibility for maintain-ing and enhancing their fitness and labor power. By the same token, concern for one's body and its potential is, more than ever, regarded as an indication of our willingness to perform at work.

Second, in addition to work, sex is a key field of civil practice and rec-ognition. This has been evident at least since the emergence of the gay and lesbian movement, the writings of Michel Foucault, and, finally, the rise of queerness and queer studies. As early as the nineteenth century, the "right" relationship to sex was of crucial importance if one wished to be regarded as a full member of society. The key requirement was to show moderation and to be reproductive. Yet around 1900 (and it is no coincidence that the first fitness wave coincided with the first sexual revolution), the ability to perform the act of sex became the best proof of a functioning male body. One's procreative powers faded into the background. The logic of enhancement inherent in fitness came to encompass sex; limitations on one's potential could not simply be accepted. From the rejuvenating operations of the early twentieth cen-tury to the invention of Viagra on the eve of the twenty-first century, the history of sexual fitness shows that the body is entangled with an entire, diverse arsenal of forces and resources. These limit or foster the body's performative potential and ability. The age of fitness is also the age of the pharmaceutical industry. Its products often convey the promise of improved performance, not only with regard to sex, but also when it comes to working longer, training harder, or losing weight faster.

Third, the fit body signals a readiness to fight, a willingness to make sacrifices, and, if need be, to go to extremes in the "struggle for survival." Historically, full civil recognition has required a defensive capability, that is, individuals who are ready and able to go to war. Furthermore, it was through extraordinary physical performance in combat and war that men could become heroes. The sphere of the heroic is traditionally martial and masculine in character, and from the nineteenth century onward, it was closely linked with notions of trained, fit bodies. Having died away almost entirely after the two world wars, the heroic has undergone a revival in recent times. Now, though, its wellspring and key point of reference are the battles of everyday life. In the twenty-first century, in the world of fitness as elsewhere, the heroic is almost omni-present when it comes to identifying and mastering challenges (and it is increasingly genderless). Ever more fitness practices are grounded in martial concepts, such as warrior workouts and hero runs. The focal point for these new fitness heroes and heroines is no longer the nation, let alone the "people," in the exclusionary and racist sense of the term, but their own success. The trained body is emblematic of the ability to rack up exceptional achievements, and this includes the battles of our everyday lives.

The Age of Fitness operates via the promise that we can all become heroes and heroines if we master the workout in the gym or run a marathon. Yet this is not a matter of a specific, measurable success, but success as a principle; it entails activating oneself, exploiting one's opportunities, and enhancing one's potential. At the core of fitness lies work on oneself and on one's own limits. We should be motivated and committed in every respect, productive, potent, willing to fight, capable of the extraordinary, and always willing to improve ourselves in order to survive in conditions of omnipresent competition.

Nevertheless, to emphasize the great power of fitness is not necessarily to assert that all of us are perpetually within its grip. There are people who resist the strict regime of fitness, who evade it or at least try to. There may even be people who are not affected by it at all. This might, for example, mean eating burgers and cream cake not as an act of conscious resistance, but for the sheer pleasure and enjoyment of it. Sometimes people laze around on the sofa simply because they feel like it; it is just what they happen to be doing. Likewise, not every sporting activity has to be an act of submission to the fitness regime. Sometimes it is simply a matter of the sheer pleasure of moving, the enjoyment of one's own body and, yes, of the challenge involved. Yet we are of course aware that the pleasure we get from things we have or do does not exist outside the realm of history or beyond social and cultural conditions.

NOTES

Introduction: The Age of Fitness

1 On "sport as an economic factor," see *Informationen aus dem Institut der deutschen Wirtschaft* #12/2018, June 7, 2018, https://www.iwd. de/archiv/2018/; see also the Instagram account of Kayla Itsines, https://www.instagram.com/kayla_itsines/?hl=en.

2 Gruneau, *Sport & Modernity*; Eisenberg, *"English Sports" und deutsche Bürger*; Eisenberg, "Die Entdeckung des Sports."

3 In using the phrase "pursuit of fitness," I borrow from the American Declaration of Independence, which refers to the "pursuit of happiness"; see esp. chapter 2 and Martschukat, "The Pursuit of Fitness."

4 See, for example, Werner Bartens, "Krankhaft sesshaft. Der Bewegungsmangel hat weltweit erschreckende Ausmaße angenommen," *SZ*, September 6, 2018, 14; on Germany, see Froböse et al., *Der DKV-Report 2018*; Guthold et al., "Worldwide Trends in Insufficient Physical Activity."

5 Editorial, *Geschichte der Gegenwart*.

6 See esp. Netzwerk Körper (ed.), *What Can a Body Do?* See also many of the articles in *Body Politics: Zeitschrift für Körpergeschichte*, http://bodypolitics.de/de/uber-die-zeitschrift/; Lorenz, *Leibhaftige Vergangenheit*, was pioneering in its day.

7 Brown, *Undoing the Demos*, 15–50; Rödder, *21.0*, 54–5. In those parts of the book where I write about fitness, the economy, and the world of work, I also use the term "flexible capitalism" to refer to the last 50 years because it more accurately captures the specific historical shifts and challenges involved; Lessenich, *Die Neuerfindung des Sozialen*, 9–19.

8 Foucault, "Confessions of the Flesh"; Ganahl, "Ist Foucaults dispositif ein Akteur-Netzwerk?"; van Dyk, "Was die Welt zusammenhält."

9 Alkemeyer, *Zeichen, Körper und Bewegung*, 212; Mayer, *Wissenschaft vom Gehen*.

10 Krasmann, "Regieren über Freiheit"; Rose, *Powers of Freedom*.

11 Honneth, *Anerkennung*, 182–234; Butler, *Psychic Life of Power*.

12 Gumbrecht, "Modern, Modernität, Moderne"; Dipper, "Moderne, Version: 2.0"; Gruneau, *Sport & Modernity*, 1–14; Villa, "Einleitung – Wider die Rede vom Äußerlichen," 8.

13 Hall, "The West and the Rest."

1. "Fit or Fat"? Fitness in Recent History and the Present Day

1 Gamper, "Radrennfahrer," 197–202.

2 However, this also includes those who, for example, step onto the scales regularly. Around 20 percent of Americans are said to practice self-tracking in the narrower sense, with this figure referring to 2013. Not least due to the many different forms tracking may take, the numbers vary greatly; Fox and Duggan, "Tracking for Health."

3 QS: Quantified Self: Self Knowledge Through Numbers – Deutsche Community, http://qsdeutschland.de/info/ (accessed May 9, 2016).

4 Rippberger, "Fitness-Apps"; Schmedt, "Fitness-Tracker"; Swan, "Quantified Self"; Crawford et al., "Our Metrics, Ourselves," 490–4. For a summary, see also Duttweiler et al., *Leben nach Zahlen*.

5 Lupton, *Quantified Self*, 3; Lupton, "Self-Tracking Citizenship"; for a concept of citizenship that has been expanded in a particularly productive way, see Rose and Novas, "Biological Citizenship"; Honneth, *Anerkennung*; see also Cooper, *Citizenship, Inequality, and Difference*.

6 Volkwein, "Introduction"; Volkwein quotes from, among other things, 1996 guidelines issued by the US Department of Health

and Human Services. Bauman, *Liquid Modernity*; Sloterdijk, *You Must Change Your Life*.

7　Volkwein, "Introduction," xi, xv.

8　Bröckling, "Prävention," 214. See also Bröckling, *Gute Hirten führen sanft*, 73–112, on prevention and "the power of prophylaxis." On prevention as a "cultural technology of modernity," see Lengwiler and Madarász, "Präventionsgeschichte."

9　See Judith Butler's performance concept, as explained in Butler, "Performative Acts."

10　Biltekoff, *Eating Right*, 5–6.

11　Crawford et al., "Our Metrics, Ourselves," 487. On the Microsoft ad from 2014, see Rubino, "Microsoft Band"; Mackert and Martschukat, "Introduction: Critical Ability History."

12　Butler, *Bodies that Matter*. See also Bauman, "Postmodern Uses of Sex."

13　See Metzl and Kirkland (eds.), *Against Health*; Guthman, *Weighing In*, which also addresses the debate on "healthism" and the normative elements in the pursuit of health; on this topic, see also Crawford, "Healthism."

14　On participation under dictatorships and state socialism, see, for example, Lüdtke, "Deutsche Qualitätsarbeit," or Offermann, "Socialist Responsibilization."

15　McRuer, "Compulsory Able-Bodiedness"; McRuer, *Crip Theory*; Mackert, "Writing the History."

16　Anon., "Deutschland verfettet"; Fröböse et al., *Der DKV-Report 2018*. On performance or efficiency as a modern paradigm, see Verheyen, *Die Erfindung der Leistung*.

17　There is a wealth of references to choose from, such as Saguy, *What's Wrong With Fat?*, 107ff.; Gilman, *Obesity*; Biltekoff, *Eating Right*. See also, for example, Pollack, "A.M.A. Recognizes Obesity"; Bakalar, "Obesity Rates"; Anon, "Übergewicht in Deutschland"; CDC Centers for Disease Control and Prevention, National Center for Health Statistics, "Obesity and Overweight," http://www.cdc.gov/nchs/fastats/obesity-overweight.htm (May 11, 2016); "The State of Obesity – Better Policies for a Healthier America, Obesity Rates and Trends," http://stateofobesity.org/rates/ (May 11, 2016); Hales et al., "Differences in Obesity."

18 Kim et al., "Causation or Selection."

19 See, for example, Gard, *End of the Obesity Epidemic*; Saguy, *What's Wrong?*; Frommeld, "Fit statt fett"; and on "excess weight" and life expectancy, see Afzal et al., "Change in Body Mass Index."

20 Wirtz, "Fit statt fett"; Geyer, "Fit statt fett"; for an early campaign, see *Essen und Trimmen – beides muß stimmen*, Frankfurt am Main: Deutsche Gesellschaft für Ernährung (*c.* 1976), and Bundeszentrale für Gesundheitliche Aufklärung, *Essen und trimmen, beides muß stimmen*. On nudging, see Thaler and Sunstein, *Nudge*; Hildebrandt, "Stups zum Glück." Just how paradigmatic "nudging" is to the governance of liberal societies becomes clear if one reads the book by Thaler and Sunstein together with Michel Foucault's studies of governmentality: Foucault, *Security, Territory, Population*, and Foucault, *The Birth of Biopolitics*. See also Foucault's remarks on power as decentral and as action that acts upon the action of others; Foucault, "Subject and Power."

21 Sutton, "First Lady"; see also the website of "Let's Move" at https://letsmove.obamawhitehouse.archives.gov/ (May 12, 2016); for a summary, see Martschukat, "On Choice."

22 The UK, for example, introduced a sugar tax in 2016: Triggle, "Sugar Tax"; similar taxes have been imposed in the United States, for example in Philadelphia and parts of California; "Tax Soda to Help Fight Obesity," *Bloomberg Opinion*, May 14, 2018, https://www.bloomberg.com/opinion/articles/2018-05-14/tax-soda-and-other-sugary-drinks-to-fight-obesity (accessed November 13, 2018).

23 Foucault, *Society Must Be Defended*.

24 Mollow and McRuer, "Fattening Austerity"; Scholl (ed.), *Körperführung*.

25 Mollow and McRuer, "Fattening Austerity"; Kreisky, "Fitte Wirtschaft"; Graf, "Leistungsfähig."

26 Brown, *Undoing the Demos*, 15–50, quote on 21, "portfolio value" on 33, *homo oeconomicus* and *politicus* on 87.

27 Rose, "Molecular Biopolitics," 11; Rose, *Powers of Freedom*; Rose and Novas, "Biological Citizenship"; Dean, *Governing Societies*.

28 Rose and Novas, "Biological Citizenship," 451.

29 Pateman, *Sexual Contract*; Mills, *Racial Contract*.

30 Willard, *A Wheel within a Wheel*.

31 A change of this kind has also taken place in the cultural and social sciences, where malleability and performativity have gradually gained acceptance as paradigms, in the shape of "doing gender," "doing race," and "doing sex." A crucial text here is Butler, *Gender Trouble*; for a multiperspectival account that provides an overall assessment, see Netzwerk Körper (ed.), *What Can a Body Do?*

32 It seems no more than logical that critical voices in disability and fat studies have distanced themselves from constructivist views; see Mollow, "Disability Studies Gets Fat"; Mollow and McRuer, "Fattening Austerity."

33 Guthman, *Weighing In*, 47–63; Moran, *Governing Bodies*, 112–54.

34 Dilley (ed.), *Darwinian Evolution*; Mackert, "I Want to Be a Fat Man"; Gilman, *Fat Boys*; Farrell, *Fat Shame*.

35 Wildt, *Beginn der Konsumgesellschaft*, 73–108; Cohen, *Consumers' Republic*, 111–65; Levenstein, *Paradox of Plenty*, 101–30; Moran, *Governing Bodies*, 112–31.

36 Biltekoff, *Eating Right*, 115; Levenstein, *Fear of Food*, 136; Ehrenreich, *The Hearts of Men*; Kury, *Der überforderte Mensch*, 109–75.

37 Levenstein, *Fear of Food*, 124–35; Möhring, "Ethnic Food," 320.

38 Biltekoff, *Eating Right*; Dufty, *Sugar Blues*; Möhring, "Ethnic Food," 320.

39 Davis, *From Head Shops to Whole Foods*; Pollan, *Omnivore's Dilemma*; Belasco, *Appetite for Change*; Möhring, "Ethnic Food," 322.

40 Cowie, *Great Exception*, 182, 202; Simon, *Hamlet Fire*; Doering-Manteuffel and Raphael, *Nach dem Boom*.

41 Guthman, *Weighing In*, 116–39; Pollan, *Omnivore's Dilemma*; Simon, "Geography of Silence."

42 Allcott et al., "Geography of Poverty"; Florida, "Food Deserts"; Reynolds and Mirosa, "Want Amidst Plenty"; Coleman-Jensen, "U.S. Food Insecurity Status"; Barrett, "Measuring Food Insecurity."

43 Guthman, *Weighing In*, 163–84; Martschukat, "On Choice."

44 Biltekoff, *Eating Right*, 94–5; Wolfe, "The 'Me' Decade." The quote comes from a letter cited in Edgely et al., "Rhetoric of Aerobics," 188.

45 Davis, *From Head Shops to Whole Foods*, 176–223; Belasco, *Appetite for Change*; Levenstein, *Fear of Food*, 116–24; on the overlap between

counterculture and flexible capitalism, see Reichhardt, *Authentizität und Gemeinschaft*.

46 Zukin, *Naked City*.

47 Serazio, "Ethos Groceries"; Pollan, *Omnivore's Dilemma*; Levenstein, *Fear of Food*, 123.

48 *Handelsblatt*, December 30, 1985, quoted in Möhring, "Ethnic Food," 322.

49 Elliott, *Better Than Well*; Biltekoff, *Eating Right*, 84–91, 94; Levenstein, *Fear of Food*, 142–59; MarketsandMarkets, "Weight Loss Management."

50 Crawford, "Boundaries of the Self," 1356; Kingsolver, *Animal, Vegetable, Miracle*, 130: "Cooking is good citizenship"; Paul Nolte, "Das große Fressen"; Biltekoff, *Eating Right*, 99–108; Belasco, *Appetite for Change*, 196–7; Moran, *Governing Bodies*, 132–54.

51 On the concept of sport, see Eisenberg, *"English Sports" und deutsche Bürger*; Guttmann, *From Ritual to Record*; on the distinction between sport and fitness, see Graf, "Leistungsfähig," 139–40; Bette, *Sportsoziologie*, 5–6. The term "fitness," described as "Germanized" American English, first appeared in Duden in 1976, which defined it as a "good physical condition, performance capacity [based on the methodical practice of sport]," and provided the following example: "to maintain one's fitness through recreational sport": *Duden: Das große Wörterbuch*, 851. Dilger, *Fitnessbewegung in Deutschland*, 238–45; Müllner, "Sich in Form bringen"; Scholl, "Europäische Biopolitik?"

52 See DSB ads associated with the get-fit campaign "Ein Schlauer trimmt die Ausdauer" ("The Smart Ones Get Fit through Endurance") (1975–8) on YouTube at https://www.youtube.com/watch?v=Z7n-lUy1dAs and https://www.youtube.com/watch?v=kWkjnPiXlJ0 (July 2, 2016); Pfütsch, "Zwischen Gesundheit und Schönheit."

53 Ninety percent of respondents in a representative municipal survey carried out by K. Bös and A. Woll in the 1980s were familiar with Trimmy; see Mörath, *Trimm-Aktionen*, 11.

54 *Essen und Trimmen – beides muß stimmen*, Frankfurt am Main: Deutsche Gesellschaft für Ernährung; in 1980, the Federal Center

for Health Education published a workbook on the topic "eat well and get fit – you need both."

55 Reed, "America Shapes Up."

56 Barney, "Book Review: Whorton," here 104; Wolfe, "The 'Me' Decade."

57 New-York-City-Marathon, in Wikipedia, https://de.wikipedia.org/wiki/New-York-City-Marathon (accessed July 5, 2016) and Berlin-Marathon, in Wikipedia, https://de.wikipedia.org/wiki/Berlin-Marathon (accessed July 5, 2016).

58 *Runner's World* was launched in 1966 as a homemade magazine published by a running fan with two issues a year and a print run of 500 copies. By the end of the 1970s, the magazine had long since attained a professional editorial staff and appeared monthly, with a print run of 500,000 copies; Black, *Making the American Body*, 77; McKenzie, *Getting Physical*, 129.

59 Sheehan, "Medical Advice"; on the agency of fat, see Forth, "On Fat."

60 Martschukat, "What Diet Can Do."

61 Hanner, "Beginning Running": "[running] has really changed my entire existence around"; Fischer, *Mein langer Lauf.*

62 Corbitt, "Adjusting to Advancing Age."

63 On the 1970s as an era characterized by both the counterculture and neoliberalism, see Tuck, "Introduction," and the other contributions to the journal issue. On European history in this regard, see the special issue of *Zeithistorische Forschungen* on "Die 1970er Jahre."

64 Luciano, *Looking Good*, 121.

65 On this recent history of fitness in the United States, see McKenzie, *Getting Physical*. On the running movement, see Plymire, "Positive Addiction"; on the spirituality of this movement, see Edgely et al., "Rhetoric"; on the search for moral leadership as a driving force of the transformation of the United States since the 1970s, see Krämer, *Moral Leaders*; on the new morality and physicality, see Metzl and Kirkland (eds.), *Against Health*.

66 Cooper, *Aerobics*. Cooper, *The New Aerobics*, was hugely successful.

67 Bassler, "Live Like a Marathoner." For an overview, see Rader, "The Quest."

68 On the body and health as key issues of the women's movement, see Kline, *Bodies of Knowledge*. Initially, the feminist movement was predominantly white. From the mid-1970s on, however, black women increasingly highlighted issues emerging at the intersection of feminism and antiracism. For a summary of Black feminism and intersectionality, see Mackert, "Kimberlé Crenshaw."

69 Women's advocates' relationship to competitive sports was somewhat more ambivalent. On the one hand, many aspects of such sports now opened up to women that had previously been denied them, and female athletes became role models in part because they incorporated themselves proactively into a competitive order. On the other hand, feminists criticized competitive sports as a typical embodiment of aggressive masculinity. Cahn, *Coming on Strong*; Schultz, *Qualifying Times*, 123–48; Theberge, "A Critique of Critiques." On feminist fitness in the nineteenth century, see Vertinsky, "Feminist Charlotte Perkins Gilman." For an overview, see Thorpe and Olive (eds.), "Forum: Feminist Sport History."

70 Fraser, "How Feminism Became Capitalism's Handmaiden"; Fraser, "Feminism."

71 Villa, "Habe den Mut"; Luciano, *Looking Good*; Pfütsch, "Zwischen Gesundheit und Schönheit."

72 Butler, *Psychic Life of Power*; Reckwitz, *Subjekt*; Schultz, *Qualifying Times*, 139–46; Hargreaves, *Sporting Females*, 160; Woitas, "Vom männlichen Elitetraining"; Markula, "Firm but Shapely"; Bradshaw, "Empowerment and Sport Feminism."

73 McKenzie, *Getting Physical*, 164; Schultz, *Qualifying Times*, 136–8.

74 Jane Fonda, Workout (VHS; USA, 1982); Black, *Making the American Body*, 79–87; Woitas, "Go for the burn!"

75 Woitas, "Vom männlichen Elitetraining."

76 See Gustav-Wrathall, *Take the Young Stranger*, on YMCA sports facilities as dating sites.

77 McKenzie, *Getting Physical*, 168–72; Dilger, *Die Fitnessbewegung in Deutschland*, 245–366; "cathedrals" in Reed, "America Shapes Up."

78 Scheller, *No Sports!*; *Pumping Iron* (USA, 1977).

79 Bailey, *Fit or Fat?*, 101.

80 Rader, "The Quest."

81 Roosevelt, "The Strenuous Life"; Möhring, "Ethnic food," 327–8.

2. Fitness. Trajectories of a Concept Since the Eighteenth Century

1 Fielding, *The History of Tom Jones, A Foundling* (1749), Book 3, Chapter 3, 128 and Chapter 5, 134. On the contemporary conceptual field, see the entry on "fitness" in the *Oxford English Dictionary*, www.oed.com (accessed April 8, 2016); Humphreys, "Eternal Fitness"; Ruthven, "Fielding, Square, and the Fitness of Things."

2 Fielding, *Historie des menschlichen Herzens*, Book 3, Chapter 3, 147; Fielding, *Geschichte des Thomas Jones*, vol. 1, Book 3, Chapter 3, 149; Fielding, *Die Geschichte des Tom Jones*, Book 3, Chapter 5, 116.

3 Humphreys, "Eternal Fitness," 190–4. Humphreys highlights the importance of the Cambridge Platonists and quotes from Cudworth, *Treatise* (1731, written before 1680), 14, which states that "things are what they are not by will but by nature. [. . .] Things are white by whiteness and black by blackness, triangular by triangularity and round by rotundity, like by likeness and equal by equality. Omnipotence itself cannot by mere will make a body triangular without having the nature and properties of a triangle in it."

4 Heater, *Brief History of Citizenship*, 64, 72–9; Lombard, *Making Manhood*.

5 McMahon, *Happiness*, 312–31. Among other things, McMahon highlights the obligating connotations of the verb "to pursue" in the eighteenth century. On the importance of consumption to this new society, see Breen, *Marketplace of Revolution*; Shachak and Illouz, "Pursuit of Happiness."

6 McMahon, *Happiness*, 312–31.

7 In the early United States, the meanings of freedom varied significantly, depending on whose freedom was at issue; Foner, "Meaning of Freedom"; Nelson, *National Manhood*.

8 Gerstle, *Liberty and Coercion*, 17–36.

9 Rorabaugh, *Alcoholic Republic*; Martschukat, *American Fatherhood*, 7–23; Kleeberg (ed.), *Schlechte Angewohnheiten*.

10 On the reform movement, see Dorsey, *Reforming Men and Women*. On the transformation of the punitive ratio in the European Enlightenment, see Foucault, *Discipline and Punish*. On the United States, see Rothman, *Discovery of the Asylum*; Meranze, *Laboratories*

of Virtue. One should also bear in mind that the paradigmatic punitive instrument of slavery remained the whip, and its target the body.

11 Alkemeyer, *Zeichen, Körper und Bewegung*; Sarasin, *Reizbare Maschinen*; Verheyen, *Erfindung der Leistung*, 123–6; Goltermann, *Körper der Nation.* More on *Turnen* in chapter 5.

12 Quotations in Anon., "Art. III: Gymnastics," and Lewis, "The New Gymnastics," 129. See also Park, "Muscles, Symmetry, and Action"; Martschukat, "Necessity for Better Bodies."

13 Weber, *Protestant Ethic*; Putney, *Muscular Christianity.*

14 Park, "Biological Thought"; Sarasin and Tanner, "Physiologie"; Stoff, "Leistungsprinzip."

15 Saldern, *Amerikanismus*, 75.

16 Page, "Our Artists in Italy," 130.

17 Eliot, "New Education, II," 362, on "natural fitness"; Hale, "What Shall We Have," 370; Parker, "Freedman's Story," 152.

18 Isenmann, "Die langsame Entstehung eines ökonomischen Systems"; Claeys, "Survival of the Fittest"; Sarasin, *Darwin und Foucault.*

19 Spencer, *Principles of Biology*; Darwin, *Origin of Species or the Preservation*, 1859; see also Darwin, *Origin of Species by Means*, 5th edn. 1869, 92 for the quote.

20 Darwin, *Über die Entstehung der Arten*, 1876, 83; Spencer, *Principien der Biologie*, vol. 1, 499.

21 Kleeberg, *Theophysis*, 189–90; Kleeberg, "Schlechte Angewohnheiten."

22 Rotteck and Welcker (eds.), *Staats-Lexikon*, vol. 9, 713–30; see Langewiesche, *Liberalism in Germany.*

23 McKendrick et al., *Birth of a Consumer Society.* Isenmann, "Die langsame Entstehung eines ökonomischen Systems," brings out the fact that Smith was concerned chiefly with French debates; Smith, *Wealth of Nations* (1776).

24 Mill, *Principles of Political Economy* (1848); Mill, *On Liberty.*

25 Wayland, "An American in the House," 147.

26 Merwin, "Ethics of Horse-Keeping," 635.

27 Anon., "Three Typical Workingmen," 722, with reference to the cultivation of nature; Shaler, "Use and Limits of Academic Culture,"

160, 167 on fitness as a product of labor; Stedman, "Edwin Booth," 585.

28 Blackie, *Self-Culture*; Sargent, "Physical Proportions"; Collier, "Sport's Place"; Müller, *Mein System*. On expertise in physical culture, see Berryman and Park, *Sport and Exercise Science*. On Sargent, see, for example, Peña, *Body Electric*, 50–72. For an overview, see Sarasin, *Reizbare Maschinen*, 324–36; Möhring, *Marmorleiber*, 65 on Müller; Müllner, "Sich in Form bringen."

29 Sargent, "Physical Development of Women," 174; quote on physique in Hutchinson, "Physical Basis of Brain-Work," 523; Collier, "Sport's Place," 383–4; Bederman, *Manliness & Civilization*; Sarasin, *Reizbare Maschinen*, 251; Verheyen, *Die Erfindung der Leistung*, 84.

30 Saldern, *Amerikanismus*; Verheyen, *Die Erfindung der Leistung*, 46.

31 Roosevelt, "The Strenuous Life."

32 Foucault, *Society Must Be Defended*, 239–63; Scholl, "Einleitung: Biopolitik."

33 Mills, *The Racial Contract*; Dean, *Governing Societies*, 118; Butler, *Bodies that Matter*, on the "constitutive other." See also Hunt, *Inventing Human Rights*.

34 Foucault, *Society Must Be Defended*, 255; Gunkel and Stieglitz, "Verqueerte Laufwege."

35 Butler, *Bodies that Matter*, 3, on banishment to "those 'unlivable' and 'uninhabitable' zones of social life which are nevertheless densely populated by those who do not enjoy the status of the subject."

36 An early text that refers to "fitness for self-government" is Frothingham, "Sam Adams Regiments," 182. Verheyen, *Die Erfindung der Leistung*, 9.

37 On the interlocking of rights and obligations in the concept of citizenship, see Heater, *Brief History of Citizenship*, or Gosewinkel, "Staatsbürgerschaft"; Cooper, *Citizenship, Inequality, and Difference*.

38 Möhring, *Marmorleiber*, 145; Zweiniger-Bargielowska, *Managing the Body*; Honneth, *Anerkennung*; Cooper, *Citizenship, Inequality, and Difference*.

39 Parker, "Freedman's Story," 152; King, "Pioneers of Ohio," 559; Thayer, "Dawes Bill and the Indians," 320; Clark, "Woman Suffrage"; Shaler, "European Peasants"; Claghorn, "Our Immigrants and Ourselves," 547.

40 Riis, "Reform by Humane Touch," 753; see also Anon., "An Englishwoman," 246; Adams, "The United States."

41 Lears, *Rebirth of a Nation*; Wiebe, *Search for Order*. Similar analyses of European societies can be found in Sarasin and Tanner (eds.), "Physiologie," and Rabinbach, *The Human Motor*.

42 Möhring, *Marmorleiber*, 15.

43 Bederman, *Manliness & Civilization*; Lutz, *American Nervousness*; Radkau, *Zeitalter der Nervosität*; Stoff, "Degenerierte Nervenkörper"; Kury, *Der überforderte Mensch*, 37–54.

44 Of the extensive literature, see Bederman, *Manliness & Civilization*; Kasson, *Houdini*; Roediger, *Working Toward Whiteness*; Lüthi, *Invading Bodies*.

45 On the significance of the swimming pool as a site of physical exercise, see Wiltse, *Contested Waters*, 31.

46 Vester, *A Taste of Power*, 80; Veit, *Modern Food*; on the significance of physical exercise in Germany, see Möhring, *Marmorleiber*.

47 Vertinsky, "Weighs and Means"; Mackert, "I want to be a fat man"; Farrell, *Fat Shame*.

48 On Sandow in the United States, see Kasson, *Houdini*. On Sandow on the global stage, see Daley, *Leisure & Pleasure*. On Macfadden, see Adams, *Mr. America*; Stieglitz, "A Man of Your Years."

49 Theiss, "Measuring Physical Fitness," 350; see also Anon., "The Oldest Games," or Raine, "Taming the Frontier."

50 Butler, *Giving an Account of Oneself*, 19. For a similar argument with respect to contemporary dietary practices, see Vester, "Regime Change"; Vester, *Taste of Power*.

51 Dubois, "The Problem of Amusement (1897)," and Scott, "Leisure Time (1925)"; Martschukat, "His Chief Sin"; Purkiss, "Beauty Secrets"; Stieglitz, "American Crawl."

52 Kugelmass (ed.), *Jews, Sports, and Rites of Citizenship*; see also the special issue of the *Journal of Sport History* 26, 2 (1999) on "One Hundred Years of 'Muscular Judaism'"; Zimmermann, "Muskeljuden"; Stieglitz et al., "Sportreportage."

53 Henne, *Training Citizenship*.

54 Willard, *A Wheel within a Wheel*; Strange and Brown, "The Bicycle"; Vertinsky, "Feminist Charlotte Perkins Gilman"; Verbrugge, *Active Bodies*.

55 Darwin, *Die Entstehung der Arten* 1902, vol. 1, 126ff. The word "fitness" first appeared in the iconic *Duden* dictionary in 1976. See also the entry on "tüchtig" in the *Deutsches Wörterbuch von Jacob Grimm und Wilhelm Grimm*.

56 Adler, "Spartan Stuff," 303; for a general account, see also Biltekoff, *Eating Right*; Mackert, "Feeding Productive Bodies."

57 Wells, "Social Darwinism," esp. 706. On the history of scientific racism in the United States, see Degler, *In Search of Human Nature*; Tucker, *The Science and Politics*; Finzsch, "Wissenschaftlicher Rassismus"; on international eugenics, see Kühl, *Die Internationale der Rassisten*; on the historical backdrop, see Lorenz, *Menschenzucht*.

58 Alkemeyer, "Aufrecht und biegsam"; Becker and Schäfer (eds.), *Sport und Nationalsozialismus*, esp. Becker and Schäfer, "Einleitung," 9–23; Diehl, "Körperbilder und Körperpraxen"; Wildt, "Volksgemeinschaft, Version: 1.0"; Wildt, *Volk, Volksgemeinschaft, AfD*.

59 Goltermann, *Körper der Nation*.

60 On the participation, see Lüdtke, *Eigen-Sinn*; Lindenberger, "Eigen-Sinn."

61 Cowie and Salvatore, "The Long Exception"; Cowie, *Great Exception*. Against this background it is hardly surprising that the New Deal has aroused so much interest among historians, particularly in Germany, prompting a large number of comparative observations; see Schild, *Zwischen Freiheit*; Patel, *The New Deal*; Gräser, *Wohlfahrtsgesellschaft*.

62 Stieglitz, *100 Percent American Boys*, 184–222; Patel, *Soldiers of Labor*; Suzik, "Building Better Men"; Henne, *Training Citizenship*, 14–20; Moran, *Governing Bodies*, 38–63.

63 Melosh, *Engendering Culture*.

64 Jarvis, *Male Body in War*; Macdonald, *Strong, Beautiful, and Modern*.

65 Wildt, *Beginn der "Konsumgesellschaft*," 76–109; see also Briesen, *Das gesunde Leben*, 190–3.

66 Cohen, *Consumers' Republic*; Steigerwald, "All Hail the Republic."

67 McKenzie, *Getting Physical*, 9; Stearns, *Fat History*, on body fat and overconsumption; Dean, *Imperial Brotherhood*; Moran, *Governing Bodies*, 112–31.

68 McKenzie, *Getting Physical*, 14–53; for the findings of the comparative

youth fitness study, see Kraus and Hirschland, "Muscular Fitness"; Kraus and Hirschland, "Minimum Muscular Fitness." On the PCYF, see Moran, *Governing Bodies*, 84–111, and Bowers and Hunt, "President's Council."

69 McKenzie, *Getting Physical*, 82–108; on the risk factor model, see Rothstein, *Public Health*, and Timmermann, "Risikofaktoren"; on prevention, see Bröckling, "Prävention"; Bröckling, *Gute Hirten*, 73–112 on prevention and "the power of prophylaxis"; see also Hannig and Thießen (eds.), *Vorsorgen in der Moderne*.

70 McKenzie, *Getting Physical*, 90–2; Martschukat, *American Fatherhood*, 182–99; Gilbert, *Men in the Middle*.

71 Meuser, "Hegemoniale Männlichkeit."

72 Ehrenreich, *Hearts of Men*.

73 McKenzie, *Getting Physical*, 54–81 on the ideal female body; on the normality of stout men in the 1950s, see Gilman, *Fat Boys*, 5; Luciano, *Looking Good*, 37–74; for a broader historical perspective, see Farrell, *Fat Shame*.

74 On softness and fitness in Kennedy's discourse, see the works of Robert Dean, and Black, *Making the American Body*, 47, here esp. on Kennedy's text concerning "The Soft American" in *Sports Illustrated* of December 1960.

75 Esquire (ed.), *The Art of Keeping Fit*.

3. Working

1 Anon., "Trimmen am Arbeitsplatz."

2 Anon., "Number of Health Clubs & Fitness Centers."

3 Peters, "In America, Corporate Fitness"; see also Gambacchini, "The Bottom Line on Fitness"; Cooper, *Aerobics*, Appendix, 165–73.

4 Sennett, *The Corrosion of Character*; Sennett, *The Culture of the New Capitalism*. Among the most important races specifically for company teams were the "Corporate Cup Championships," with their relay teams; see, for example, Post, "The Corporate Cup."

5 Such claims appeared, for example, in very different specialist magazines such as *Runner's World* and *Forbes*, and even *TIME Magazine*. See Peters, "In America, Corporate Fitness"; Anon., "Getting a Move On"; Reed, "America Shapes Up."

6 Anon., "Trimmen am Arbeitsplatz."

7 Lessenich, *Die Neuerfindung des Sozialen*, 12–17; Bröckling, *Gute Hirten*, 100; Chappell, *The War on Welfare*.

8 Reed, "America Shapes Up," 94; see also Byrne, "Executive Sweat," on the qualities that sports careers foster in leading economic and political figures, and Waters, "Defining the Runner's Personality."

9 Stress, above all at work, was another risk factor that was often mentioned, though some commentators were soon suggesting that its importance was being overstated; see Kury, *Der überforderte Mensch*; see also Jackson, *The Age of Stress*.

10 According to Zink, "At Texas Instruments."

11 Bröckling, *Gute Hirten*, 73–112; see also Singer, "Entstehung des Betrieblichen Gesundheitsmanagements."

12 On the increasing marketization of previously alternative practices, see Davis, *From Head Shops to Wholefoods*. With respect to Germany, Sven Reichardt has put forward a similar argument regarding "project work," which initially emerged in the alternative milieu: Reichardt, *Authentizität und Gemeinschaft*, 319–50.

13 Bernet, "Insourcing und Outsourcing," 273.

14 Bröckling, *Gute Hirten*, 100; see also Kreisky, "Fitte Wirtschaft."

15 Verheyen, *Die Erfindung der Leistung*, underlines the productive vagueness of the concept of productivity.

16 Gramsci, "Rationalization of Production and Work," 291; Bänziger, "Fordistische Körper in der Geschichte des 20. Jahrhunderts – eine Skizze."

17 Owen, "A New View of Society"; Chance, "Mobilising the Modern Industrial Landscape."

18 Bates and Riess, "Industrial Sports"; Gems, "Welfare Capitalism"; Park, "Blending Business and Basketball"; Kleeberg, "Schlechte Angewohnheiten."

19 Putney, *Muscular Christianity*; Henne, *Training Citizenship*.

20 Pesavento, "Sport and Recreation"; Chance, "Mobilising the Modern Industrial Landscape"; Pfister, "Stählung der Arbeiterschaft," 22–8; Sachse, *Siemens, der Nationalsozialismus*.

21 Pesavento, "Sport and Recreation."

22 See esp. Luh, *Betriebssport*.

23 Park, "Blending Business and Basketball"; Chance, "Mobilising the

Modern Industrial Landscape"; Burnap, *Parks*, 116ff. was less than thrilled by the growth in sporting activities in parks.

24 The reference to "sound physical culture" as the "basis of a rational way of working" comes from a letter from Carl Diem to the Reichsminister of the interior, Carl Wilhelm Severing, of November 16, 1929 (copy), 8, quoted in Dinçkal, "Sport ist die körperliche," 71. Berlin mayor Böß is quoted in Pfister, "Stählung der Arbeiterschaft," 28.

25 This was, for example, the way the body was viewed in the *Brockhaus* encyclopedia in the late nineteenth century, according to Verheyen, *Erfindung der Leistung*, 134.

26 Sarasin and Tanner, "Physiologie und industrielle Gesellschaft."

27 See, for example, Wheeler, *The American Diseases*; Radkau, *Das Zeitalter der Nervosität*.

28 See esp. Rabinbach, *The Human Motor*, 19–44 on fatigue; Vatin, "Arbeit und Ermüdung," on the connection between physical and mental fatigue. On the concept of *Leistung*, see Verheyen, *Erfindung der Leistung*, 130–9. On the surge in interest in the body, see Martschukat, "The Necessity for Better Bodies"; Möhring, *Marmorleiber*.

29 See, for example, Mackert, "Feeding Productive Bodies."

30 On Marey, see Rabinbach, *Human Motor*, 84–119; Fleig, *Körperkultur und Moderne*, 50.

31 On Marey, see Rabinbach, *Human Motor*, 84–119; on Muybridge, see the recent complete edition of his photographs of movement by Adam, *Eadweard Muybridge*. On working conditions, see Bernet, "Insourcing und Outsourcing."

32 Smith, *The Wealth of Nations* (1776), Book 1, Chapter 1, 4: "The greatest improvement in the productive powers of labour, and the greater part of the skill, dexterity, and judgment with which it is anywhere directed, or applied, seem to have been the effects of the division of labour"; Taylor, *Principles of Scientific Management*.

33 In addition to the practicing of operations, Foucault, *Discipline and Punish*, Part 3, Chapter 1, also describes the decomposition and recomposition of procedures as one of the mechanisms of discipline. On the history of Fordism, the assembly line, and their critique, see

Nye, *America's Assembly Line*; Hachtmann and von Saldern, "Das fordistische Jahrhundert."

34 Honisch, "Wirtschaft und Leibesübungen," 532, quote in Becker, "Sport bei Ford," 212. On Taylor as sportsman, see Fleig, *Körperkultur und Moderne*, 57–67.

35 Diem quoted in Pfister, "Stählung der Arbeiterschaft," 31; see also Dinçkal, "Sport ist die körperliche."

36 Mills, *White Collar*, xix–xx; Kocka, *Angestellte zwischen Faschismus und Demokratie*.

37 Kwolek-Folland, *Engendering Business*. The white-collar woman worker was also a figure in many novels, from Sinclair Lewis's Una Golden in *The Job* of 1917 to Christopher Morley's eponymous Kitty Foyle of 1939.

38 Rosa, *Beschleunigung*; Verheyen, *Die Erfindung der Leistung*; Kracauer, *Salaried Masses*; Mills, *White Collar*; Reckwitz, *Das hybride Subjekt*, 282–8. "Cage-like offices" in Marcuse, *Körperpflege*, 113, "cerebral cripples" in Nordhausen, *Moderne Körperkultur*, 2, both cited in Fleig, *Körperkultur und Moderne*, 33.

39 Blackford and Newcomb, *Analyzing Character*, 159; Martschukat, "The Necessity for Better Bodies," 480. On the development of analogous perspectives in Germany, see Verheyen, *Erfindung der Leistung*, 166–71; Stoff, "Der erfolgreiche Mensch."

40 Hutchinson, "The Physical Basis of Brain-Work"; Martschukat, "The Necessity for Better Bodies," 480.

41 Luh, *Betriebssport*, 124, 144.

42 On petit bourgeois white-collar workers as key agents of German fascism, see Kocka, *Angestellte zwischen Faschismus und Demokratie*.

43 Luh, *Betriebssport*, 208–337; Hachtmann, "Bäuche wegmassieren," which also contains the Ley quotations; Verheyen, *Erfindung der Leistung*, 182–90; Planert, "Der dreifache Körper"; Wildt, "Volksgemeinschaft."

44 Dabakis, *Visualizing Labor*; Jarvis, *The Male Body at War*.

45 Bates and Riess, "Industrial Sports," 482.

46 Martschukat, *American Fatherhood*, 182–99; McKenzie, *Getting Physical*, 3; Mills, *White Collar*, 63; Kracauer, *Salaried Masses*, 29.

47 Whyte, *The Organization Man*; Riesman, *The Lonely Crowd*; Ehrenreich, *The Hearts of Men*.

48 Mills, *White Collar*, 80, 197.
49 Cuordileone, *Manhood and American Political Culture*; Kimmel, *The Gendered Society*, 117 refers to "corporate clones." Lüdtke, "Helden der Arbeit"; Budde, "Der Körper der sozialistischen Frauenpersönlichkeit."
50 Whyte, *Is Anybody Listening?*, 168; Riesman, *The Lonely Crowd*, 141.
51 McKenzie, *Getting Physical*, 71–8; see the *Jack LaLanne Show*, episode 1, YouTube, https://www.youtube.com/watch?v=y4A3mdG 5zbQ&t=81s (accessed April 27, 2018).
52 McKenzie, *Getting Physical*, 98–108; Miller, *Death of a Salesman*.
53 See, for example, Anon., "Medicine."
54 Kury, *Der überforderte Mensch*, 109–75; Kury, "Von der Neurasthenie zum Burnout."
55 I thus follow the reading expounded by Haller et al., "Stress – Konjunkturen eines Konzepts," but with certain qualifications.
56 Esquire (ed.), *The Art of Keeping Fit*; McKenzie, *Getting Physical*, 103, on the warnings about fitness training.
57 See, for example, from 1968, the *Executive Health Report*; for a book, see also Anon., *Executive Health Report Fitness Guide*.
58 While the NASDAQ (National Association of Securities Dealers Automated Quotations) in the United States opened for business in February 1971 as the world's first electronic stock exchange, it was not until 1997 that the Deutsche Börse established its so-called New Market, where companies associated with the new technologies could acquire capital through flotation.
59 Anon., "Watch That Waistline!"
60 To quote the assessment provided at the turn of the century by Tuma, "Körperkult," 135.
61 Doering-Manteuffel and Raphael (eds.), *Nach dem Boom*; Hachtmann and von Saldern, "Gesellschaft am Fließband."
62 On Toyota production methods, see Womack et al., *The Machine That Changed the World*; see also Elis, "Von Amerika nach Japan." On fitness training in Japanese firms, see Anon., "Getting a Move On." On the political and economic metaphors of leanness, see Kreisky, "Fitte Wirtschaft"; Bernet, "Insourcing und Outsourcing."

63 Reichardt, *Authentizität und Gemeinschaft*, 319–50; Bröckling, *Das unternehmerische Selbst*, 248–82.

64 See, for example, Simon, *The Hamlet Fire*.

65 Bröckling, *Das unternehmerische Selbst*, 9; Reckwitz, *Das hybride Subjekt*, 282, sees the initial rise of the white-collar worker in the early twentieth century, its apogee in the 1950s, and its erosion in the 1970s. The "economization of the social" joined the much-invoked "scientification of the social" around the turn of the century: Raphael, "Die Verwissenschaftlichung des Sozialen."

66 Voß and Pongratz, "Der Arbeitskraftunternehmer."

67 Bröckling, *Das unternehmerische Selbst*, 65.

68 Rose, "Governing the Enterprising Self."

69 Bröckling, *Gute Hirten*, 243–59; on coaching and the meaning of sport, see Ribbat, *Deutschland für eine Saison*; Anon., "Getting a Move On"; Tuma, "Körperkult," 138.

70 See, for example, Anon., "Manager: Erfülltes Leben."

71 Meusel, *Trimm Dich im Büro!* (1971): the brochure went through several print runs. Anon., "Gymnastik – Bürotraining"; Spangenberg, "Betriebssport." There were, however, companies such as Nixdorf in Paderborn, which were already investing millions in staff fitness in the 1970s and, above all, created a training infrastructure; see Luh, *Betriebssport*, 385.

72 Anon., "Kuß des Todes"; Anon., "Wonniges Dahingleiten"; Kunkel, "Die dreifache totale Fitneß"; Caysa, "Krieg der Körper" in a special issue of *Der Spiegel* on the topic of "Beauty: Physical Drive: The Discovery of the Body."

73 Anon., "Brutale Harmonie"; Anon., "Lockeres Sitzfleisch"; the theme of the *Spiegel* issue was "Fat Chance! Eating, Drinking, and Enjoying"; Anon., "Fit für die Firma."

74 Luh, *Betriebssport*, 386; Singer, "Entstehung des Betrieblichen Gesundheitsmanagements."

75 Tuma, "Körperkult." Anon., "Fit durch Cyber-Sport"; Bundesministerium für Gesundheit, *Arbeitsunfähigkeit: Monatlicher Krankenstand – 1970 bis Oktober 2014*, https://www.bundesges undheitsministerium.de/fileadmin/Dateien/3_Downloads/Statist iken/GKV/Geschaeftsergebnisse/Krankenstand_Okt_2014.pdf

(accessed December 11, 2018); Bureau of Labor Statistics, *Labor Force Statistics from the Current Population Survey*, https://www.bls.gov/cps/tables.htm#absences (accessed December 11, 2018), available data extends back to 1995.

76 Madarász-Lebenhagen, "Geschlechterbilder in Präventionskonzepten"; see also – with rather different results – Linek, *Gesundheitsvorsorge in der DDR*.

77 Bernet, "Insourcing und Outsourcing." Stefan Offermann identifies incentives for self-management in the East German health system: Offermann, "On Responsibilization."

78 Martschukat, "On Choice."

79 Analysis of the literature on the relationship between body shape, education, and income is provided by Kim and von dem Knesebeck, "Income and Obesity"; Kim et al., "Causation or Selection."

80 Graefe, "Subjektivierung"; Graefe, *Resilienz*; see also Bröckling, *Gute Hirten*, 113–39 on resilience.

81 An insight gleaned from Haller et al., "Stress – Konjunkturen eines Konzepts."

4. Having Sex

1 Alison Keith of Pfizer referred to 300,000 in the first week and 30 million in the first one and a half years; see Keith, "The Economics of Viagra," 148.

2 Anon., "Schau mal, hier steht was." Also in *Der Spiegel*: Anon., "Viagra ist eine Bombe"; on the consumption of Viagra in the United States, see Martin, "Thanks a Bunch, Viagra"; Anon., "Viagra: The Potency Pill," cover. Of the literature, see esp. Loe, *Rise of Viagra*; McLaren, *Impotence*, chs. 9 and 10, 208–62.

3 Tiefer, "Doing the Viagra Tango," 3.

4 Weingarten, "Ein Lob dem Mann, der nicht kann."

5 Levy, "Pill Culture Pops"; Mamo and Fishman, "Potency in All the Right Places," 16; David Bell and Joanne Hollows also underline the tremendous significance of lifestyle in the late twentieth century, but describe this as the culmination of a lengthy development over the course of the twentieth century; Bell and Hollows, "Towards a History of Lifestyle." See also Spreen, *Upgradekultur*.

6 Elliott, *Better Than Well*; van Dyk, *Soziologie des Alters*; Levy, "Pill Culture Pops"; Marshall and Katz, "Forever Functional," 59.

7 Mamo and Fishman, "Potency in All the Right Places," 14; Marshall, "Hard Science," 132; Glick, "Of Sodomy and Cannibalism."

8 Harrasser, *Körper 2.0.*

9 Baglia, *Viagra Ad Venture*; Loe, *Rise of Viagra*; van Dyk, *Soziologie des Alters*, 25, 97–101; van Dyk and Graefe, "Fit ohne Ende"; Rowe and Kahn, *Successful Aging*; Wellman-Stühring, "Silber-Sex."

10 Elliott, *Better Than Well*, 124–7; Tiefer, "Sexology and the Pharmaceutical Industry." Pfizer pushed the concept of "erectile dysfunction," which could then be treated in "masculinity clinics" financed by none other than Pfizer; Loe, *Rise of Viagra*, 18, 48.

11 McLaren, *Impotence*, 243, 252; Marshall, "Hard Science," 139; Feldman et al., "Impotence"; on the MMAS and the marketing of pharmaceuticals, see Lexchin, "Bigger and Better"; Rosen et al., "International Index: Multidimensional Scale"; Rosen et al., "International Index: State-of-the-Science."

12 Bordo, *The Male Body*, 59–64.

13 A brief overview is provided by Crouch, "Viagra Returns."

14 McLaren, *Impotence*, 255; Faludi, *Stiffed*; Trebay, "Longer Harder Faster."

15 Much has been written about the crisis of masculinity. For a summary, see Martschukat and Stieglitz, *Geschichte der Männlichkeiten*; di Blasi, *Der weiße Mann*; Nünning, "Krise als Erzählung." On hegemony, see Connell, *Masculinities*; on the importance of control, particularly in the field of sex, see Potts, "Essence of the Hard On," 92–3.

16 Weeks, "Sexual Citizen"; for an overall take, see also Canaday, *The Straight State*.

17 Jagose, *Orgasmology*, 25; Koedt, "The Myth of the Vaginal Orgasm"; Fahs, *Performing Sex*, 38–43; Rich, "Compulsory Heterosexuality."

18 This, of course, also applies to egg cells and human organs, as Paula-Irene Villa emphasizes in Ramsbrock et al., "Menschliche Dinge"; Schmincke, "Sexualität als Angelpunkt."

19 Sherman, "Little Blue Miracle"; Jeffords, *Remasculinization of America*; Martschukat, *American Fatherhood*, 224–42; Melzer, *Gun Crusaders*; Krämer, "Playboy tells his story"; Potts, "Essence of the

Hard On," 92–3; Luciano, *Looking Good*, 97–9; Loe, *Rise of Viagra*, 13, 63–93.

20 Foucault, "Confessions of the Flesh," 194–5.

21 Greene and Siegel Watkins, "Introduction"; Elliott, *Better Than Well*; Terzian, "Direct-to-Consumer Prescription Drug"; Loe, *Rise of Viagra*, 23.

22 Elliott, *Better Than Well*, 102–7.

23 Danoff, *Superpotency*, 158; "consumerist erectile economy" in Marshall and Katz, "Forever Functional," 45.

24 On the vagueness of the concept of doping, see Reinold, *Doping als Konstruktion*, 71–124; Harrasser, *Körper 2.0*, 12; Harrasser et al., "Wieviel Technology ist im Laufschuh?"

25 A logic that has enabled many convicted dopers in sports with major doping problems to deny having ever cheated; see also Reinold, *Doping als Konstruktion*, 127. For an example of a definition of doping, see the first one produced by the Council of Europe in 1963, which describes doping as "the administration, by any means, to an individual in good health of a substance foreign to the body or of abnormal quantities of physiological substances, with the sole aim of artificially and unfairly enhancing individual performance in a competition." On the entanglement of everyday doping and doping in sport, see also Hoberman, *Testosterone Dreams*.

26 Møller, *The Doping Devil*. On the distinction between sport and fitness, see Scholl, "Einleitung: Biopolitik."

27 On the social history of doping, in addition to Møller, *The Doping Devil*, and Hoberman, *Testosterone Dreams*, see esp. Hoberman, *Mortal Engines*; Dimeo, "A Critical Assessment"; Dimeo, *A History of Drug Use*; Schneider, "The Concept of Doping," and Ritchie, "Understanding Performance-Enhancing Substances."

28 Kläber, *Doping im Fitness-Studio*; Martschukat, "What Diet Can Do."

29 Barker-Benfield, "The Spermatic Economy"; Mumford, "Lost Manhood."

30 See Martschukat, *American Fatherhood*.

31 White, *First Sexual Revolution*; Daley, *Leisure & Pleasure*; Kasson, *Houdini*; on Sandow's erotic charm, see Poole, "Männer im Pelz."

32 Beard, *Sexual Neurasthenia*; Mumford, "Lost Manhood," 43.

33 Reinold, *Doping als Konstruktion*, 83.

34 McLaren, *Impotence*, 126–48; Gilman, *Making the Body Beautiful*; Ramsbrock, *Science of Beauty*.

35 Stoff, *Ewige Jugend*, 37–43.

36 Stoff, *Ewige Jugend*, 16; see also p. 80 on the emerging productivist ideology of sex and on the distinction between bodies of production and consumption; on the female body of consumption, see also Stoff, "Janine"; in addition to Stoff, see esp. Birken, *Consuming Desire*; Marshall and Katz, "Forever Functional," 49.

37 Freud, "Vorwort" (1913); McLaren, *Impotence*, 181–207.

38 Cushman, *Constructing the Self*; Moskowitz, *In Therapy We Trust*.

39 Spark et al., "Impotence Is Not Always Psychogenic"; Toufexis, "It's Not All in Your Head." On the turn toward the body, see also Bänziger et al., *Sexuelle Revolution?*; in this volume particularly Eder, "Lange Geschichte der Sexuellen Revolution." On the engines of research in the life sciences, see Rheinberger, *Experimentalsysteme*.

40 Following Gilles Deleuze and Félix Guattari, we would refer to an assemblage, while Michel Foucault spoke of a *dispositif*, and Bruno Latour emphasized the network: Deleuze and Guattari, *Mille Plateaux*; Foucault, "Confessions of the Flesh"; Ganahl, "Foucaults dispositif"; van Dyk, "Was die Welt zusammenhält"; Bennett, *Vibrant Matter*, 20–38.

41 Latour, *Reassembling the Social*, 46, 71; Coole and Frost, "Introducing the New Materialisms"; Mackert and Martschukat, "Introduction: Fat Agency."

42 Loe, *Rise of Viagra*, 79. For an illuminating account of the relationship between body and prosthesis, see Kienitz, "Schöner gehen?", which considers the agency of the stump. Harrasser, *Prothesen*.

43 Paula-Irene Villa in Ramsbrock et al., "Menschliche Dinge."

44 Marshall and Katz, "Forever Functional"; Potts, "Deleuze on Viagra"; Mamo and Fishman, "Potency in All the Right Places."

45 Latour, *Reassembling the Social*.

46 Here I have benefited above all from the studies of Sontowski, *Viagra im Alltag*; Potts et al., "Viagra Stories"; Potts et al., "Sex for Life"; Potts et al., "Downside of Viagra"; Loe, *Rise of Viagra*.

47 Hultling, "Partners' Perceptions"; Potts et al., "Downside of Viagra."

48 Sontowski, *Viagra im Alltag*, 92, 95, 144–5; Loe, *Rise of Viagra*, 65, 70–1, 79. The effect of prostheses has been a more controversial topic in debates on disability than the respondents were able to appreciate; see, for example, Spöhrer, "Wie ich zum Cyborg wurde."

49 Sontowski, *Viagra im Alltag*, 119, 153, 187–8; on performance and the modern logic of enhancement, see Verheyen, *Erfindung der Leistung*, 127ff.; on the loss of agency, see also Harrasser, *Körper 2.0*, 13.

50 Sontowski, *Viagra im Alltag*, 92–3, 95, 143, 149, 168; Potts et al., "Sex for Life."

51 Sontowski, *Viagra im Alltag*, 95–6, 147, 172–6.

52 Sontowski, *Viagra im Alltag*, 155, 161, 180, 201, 208–10; Weeks, "Sexual Citizen."

53 Potts et al., "Downside of Viagra," 701–2; Riley, "Role of the Partner"; Loe, *Rise of Viagra*, 95–123.

54 Potts et al., "Downside of Viagra," 703–6, 708; Riley and Riley, "Behavioural and Clinical Findings."

55 Potts et al., "Downside of Viagra," 712.

56 Potts et al., "Downside of Viagra," 713.

57 Loe, *Rise of Viagra*, 125–65.

58 Foucault, *History of Sexuality*; Jagose, *Queer Theory*; Stieglitz and Martschukat, *Race & Sex*.

59 For a summary, see Martschukat and Stieglitz, "Race & Sex."

60 Baglia, *Viagra Ad Venture*, 80–2.

5. Fighting

1 http://www.urbanheroes.com/die-urban-heroes-trainer/ – these appeals quote from or paraphrase statements found on the webpage.

2 http://www.urbanheroes.com/heronation/

3 For the interview, see http://www.urbanheroes.com/too-busy-to-work-out-5-tipps-von-johannes-b-kerner/

4 http://www.urbanheroes.com/preise-urban-heroes/

5 For Fitness Hero, see http://www.fitnessheroinc.com/; for Heroes Fitness, see https://www.herofitnessgyms.com/; for the training camp in Spain, see http://heldensphaere.de/; for the Hamburg race, see https://www.heldenlauf.de/ and for the "cycling heroes," see https://www.facebook.com/stuttgartervelohelden/.

6 On "post-heroic societies," see esp. Münkler, *Kriegssplitter*; on the definition of the hero, see Hoff et al., "Helden – Heroisierungen – Heroismen," 10. On the figure of the hero and difference, see the recent contribution by Wendt (ed.), *Warring over Valor*.

7 Goltermann, *Opfer*.

8 Mosse, *The Image of Man*; Probst, "Held auf dem Sprung"; Gibson, *Warrior Dreams*.

9 Jones, "What Should Historians Do"; Frevert, "Das Militär als Schule der Männlichkeiten," 70, on heroism's martial grounding; Frevert, "Vom heroischen Menschen." In this special issue of *Merkur* on "Heldengedanken. Über das heroische Phantasma" ("Ideas of the Hero: On the Heroic Imaginary"), see also Tetzlaff, "Wie Jugendliche heute Helden sehen"; Hoff et al., "Helden – Heroisierungen – Heroismen"; Bröckling, "Negationen des Heroischen." On the complexity of the post-heroic, see also Tanrisever, *Fathers*.

10 Bette, *Sporthelden*.

11 Teleky, "Post-Heroism?", 44; Schlechtriemen, "The Hero."

12 On the "citizenship of civic practices," see Snyder, *Citizen-Soldiers*; Bradburn, *Citizenship Revolution*; Martschukat, *American Fatherhood*, 7–23 on the process of becoming a man.

13 Frevert, "Bürgersoldaten"; Frevert, *A Nation in Barracks*; Nelson, "Citizen Soldiers"; Herrera, *For Liberty*; Crépin, *Défendre la France*, esp. chapter III, 173–99.

14 Wendt, "Reconsidering Military Heroism," 3.

15 Hagemann, "Tod für das Vaterland," also "act of heroism" from the decree of May 5, 1813, on p. 307, reprinted in *der Preußische Correspondent*, Berlin, no. 37, June 4, 1813; "valor" on p. 33, from the official document on the establishment of the Iron Cross of March 10, 1813; see also Hagemann, *Revisiting Prussia's Wars*.

16 Jahn in March 1813, quoted in Hagemann, "Tod für das Vaterland," 328.

17 Frevert, "Das Militär als Schule der Männlichkeiten," 68.

18 Cullen, "I's a Man Now."

19 Hoganson, *Fighting for American Manhood*; Jünger, *Storm of Steel*; for a nuanced account, see Münch, *Bürger in Uniform*.

20 Foucault, *Discipline and Punish*, 137.

21 Steuben, *Regulations for the Order.*

22 Goltermann, *Körper der Nation*; Krüger, *Körperkultur*; for a summary, see Pfister, "200 Jahre Turnbewegung."

23 According to Pilcher, "Building of the Soldier"; East, *A Historical Review*, 15; Pfister, "Role of German Turners."

24 Koehler, *Manual of Gymnastic Exercises*, 10–12, quoted in East, *A Historical Review*, 41.

25 Campbell, "Training for Sport," 21, 36 and 41f. on the similar requirements found in sport and military service; Goltermann, *Körper der Nation*, 114; East, *A Historical Review*, 26–42, quote on p. 39; Pfister, "Role of German Turners."

26 Wood in foreword to Koehler, *Manual for Physical Training*, 3; Roosevelt, *America and the First World War*, 209; see also East, *A Historical Review*, 49–50.

27 Bristow, *Making Men Moral*; Veit, *Modern Food, Moral Food*, 11–36; Fosdick, "War and Navy Departments"; Fosdick, "Commission on Training Camp Activities."

28 "No nation" from the *US Army Training Manual No. 2: Studies in Citizenship for Recruits*, Washington, DC: Government Printing Office. 1922, 33, quoted in East, *A Historical Review*, 67–8; Stieglitz, *100 Percent American Boys*; Patel, *Soldiers of Labor*, on the militarization of conceptions of work in Germany; Jarvis, *The Male Body at War*, 26–7.

29 Jarvis, *The Male Body at War*, 19–20, 57; Moran, *Governing Bodies*, 64–83; the quote is from Lieutenant General Brehon B. Somervell, Commanding General of the Army Services Forces, quoted in Spencer, *Youth Goes to War*, cover; East, *Historical Review*, 93.

30 Theweleit, *Male Fantasies*; Reichardt, "Klaus Theweleits 'Männerphantasien'."

31 Jarvis, *The Male Body at War*, 44–5; Mirzoeff, *Bodyscape*; Mangan (ed.), *Shaping the Superman*; Wildmann, *Begehrte Körper*; Foucault, *Society Must Be Defended*, 239–63.

32 Sombart, *Händler und Helden*, quoted in Frevert, "Herren und Helden," 339.

33 Anderson, "Mutilation and Disfiguration"; Kienitz, *Beschädigte Helden*; Kienitz, "Krieg der Invaliden"; Kienitz, "Körper – Beschädigungen"; Harrasser, *Prothesen*, 100–21; Linker, *War's*

Waste; Stagner, "Healing the Soldier"; Bourke, *Dismembering the Male*; Cowan and Sicks, "Technik, Krieg und Medien," 19 for the Benjamin quote; see also Benjamin, "Erfahrung und Armut." For an overview of this field, see also Mosse, *Image of Man*.

34 Frevert, *A Nation in Barracks*, 238–47.

35 Quoted in Frevert, "Herren und Helden," 342; MacDonogh, "Helden und Patrioten," 783.

36 Sebastian Haak, *Making of the Good War*.

37 Still worth looking at are Engelhardt, *The End of Victory Culture*; Greiner, *War Without Fronts*; Turse, *Kill Anything That Moves*; Graebner, "The Man in the Water," 519–20. On the critique of patriarchy propagated by the 1968 protest movements, see Hodenberg, *Das andere Achtundsechzig*.

38 Graebner, "The Man in the Water"; see, for example, Warren, "A Dearth of Heroes," whose text also appeared as foreword to the second edition of Wecter, *The Hero in America*; Plumb, "Disappearing Heroes"; Anon., "The Vanishing American Hero"; Egan, "Changing Faces of Heroism"; Jones, "What Should Historians Do," 441; Frevert, "Vom heroischen Menschen," 811.

39 Mills, *White Collar*, xii; Martschukat, *Ordnung des Sozialen*, 263–92. On the civilian hero in US history, see Houchin Winfield and Hume, "The American Hero."

40 Mailer, "The White Negro"; Mailer, "Superman"; Depoe, *Arthur M. Schlesinger, Jr.*; Moran, *Governing Bodies*, 98–111.

41 Reagan, "Inaugural Address."

42 Schlechtriemen, "The Hero," 17, 27; Lehmann, "Wunsch nach Bewunderung," 774.

43 See also Wolfe, "The Me Decade," on the 1970s as the start of a new "age of me."

44 Scheller, *No Sports!*, 13. In the film *Pumping Iron*, Arnold Schwarzenegger compares himself to a sculptor.

45 See, for example, Reagan, "How to Stay Fit," in *Parade* magazine, a weekend supplement in numerous newspapers.

46 Jeffords, *The Remasculinization of America*; Jeffords, *Hard Bodies*; Heywood, *Bodymakers*; Poole, "Preface"; Wacquant, "Why Men Desire Muscles."

47 Gibson, *Warrior Dreams*; Melzer, *Gun Crusaders*; Carlson,

Citizen-Protectors; Kieran and Martini (eds.), *At War*. Kathrin Hartmann notes the upsurge of the autonomous warrior as cultural and political phenomenon in post-Soviet Russia, coupled with the perception of a disintegrating state: Hartmann, "Kontinuität und Wandel."

48 Kieran and Martini (eds.), *At War*; Dudziak, *War Time*, 30.

49 Warren, "US Special Forces."

50 Luciano, *Looking Good*, 121.

51 Underhill, "Converting the Non-Runner"; Higdon, "Is Running a Religious Experience?", quote on 78; Anon., "Year of the Marathon," on the growth of organized events; Mickel, "The True Runner"; Pinkerton, "Running Can Be Your Substitute." Sloterdijk, *You Must Change Your Life*, underlines the sacred element of the fitness and self-improvement movements.

52 Tymn, "Trauma of Turning Forty"; Warde, "Coming On Strong," quote on 44; Benyo, "Running Is a Tough Act," 73 on life as a kind of marathon; Wischnin, "Alex Ratelle Wants to Go Forever."

53 Higdon, "A Race with Texture"; see also Anon., "Year of the Marathon"; Henderson, "The Year Running Became the Sport."

54 Fischer, *Mein langer Lauf*.

55 Fixx, *Complete Book of Running*, xviii; Burfoot, "Going for It!"; Anon., "Byline," on the massification of the marathon; Waters, "Defining the Runner's Personality"; Shangold, "The Woman Runner"; Osler, "The Easy Way"; Horning, "Cold, Wet and Wild"; Henderson, "Tips For the First-Time Marathoner"; Burfoot, "You Should be Committed"; Burfoot: "The Old and the Renewed"; Hogan, "Total Fitness '89"; Delhagen, "Ironmania"; Burfoot, "Heads Above the Crowd"; Kowalchick and Will-Weber, "Extraordinary People"; Lynch, "Mind Over Marathon"; Lewis, "Mapping the Way"; Higdon, "The Master Plan."

56 Anon., "Heroes of Running 2006"; on the 2005 awards, see also Unger Hahn, "Heroes of Running 2005."

57 Spiker, "The Mudder Report"; Megroz, "Down and Dirty."

58 Gelz et al., "Phänomene der Deheroisierung," 136; Wacquant, "Why Men Desire Muscles," 174.

59 Because fitness is just as ephemeral as the hero's renown; see Gelz et al., "Phänomene der Deheroisierung," 137.

60 Bortz, "Primitive Man and Athletics," quote on 90.

61 Bröckling, "Negationen des Heroischen," 9–12; on the relationship between fat and agency, see the contributions in Mackert and Martschukat (eds.), "Fat Agency," special issue of *Body Politics* 3, 5 (2015) and various contributions to the blog *Food, Fatness, and Fitness: Critical Perspectives*, http://foodfatnessfitness.com/. On heroic metaphors and weight loss, see the self-presentation of and reportage on the TV show *The Biggest Loser*, https://www.sat1.de/tv/the-biggest-loser (July 6, 2018).

62 Werber, "Soldaten und Söldner," 797; Steiner, "Heldenposen," 930; on fat as a dogged substance, see Forth, "Materializing Fat."

63 See Biltekoff, *Eating Right*, 130–7; Mitchell and McTigue, "The US Obesity 'Epidemic'"; a text regarded as the starting point of an increasingly militarized discourse of fat is Office of the Surgeon General et al., *The Surgeon General's Call*. See also Jackson, "All Quiet on the Fat Front"; Council for a Strong America, *Unhealthy and Unprepared*; Anon., "Zu dick zum Kämpfen."

64 Haralambon, *Der Radrennfahrer*, 64, 67.

65 Hoff et al., "Helden – Heroisierungen – Heroismen," 9; Bröckling, "Wettkampf und Wettbewerb"; Bolz, "Der antiheroische Effekt," 767, 771; Lehmann, "Wunsch nach Bewunderung," 775; Drucker, "The Mediated Sports Hero."

6. Productive, Potent, and Ready to Fight?

1 The fundamental question is whether fatness should be considered the cause or consequence of educational disadvantages and poverty: Kim and von dem Knesebeck, "Income and Obesity"; Kim et al., "Causation or Selection."

2 Muttarak, "Normalization of Plus Size"; Stewart, "Why Thinking We're Fat"; Blair, "Fitness or Fatness"; Burke, "Evolving Societal Norms of Obesity."

3 Brody, "More Fitness, Less Fatness"; Fischer, "Macht Mode dick?"; see the regular column by Natalie Rosenke, "Über Gewicht: Mein dickes Leben," *SZ-Magazin online*, launched on November 29, 2018, https://sz-magazin.sueddeutsche.de/ueber-gewicht-mein-dickes-leben/natuerlich-darf-ich-gluecklich-sein-86372 (accessed December 3, 2018).

4 Albrecht, "Doppelkinn statt Doppelmoral"; see also Albrecht, *Fa(t) shionista*; Baker, "Why I Have Chosen Body Liberation Over Body Love." A quick internet search provides a very good impression of the momentum of the body positivity movement; see also #body-positive or #bodypositivity.

5 Bacon, *Health At Every Size*; Lee and Pausé, "Stigma in Practice." For a critique of the connection between health and self-responsibility with regard to tuberculosis and cancer, see Sontag, *Illness As Metaphor*.

6 Tovar, *Hot & Heavy*, 7f.; Tovar, *You Have the Right to Remain Fat*; Tovar, "Lose Hate Not Weight"; see also Baker, *Things No One Will Tell Fat Girls*; Baker, *Landwhale*; Taylor, *This Body Is Not an Apology*; Ludwig, "Selbstliebe reicht nicht."

7 Rothblum and Solovay (eds.), *The Fat Studies Reader*, 341 for the manifesto; Kreuzenbeck, "Nothing to Lose."

8 McRuer, Robert, "Compulsory Able-Bodiedness"; Wilkerson, "From the Land of the Fat to the Fat of the Land"; Wilkerson, "'Obesity,' the Transnational Plate, and the Thin Contract." Quotation in Butler, *Bodies that Matter*, 3.

9 The quote comes from the context of the German nudist movement of the early twentieth century; quoted in Möhring, "Der moderne Apoll," 32; Scheller, *No Sports!*, 12–14. A less nuanced account of the meaning of muscles is provided by Wacquant, "Why Men Desire Muscles"; on slimness and self-management, see Bordo, "Reading the Slender Body"; on fat and muscles, see Forth, "On Fat and Fattening"; for an overview, see Mackert and Martschukat, "Introduction: Fat Agency."

10 Lee and Pausé, "Stigma in Practice," 5.

11 Honneth, *Anerkennung*; Cooper, *Citizenship, Inequality, and Difference*; Rose and Novas, "Biological Citizenship."

12 Campbell, *Contours of Ableism*, 5; Goodley, *Dis/Ability Studies*; Mackert and Martschukat, "Critical Ability History."

13 See also Sloterdijk, *You Must Change Your Life*, 65.

14 Sloterdijk, *You Must Change Your Life*, 34.

15 Snyder, *Citizen-Soldiers*, 1–13 on the concept of the "citizenship of civic practices" in connection with military service.

REFERENCES

Adam, Hans-Christian, *Eadweard Muybridge: The Human and Animal Locomotion Photographs*. Cologne: Taschen, 2010.

Adams, George B., "The United States and the Anglo-Saxon Future," *Atlantic Monthly* 78, 465 (1896), 35–45.

Adams, Mark, *Mr. America: How Muscular Millionaire Bernarr Macfadden Transformed the Nation Through Sex, Salad, and the Ultimate Starvation Diet*. New York: HarperCollins, 2009.

Adler, Waldo, "Spartan Stuff in Diet," *Outing* 66 (1915), 298–303.

Afzal, Shoaib, Anne Tybjærg-Hansen, Gorm B. Jensen, and Børge G. Nordestgaard, "Change in Body Mass Index Associated with Lowest Mortality in Denmark, 1976–2013," *JAMA* 315, 18 (2016), 1989–96.

Albrecht, Magda, "Doppelkinn statt Doppelmoral. Die Body-Positivity-Bewegung ist im Mainstream angekommen. Eigentlich ein Grund zum Feiern – oder etwa nicht?" *Missy Magazin* 4 (2018), https://missy-magazine.de/blog/2018/08/23/doppelkinn-statt-doppelmoral (accessed November 15, 2018).

Albrecht, Magda, *Fa(t)shionista. Rund und glücklich durchs Leben*. Berlin: Ullstein, 2018.

Alkemeyer, Thomas, "Aufrecht und biegsam. Eine politische Geschichte des Körperkults," *Aus Politik und Zeitgeschichte* (APuZ) 18 (2007), http://www.bpb.de/apuz/30506/aufrecht-und-biegsam

-eine-politische-geschichte-des-koerperkults?p=all#fr-footnodeid
_27 (accessed July 8, 2016).

Alkemeyer, Thomas, *Zeichen, Körper und Bewegung: Aufführungen von Gesellschaft im Sport*. Berlin: Habilitationsschrift, 2000.

Allcott, Hunt, Rebecca Diamond, Jean-Pierre Dubé, et al., "Food Deserts and the Causes of Nutritional Inequality," *Quarterly Journal of Economics* 134, 4 (2019), 1793–844.

Anderson, Julie, "Mutilation and Disfiguration," in: Ute Daniel et al. (ed.), *1914–1918-online. International Encyclopedia of the First World War*. Berlin: Freie Universität Berlin, 2017.

Anon., "An Englishwoman in the New England Hill Country," *Atlantic Monthly* 46, 274 (1880), 238–48.

Anon., "Art. III: Gymnastics," *North American Review* 81, 168 (1855), 51–69.

Anon., "Brutale Harmonie. Mit Schönheitsstudios, Psychobetreuung und Sportprogrammen buhlen Hotels um Kundschaft aus dem Manager-Milieu," *Der Spiegel* 7 (1990), 245–6.

Anon., "Byline," *Runner's World* 16, 5 (1981), 5.

Anon., "Deutschland verfettet, aber raucht weniger," *Spiegel Online*, November 4, 2014, http://www.spiegel.de/gesundheit/ernaehrung/studie-zu-uebergewicht-mehr-als-jeder-zweite-deutsche-ist-zu-dick-a-1001097.html (accessed September 30, 2016).

Anon., "Fit durch Cyber-Sport: Die Branche steht vor einem Umbruch. Das Studio an der Ecke verschwindet, die Zukunft gehört den Fitneß-Supermärkten," *Der Spiegel* 18 (1998), 142.

Anon., "Fit für die Firma. Gute Chefs beugen vor und sorgen sich um das Wohlbefinden ihrer Angestellten," *Die Zeit*, October 1, 1998, https://www.zeit.de/1998/41/199841.c-gesund_.xml (accessed May 1, 2018).

Anon., "Getting a Move On," *Forbes* 113, 5 (1974), 9.

Anon., "Gymnastik – Bürotraining. Heißer Stuhl," *Der Spiegel* 17 (1971), 153.

Anon., "Heroes of Running 2006. Heroes of Running Are Everywhere," *Runner's World*, October 27, 2006, https://www.runnersworld.com/runners-stories/a20800752/heroes-of-running-2006/ (accessed July 4, 2018).

Anon., "Kuß des Todes. Wer dick ist, hat kaum Karriere-Chancen.

Übergewichtige Amerikaner klagen über Diskriminierung am Arbeitsplatz," *Der Spiegel* 1 (1978), 69–71.

Anon., "Lockeres Sitzfleisch," *Der Spiegel special* 4 zum Thema "Prost Mahlzeit! Essen, Trinken und Genießen" (1996), 60.

Anon., "Manager: Erfülltes Leben," *Der Spiegel* 8 (1970), 170.

Anon., "Medicine: The Life of Stress," *TIME Magazine* LXXII, 4 (July 28, 1958).

Anon., "Number of Health Clubs & Fitness Centers in the U.S. from 2008 to 2016," *The Statistics Portal*, https://www.statista.com/statis tics/244922/us-fitness-centers-und-health-clubs/ (accessed May 4, 2018).

Anon., "Schau mal, hier steht was," *Der Spiegel* 21 (1998), 108–26.

Anon., "Spectrum: Trimmen am Arbeitsplatz," *Der Spiegel* 34, 8 (1980), 233.

Anon., *The Executive Health Report Fitness Guide*. New York: Award Books, 1969.

Anon., "The Oldest Games of All," *Outing* 58 (1911), 662.

Anon., "The Vanishing American Hero," *U.S. News & World Report*, July 21, 1975, 16–18.

Anon., "Three Typical Workingmen," *Atlantic Monthly* 42, 254 (1878), 717–27.

Anon., "Übergewicht in Deutschland: Zahl der Fettleibigen soll bis 2030 dramatisch steigen," *Spiegel Online*, June 19, 2014, http://www.spiegel.de/gesundheit/ernaehrung/uebergewicht-und-adipositas-in-deutschland-80-prozent-mehr-fettleibige-a-981908.html (accessed May 11, 2016).

Anon., "'Viagra ist eine Bombe.' Der Hamburger Urologe Hartmut Porst über Nutzen und Gefahren der Potenzpille," *Der Spiegel* 21 (1998), 110.

Anon., "Viagra: The Potency Pill," *TIME Magazine* 115, 17 (1998), cover.

Anon., "Watch That Waistline!," *Forbes* 105, 10 (May 15, 1970), 214, 219–21.

Anon., "'Wonniges Dahingleiten, geschwind wie ein Pfeil'. Die Deutschen steigen wieder aufs Rad," *Der Spiegel* 19 (1980), 88–105.

Anon., "Year of the Marathon. No Running Sport in History Has

Grown So Quickly, So Well, Or So Enthusiastically," *Runner's World* 13, 2 (1978), 68–73.

Anon., "Zu dick zum Kämpfen," *Spiegel Online*, October 13, 2018, http://www.spiegel.de/politik/ausland/usa-fettleibigkeit-bedroht-sicherheit-des-landes-a-1233102.html (accessed November 2, 2018).

Bacon, Linda, *Health At Every Size, The Surprising Truth About Your Weight*, Dallas, TX: BenBella Books, 2008.

Baglia, Jay, *The Viagra Ad Venture. Masculinity, Marketing, and the Performance of Sexual Health*, New York: Peter Lang, 2005.

Bailey, Covert, *Fit or Fat?* (1977), London: Houghton Mifflin, 1985.

Bakalar, Nicholas, "Obesity Rates Higher in Country Than City," *New York Times*, June 21, 2018.

Baker, Jes, *Landwhale. On Turning Insults Into Nicknames, Why Body Image Is Hard, and How Diets Can Kiss My Ass*, New York: Seal Press, 2018.

Baker, Jes, *Things No One Will Tell Fat Girls. A Handbook for Unapologetic Living*, Berkeley, CA: Seal Press, 2015.

Baker, Jes, "Why I Have Chosen Body Liberation Over Body Love," *The Militant Baker*, June 25, 2018, http://www.themilitantbaker.com/2018/06/why-ive-chosen-body-liberation-over.html (accessed November 17, 2018).

Bänziger, Peter-Paul, "Fordistische Körper in der Geschichte des 20. Jahrhunderts – eine Skizze," *Body Politics* 1, 1 (2013), 11–40.

Bänziger, Peter-Paul, Magdalena Beljan, Franz X. Eder, and Pascal Eitler, "Sexuelle Revolution? Zur Sexualitätsgeschichte seit den 1960er Jahren im deutschsprachigen Raum," in: Peter-Paul Bänziger, Magdalena Beljan, Franz X. Eder, and Pascal Eitler (eds.), *Sexuelle Revolution? Zur Geschichte der Sexualität im deutschsprachigen Raum seit den 1960er Jahren*. Bielefeld: transcript, 2015, 7–24.

Barker-Benfield, Ben, "The Spermatic Economy: A Nineteenth Century View of Sexuality," *Feminist Studies* 1, 1 (1972), 45–74.

Barney, Robert Knight, "Book Review: James C. Whorton, Crusaders for Fitness: The History of American Health Reformers," *Journal of Sport History* 11, 1 (1984), 104–6.

Barrett, Christopher B., "Measuring Food Insecurity," *Science*, New Series, 327, 5967 (2010), 825–8.

Bassler, Thomas, "Live Like a Marathoner," *Runner's World* 9, 10 (1974), 26.

Bates, Christopher G. and Steven A. Riess, "Industrial Sports," in: Steven A. Riess (ed.), *Sports in America. From Colonial Times to the Twenty-First Century. An Encyclopedia*, vol. 2. London: Routledge, 2011, 479–82.

Bauman, Zygmunt, *Liquid Modernity*, Cambridge: Polity, 2000.

Bauman, Zygmunt, "On Postmodern Uses of Sex," *Theory, Culture & Society* 15, 3–4 (1998), 19–33.

Beard, George M., *Sexual Neurasthenia. Its Hygiene, Causes, Symptoms, and Treatment, with a Chapter on Diet for the Nervous*, New York: E.B. Treat, 1884.

Becker, Frank, "Sport bei Ford. Rationalisierung und Symbolpolitik in der Weimarer Republik," *Stadion* 27 (1991), 207–29.

Becker, Frank and Ralf Schäfer (eds.), *Sport und Nationalsozialismus*, Göttingen: Wallstein, 2016.

Bederman, Gail, *Manliness & Civilization: A Cultural History of Gender and Race in the United States, 1880–1917*. Chicago, IL: University of Chicago Press, 1995.

Belasco, Warren J., *Appetite for Change: How the Counterculture Took on the Food Industry*. Ithaca, NY: Cornell University Press, 2007 (1989).

Bell, David and Joanne Hollows, "Towards a History of Lifestyle," in: David Bell and Joanne Hollows (eds.), *Historicizing Lifestyle. Mediating Taste, Consumption and Identity from the 1900s to 1970s*. New York: Routledge, 2016, 1–20.

Benjamin, Walter, "Erfahrung und Armut," *Illuminationen – ausgewählte Schriften 1 (1920–1940)*, https://www.textlog.de/benjamin-erfahru ng-armut.html (accessed June 4, 2018).

Bennett, Jane, *Vibrant Matter. A Political Ecology of Things*, Durham, NC: Duke University Press, 2010.

Benyo, Rich, "Running Is a Tough Act to Follow," *Runner's World* 13, 1 (1978), 66–73.

Bernet, Brigitta, "Insourcing und Outsourcing. Anthropologien der modernen Arbeit," *Historische Anthropologie* 24, 2 (2016), 272–93.

Berryman, Jack W. and Roberta J. Park, *Sport and Exercise Science. Essays in the History of Sports Medicine*, Urbana, IL: University of Illinois Press, 1992.

Bette, Karl-Heinrich, *Sporthelden. Spitzensport in postheroischen Zeiten*, Bielefeld: transcript, 2019.

Bette, Karl-Heinrich, *Sportsoziologie*, Bielefeld: transcript, 2010.

Biltekoff, Charlotte, *Eating Right in America. The Cultural Politics of Food and Health*, Durham, NC: Duke University Press, 2013.

Birken, Lawrence, *Consuming Desire. Sexual Science and the Emergence of a Culture of Abundance, 1871–1914*, Ithaca, NY: Cornell University Press, 1988.

Black, Jonathan, *Making the American Body: The Remarkable Saga of the Men and Women Whose Feats, Feuds, and Passions Shaped Fitness History*, Lincoln, NE: University of Nebraska Press, 2013.

Blackford, Katherine M. and Arthur Newcomb, *Analyzing Character, the New Science of Judging Men: Misfits in Business, the Home and Social Life*, New York: Review of Reviews Company, 1916.

Blackie, John S., *Self-Culture, Intellectual, Physical and Moral. A Vade Mecum for Young Men and Students*, Edinburgh: Edmonston and Douglas, 1874.

Blair, Steven N., "Fitness or Fatness. Which Is More Important?," *JAMA* 319, 3 (2018), 231–2.

Blasi, Luca di, *Der weiße Mann. Ein Anti-Manifest*, Bielefeld: transcript, 2013.

Bolz, Norbert, "Der antiheroische Effekt," *Merkur* 63, 9/10 (2009), 762–71.

Bordo, Susan, "Reading the Slender Body," in: Mary Jacobus, Evelyn Fox Keller, and Sally Shuttleworth (eds.), *Body/Politics. Women and the Discourses of Science*. London: Routledge, 1990, 83–112.

Bordo, Susan, *The Male Body: A New Look at Men in Public and Private*, New York: Farrar, Straus and Giroux, 1999.

Bortz, Walter, "Primitive Man and Athletics," *Runner's World* 17, 6 (1982), 40–5, 90.

Bourke, Joanna, *Dismembering the Male. Men's Bodies, Britain, and the Great War*, London: Reaktion Press, 1996.

Bowers, Matthew T. and Thomas M. Hunt, "The President's Council on Physical Fitness and the Systematisation of Children's Play in America," *International Journal of the History of Sport* 28 (2011), 1496–511.

Bradburn, Douglas, *The Citizenship Revolution. Politics and the Creation of the American Union, 1774–1804,* Charlottesville, VA: University of Virginia Press, 2009.

Bradshaw, Alison, "Empowerment and Sport Feminism. A Critical Analysis," *International Sport Studies* 24, 1 (2005), 5–31.

Breen, T. H., *The Marketplace of Revolution. How Consumer Politics Shaped American Independence,* New York: Oxford University Press, 2004.

Briesen, Detlef, *Das gesunde Leben. Ernährung und Gesundheit seit dem 18. Jahrhundert,* Frankfurt/M.: Campus, 2010.

Bristow, Nancy K., *Making Men Moral: Social Engineering during the Great War,* New York: New York University Press, 1996.

Bröckling, Ulrich, *Das unternehmerische Selbst. Soziologie einer Subjektivierungsform,* Frankfurt/M.: Suhrkamp, 2007.

Bröckling, Ulrich, *Gute Hirten führen sanft. Über Menschenregierungskünste,* Berlin: Suhrkamp, 2017.

Bröckling, Ulrich, "Negationen des Heroischen – ein typologischer Versuch," *helden.heroes.héros.* 3, 1 (2015), 9–13.

Bröckling, Ulrich, "Prävention," in: Ulrich Bröckling, Susanne Krasmann, and Thomas Lemke (eds.), *Glossar der Gegenwart,* Frankfurt/M.: Suhrkamp, 2004, 210–15.

Bröckling, Ulrich, "Wettkampf und Wettbewerb. Konkurrenzordnungen zwischen Sport und Ökonomie," in: Ulrich Bröckling, *Gute Hirten führen sanft. Über Menschenregierungskünste.* Berlin: Suhrkamp, 2017, 243–59.

Brody, Jane E., "More Fitness, Less Fatness," *New York Times,* February 26, 2018, https://www.nytimes.com/2018/02/26/well/more-fitness-less-fatness.html (accessed November 14, 2018).

Brown, Wendy, *Undoing the Demos. Neoliberalism's Stealth Revolution,* New York: Zone Books, 2015.

Budde, Gunilla, "Der Körper der sozialistischen Frauenpersönlichkeit. Weiblichkeits-Vorstellungen in der SBZ/DDR," *Geschichte und Gesellschaft* 26, 4 (2000), 602–28.

Bundeszentrale für Gesundheitliche Aufklärung, *Essen und trimmen, beides muß stimmen. Trimmpfade zum Wohlbefinden,* Cologne, 1986.

Burfoot, Amby, "Going for It! If You Want to Reach Your Goal, You Have to Take Some Chances," *Runner's World* 15, 7 (1980), 35–7.

Burfoot, Amby, "Heads Above the Crowd," *Runner's World* 25, 7 (1990), 70.

Burfoot, Amby, "The Old and the Renewed," *Runner's World* 21, 6 (1986), 40–5.

Burfoot, Amby, "You Should Be Committed," *Runner's World* 21, 2 (1986), 44.

Burke, Mary A., "Evolving Societal Norms of Obesity: What Is the Appropriate Response?," *JAMA* 319, 5 (2018), 221–2.

Burnap, George, *Parks. Their Design, Equipment and Use*. Philadelphia, PA: J.B. Lippincott, 1916.

Butler, Judith, *Bodies that Matter: On the Discursive Limits of Sex*. New York: Routledge, 1993.

Butler, Judith, *Gender Trouble: Feminism and the Subversion of Identity*. New York: Routledge, 1990.

Butler, Judith, *Giving an Account of Oneself*. New York: Fordham University Press, 2005.

Butler, Judith, "Performative Acts and Gender Constitution: An Essay in Phenomenology and Feminist Theory," *Theatre Journal* 40, 4 (1988), 519–31.

Butler, Judith, *The Psychic Life of Power: Theories in Subjection*. Stanford, CA: Stanford University Press, 1997.

Byrne, John A., "Executive Sweat," *Forbes* 135, 11 (1985), 198–200.

Cahn, Susan, *Coming on Strong. Gender and Sexuality in Twentieth-Century Women's Sports*, Cambridge, MA: Harvard University Press, 1998.

Campbell, Fiona A. Kumari, *Contours of Ableism. The Production of Disability and Ableness*, New York: Palgrave Macmillan, 2009.

Campbell, J.D., "Training for Sport Is Training for War. Sport and the Transformation of the British Army, 1860–1914," *International Journal of the History of Sport* 17, 4 (2000), 21–58.

Canaday, Margot, *The Straight State. Sexuality and Citizenship in 20th Century America*, Princeton, NJ: Princeton University Press, 2011.

Carlson, Jennifer, *Citizen-Protectors: The Everyday Politics of Guns in an Age of Decline*, Oxford: Oxford University Press, 2015.

Caysa, Volker, "Krieg der Körper," *Der Spiegel special* 4 zum Thema "Schönheit: Lust am Leib: Die Entdeckung des Körpers" (1997), 8.

Chance, Helena, "Mobilising the Modern Industrial Landscape for Sports and Leisure in the Early Twentieth Century," *International Journal of the History of Sport* 29, 11 (2012), 1600–25.

Chappell, Marisa, *The War on Welfare. Family, Poverty, and Politics in Modern America*. Philadelphia, PA: University of Pennsylvania Press, 2010.

Claeys, Gregory, "The 'Survival of the Fittest' and the Origins of Social Darwinism," *Journal of the History of Ideas* 61, 2 (2000), 223–40.

Claghorn, Kate H., "Our Immigrants and Ourselves," *Atlantic Monthly* 86, 516 (1900), 535–48.

Clark, Charles W., "Woman Suffrage, Pro and Con," *Atlantic Monthly* 65, 389 (1890), 310–20.

Cohen, Lizabeth, *A Consumers' Republic. The Politics of Mass Consumption in Postwar America*. New York: Vintage Books, 2003.

Coleman-Jensen, Alisha Judith, "US Food Insecurity Status: Toward a Refined Definition," *Social Indicators Research* 95, 2 (2010), 215–30.

Collier, Price, "Sport's Place in the Nation's Well-Being," *Outing* 32 (1898), 382–8.

Connell, Raewyn, *Masculinities* 2. Auflage, Berkeley, CA: Polity Press, 2005.

Coole, Diana and Samantha Frost, "Introducing the New Materialisms," in: Diana Coole and Samantha Frost (eds.), *New Materialisms: Ontology, Agency, and Politics*. Durham, NC: Duke University Press, 2010, 1–45.

Cooper, Frederick, *Citizenship, Inequality, and Difference: Historical Perspectives*. Princeton, NJ: Princeton University Press, 2018.

Cooper, Kenneth H., *Aerobics*. New York: M. Evans, 1968.

Cooper, Kenneth H., *The New Aerobics*. New York: M. Evans, 1970.

Corbitt, Ted, "Adjusting to Advancing Age," *Runner's World* 6, 6 (1971), 29.

Council for a Strong America, *Unhealthy and Unprepared. National Security Depends on Promoting Healthy Lifestyles from an Early Age*. Washington, DC: Council for a Strong America, October 10, 2018, https://www.strongnation.org/articles/737-unhealthy-and-unprepared (accessed November 2, 2018).

Cowan, Michael and Kai Marcel Sicks, "Technik, Krieg und Medien. Zur Imagination von Idealkörpern in den zwanziger Jahren," in: Michael Cowan and Kai Marcel Sicks (eds.), *Leibhaftige Moderne. Körper in Kunst und Massenmedien 1918 bis 1933*. Bielefeld: transcript, 2005, 13–29.

Cowie, Jefferson, *The Great Exception. The New Deal and the Limits of American Politics*. Princeton, NJ: Princeton University Press, 2016.

Cowie, Jefferson and Nick Salvatore, "The Long Exception. Rethinking the Place of the New Deal in American History," *International Labor and Working-Class History* 74 (2008), 1–32.

Crawford, Kate, Jessa Lingel, and Tero Karppi, "Our Metrics, Ourselves: A Hundred Years of Selftracking from the Weight Scale to the Wrist Wearable Device," *European Journal of Cultural Studies* 18, 4–5 (2015), 479–96.

Crawford, Robert, "Boundaries of the Self and the Unhealthy Other: Reflections on Health, Culture and AIDS," *Social Science and Medicine* 38, 10 (1994), 1347–65.

Crawford, Robert, "Healthism and the Medicalization of Everyday Life," *International Journal of Health Services* 10, 3 (1980), 365–88.

Crépin, Annie, *Défendre la France. Les Français, la guerre et le service militaire, de la guerre de Sept Ans à Verdun*. Rennes: Presses universitaires de Rennes, 2005.

Crouch, Ian, "Viagra Returns to the Bob Dole Approach," *The New Yorker*, October 7, 2014, http://www.newyorker.com/business/currency/viagra-returns-bob-dole-approach (accessed December 9, 2016).

Cudworth, Ralph, *Treatise Concerning the Eternal and Immutable Nature of Morality*. London: James and John Knapton, 1731.

Cullen, Jim, "'I's a Man Now'. Gender and African American Men," in: Darlene Clark Hine and Ernestine Jenkins (eds.), *A Question of Manhood. A Reader in U.S. Black Men's History and Masculinity, Vol. 1: Manhood Rights. The Construction of Black Male History and Manhood, 1750–1870*. Bloomington, IN: Indiana University Press, 1999, 489–501.

Cuordileone, Kyle A., *Manhood and American Political Culture in the Cold War*. New York: Routledge, 2005.

Cushman, Philip, *Constructing the Self, Constructing America: A Cultural History of Psychotherapy*. Boston, MA: Addison-Wesley, 1995.

Dabakis, Melissa, *Visualizing Labor in American Sculpture. Monuments, Manliness, and the Work Ethic, 1880–1935*. Cambridge, MA: Cambridge University Press, 1999.

Daley, Caroline, *Leisure & Pleasure. Reshaping & Revealing the New Zealand Body 1900–1960*. Auckland: Auckland University Press, 2003.

Danoff, Dudley S., *Superpotency: How to Get It, Use It and Maintain It for a Lifetime*. New York: Warner Books, 1993.

Darwin, Charles, *Die Entstehung der Arten durch natürliche Zuchtwahl oder: Die Erhaltung der bevorzugten Rassen im Kampfe ums Dasein. Aus dem Englischen von Paul Seliger*, Leipzig and Vienna: Bibliographisches Institut, 1902.

Darwin, Charles, *On the Origin of Species by Means of Natural Selection, or The Preservation of Favoured Races in the Struggle for Life*, 5th edn. London: John Murray, 1869, http://darwin-online.org.uk/content/frameset?pageseq=1&itemID=F387&viewtype=text (accessed May 8, 2015).

Darwin, Charles, *On the Origin of Species, or The Preservation of Favoured Races in the Struggle for Life*. London: John Murray, 1859, http://www.gutenberg.org/files/1228/1228-h/1228-h.htm (accessed May 8, 2015).

Darwin, Charles, *Über die Entstehung der Arten durch natürliche Zuchtwahl oder die Erhaltung der begünstigten Rassen im Kampfe um's Dasein. Aus dem Englischen übersetzt von H.G. Bronn. Nach der sechsten englischen Auflage wiederholt durchgesehen und berichtigt von J. Victor Carus*, 6th edn. Stuttgart, 1876.

Davis, Joshua Clark, *From Head Shops to Whole Foods. The Rise and Fall of Activist Entrepreneurs*. New York: Columbia University Press, 2017.

Dean, Mitchell, *Governing Societies. Political Perspectives on Domestic and International Rule*. Maidenhead: Open University Press, 2007.

Dean, Robert D., *Imperial Brotherhood: Gender and the Making of Cold War Foreign Policy*. Amherst, MA: University of Massachusetts Press, 2001.

Degler, Carl, *In Search of Human Nature. The Decline and Revival of Darwinism in American Social Thought*. Oxford: Oxford University Press, 1991.

Deleuze, Gilles and Félix Guattari, *Mille Plateaux*. Paris: Minuit, 1980.

Delhagen, Kate, "Ironmania," *Runner's World* 24, 5 (1989), 54–61.

Depoe, Stephen P., *Arthur M. Schlesinger, Jr., and the Ideological History of American Liberalism*. Tuscaloosa, AL: University of Alabama Press, 2016.

Deutsches Wörterbuch von Jacob Grimm und Wilhelm Grimm, "tüchtig," www.woerterbuchnetz.de/DWB/?lemma=tuechtig (accessed September 20, 2018).

Diehl, Paula, "Körperbilder und Körperpraxen im Nationalsozialismus," in: Paula Diehl (ed.), *Körper im Nationalsozialismus. Bilder und Praxen.* Munich: Fink, 2006, 9–30.

Dilger, Erika, *Die Fitnessbewegung in Deutschland. Wurzeln, Einflüsse und Entwicklungen.* Schondorf: Hofmann-Verlag, 2008.

Dilley, Stephen (ed.), *Darwinian Evolution and Classical Liberalism. Theories in Tension.* Lanham, MD: Lexington Books, 2013.

Dimeo, Paul, "A Critical Assessment of John Hoberman's Histories of Drugs in Sport," *Sport in History* 27, 2 (2007), 318–42.

Dimeo, Paul, *A History of Drug Use in Sport, 1876–1976: Beyond Good and Evil.* London: Routledge, 2007.

Dinçkal, Noyan, "'Sport ist die körperliche und seelische Selbsthygiene des arbeitenden Volkes': Arbeit, Leibesübungen und Rationalisierungskultur in der Weimarer Republik," *Body Politics* 1, 1 (2013), 71–97.

Dipper, Christof, "Moderne" Version: 2.0, *Docupedia-Zeitgeschichte,* January 17, 2018, http://docupedia.de/zg/Dipper_moderne_v2_de_2018 (accessed October 3, 2018).

Doering-Manteuffel, Anselm and Lutz Raphael, *Nach dem Boom, Perspektiven auf die Zeitgeschichte seit 1970,* 3rd edn. Göttingen: Vandenhoeck & Ruprecht, 2012.

Dorsey, Bruce, *Reforming Men and Women. Gender in the Antebellum City.* Ithaca, NY: Cornell University Press, 2002.

Drucker, Susan J., "The Mediated Sports Hero," in: Susan J. Drucker and Gary Gumpert (eds.), *Heroes in a Global World.* Cresskill, NJ: Hampton Press, 2008, 415–31.

Dubois, W.E.B., "The Problem of Amusement (1897)," in: David K. Wiggins and Patrick B. Miller (eds.), *The Unlevel Playing Field: A Documentary History of the African American in Sport.* Urbana, IL: University of Illinois Press, 2003, 39–42.

Duden: Das große Wörterbuch der deutschen Sprache in 6 Vols. Mannheim: Bibliogr. Inst., 1976 (reprinted in 1977).

Dudziak, Mary, *War Time. An Idea, its History, its Consequences.* Oxford: Oxford University Press, 2012.

Dufty, William, *Sugar Blues*. New York: Chilton Book Company, 1975.

Duttweiler, Stefanie, Robert Gugutzer, Jan-Hendrik Passoth, and Jörg Strübing (eds.), *Leben nach Zahlen. Self-Tracking als Optimierungskonzept?* Bielefeld: transcript, 2016.

East, Whitfield B., *A Historical Review and Analysis of Army Physical Readiness Training and Assessment*. Fort Leavenworth, KS: Combat Studies Institute Press, 2013.

Eder, Franz, "Die lange Geschichte der 'Sexuellen Revolution' in Westdeutschland (1950er bis 1980er Jahre)," in: Peter-Paul Bänziger, Magdalena Beljan, Franz X. Eder, and Pascal Eitler (eds.), *Sexuelle Revolution? Zur Geschichte der Sexualität im deutschsprachigen Raum seit den 1960er Jahren*. Bielefeld: transcript, 2015, 25–59.

Edgely, Charles, Betty Edgely, and Ronny Turner, "The Rhetoric of Aerobics. Physical Fitness as Religion," *Free Inquiry in Creative Sociology* 10, 2 (1982), 187–96.

Editorial, *Geschichte der Gegenwart*, https://geschichtedergegenwart.ch/editorial/ (accessed September 9, 2019).

Egan, Susanna, "Changing Faces of Heroism: Some Questions Raised by Contemporary Autobiography," *Biography* 10, 1 (1987), 20–38.

Ehrenreich, Barbara, *The Hearts of Men. American Dreams and the Flight from Commitment*. Garden City, NY: Anchor Press, 1983.

Eisenberg, Christiane, "Die Entdeckung des Sports durch die moderne Geschichtswissenschaft," *Historical Social Research* 27, 2/3 (2002), 4–21.

Eisenberg, Christiane, *"English Sports" und deutsche Bürger. Eine Gesellschaftsgeschichte 1800–1939*. Paderborn: Schöningh, 1999.

Eliot, C.W., "The New Education, II," *Atlantic Monthly* 23, 137 (1869), 358–67.

Elis, Volker, "Von Amerika nach Japan – und zurück. Die historischen Wurzeln und Transformationen des Toyotismus," *Zeithistorische Forschungen* 6, 2 (2009), 255–75.

Elliott, Carl, *Better Than Well. American Medicine Meets the American Dream*. New York: W.W. Norton & Company, 2003.

Engelhardt, Tom, *The End of Victory Culture. Cold War America and the Disillusioning of a Generation*. Amherst, MA: University of Massachusetts Press, 1995.

Esquire (ed.), *The Art of Keeping Fit, Or How the Successful Male Can Avoid Going to Seed.* New York: Harper, 1959.

Essen und Trimmen – beides muß stimmen. Frankfurt/M.: Deutsche Gesellschaft für Ernährung, *c.* 1976.

Fahs, Breanne, *Performing Sex: The Making and Unmaking of Women's Erotic Lives.* Albany, NY: SUNY Press, 2011.

Faludi, Susan, *Stiffed: The Betrayal of the American Man.* New York: W. Morrow, 1999.

Farrell, Amy E., *Fat Shame. Stigma and the Fat Body in American Culture.* New York: New York University Press, 2011.

Feldman, H.A., Irwin Goldstein, Dimitrios G. Hatzichristou, Robert J. Krane, and John B. McKinlay, "Impotence and Its Medical and Psychosocial Correlates: Results of the Massachusetts Male Aging Study," *Journal of Urology* 151, 1 (1994), 54–61.

Fielding, Henry, *Die Geschichte des Tom Jones, eines Findlings,* transl. by U. Diezmann. Part 1, Braunschweig: Westermann, 1841.

Fielding, Henry, *Geschichte des Thomas Jones, eines Fündlings.* Previously transl. from the English of Henry Fielding and now completely revised by U. Diezmann on the basis of the most recent original edition. Part 1, Hamburg and Leipzig: F.L. Gleditsch, 1771.

Fielding, Henry, *Historie des menschlichen Herzens, nach den Abwechselungen der Tugenden und Laster in den sonderbaren Begebenheiten Thomas Jones, eines Fündlings: Moralisch und satyrisch beschrieben.* From the English. Part 1, Hamburg: In der Hertelischen Handlung, 1750.

Fielding, Henry, *The History of Tom Jones, A Foundling* (1749). Harmondsworth: Penguin Classics, 1966.

Finzsch, Norbert, "Wissenschaftlicher Rassismus in den Vereinigten Staaten, 1850 bis 1930," in: Heidrun Kaupen-Haas and C. Saller (eds.), *Wissenschaftlicher Rassismus. Analysen einer Kontinuität in den Human- und Naturwissenschaften.* Frankfurt/M.: Campus, 1999, 84–110.

Fischer, Joschka, *Mein langer Lauf zu mir selbst.* Cologne: Kiepenheuer & Witsch, 1999.

Fischer, Linda, "Macht Mode dick?" *Die Zeit,* July 5, 2018, 38.

Fixx, Jim, *The Complete Book of Running.* New York: Random House, 1977.

Fleig, Anne, *Körperkultur und Moderne. Robert Musils Ästhetik des Sports.* Berlin: de Gruyter, 2008.

Florida, Richard, "Food Deserts Exist. But Do They Matter?," *The Atlantic*, January 22, 2018, https://www.theatlantic.com/business/archive/2018/01/food-deserts/551138 (accessed July 27, 2018).

Foner, Eric, "The Meaning of Freedom in the Age of Emancipation," *Journal of American History* 81, 2 (1994), 435–60.

Forth, Christopher E., "Materializing Fat," in: Christopher E. Forth and Alison Leitch (eds.), *Fat. Culture and Materiality.* London: Bloomsbury, 2014, 3–16.

Forth, Christopher E., "On Fat and Fattening: Agency, Materiality and Animality in the History of Corpulence," *Body Politics* 3, 5 (2015), 51–74.

Fosdick, Raymond B., "The Commission on Training Camp Activities," *Proceedings of the Academy of Political Science in the City of New York* 7, 4 (1918), 163–70.

Fosdick, Raymond B., "The War and Navy Departments Commission on Training Camp Activities," *Annals of the American Society of Political and Social Science* 79, 1 (1918), 130–42.

Foucault, Michel, *Discipline and Punish: The Birth of the Prison*, 1975, transl. by A. Sheridan. New York: Vintage, 1995.

Foucault, Michel, *Security, Territory, Population. Lectures at the Collège de France, 1977–78.* New York: Palgrave Macmillan, 2009.

Foucault, Michel, *Society Must Be Defended. Lectures at the Collège de France*, transl. by David Macey. New York: Picador, 2003.

Foucault, Michel, *The Birth of Biopolitics. Lectures at the Collège de France, 1978–79.* New York: Palgrave Macmillan, 2008.

Foucault, Michel, "The Confessions of the Flesh" (1977) interview, in: *Power/Knowledge Selected Interviews and Other Writings* (ed. Colin Gordon). New York: Pantheon, 1980, 194–228.

Foucault, Michel, *The History of Sexuality, Vol. 1: An Introduction* (1976), transl. by Robert Hurley. New York: Vintage, 1990.

Foucault, Michel, "The Subject and Power," *Critical Inquiry* 8, 4 (1982), 777–95.

Fox, Susannah and Maeve Duggan, "Tracking for Health," *Pew Research Center*, January 28, 2013, http://www.pewinternet.org/2013/01/28/tracking-for-health/ (accessed May 9, 2016).

Fraser, Nancy, "Feminism, Capitalism and the Cunning of History," *New Left Review* 56 (2009), 97–117.

Fraser, Nancy, "How Feminism Became Capitalism's Handmaiden – and How to Reclaim It," *The Guardian*, October 14, 2013, https://www.theguardian.com/commentisfree/2013/oct/14/feminism-capitalist-handmaiden-neoliberal (accessed July 6, 2016).

Freud, Sigmund, "Foreword to Steiner, Maximilian: Die psychischen Störungen der männlichen Potenz" (1913), in: Sigmund Freud, *Gesammelte Werke*, vol. 10, ed. Anna Freud et al. Frankfurt/M.: Fischer, 1980, 451–2.

Frevert, Ute, *A Nation in Barracks: Modern Germany, Military Conscription and Civil Society*, transl. by Andrew Boreham with Daniel Brückenhaus. New York: Berg, 2004.

Frevert, Ute, "Bürgersoldaten. Die allgemeine Wehrpflicht im 19. und 20. Jahrhundert," in: Ines-Jacqueline Werkner (ed.), *Die Wehrpflicht und ihre Hintergründe. Sozialwissenschaftliche Beiträge zur aktuellen Debatte*. Wiesbaden: VS-Verlag, 2004, 45–64.

Frevert, Ute, "Das Militär als Schule der Männlichkeiten," in: Ulrike Brunotte and Rainer Herrn (eds.), *Männlichkeiten und Moderne. Geschlecht in den Wissenskulturen um 1900*. Bielefeld: transcript, 2008, 57–75.

Frevert, Ute, "Herren und Helden. Vom Aufstieg und Niedergang des Heroismus im 19. und 20. Jahrhundert," in: Richard van Dülmen (ed.), *Erfindung des Menschen. Schöpfungsträume und Körperbilder 1500–2000*. Cologne: Böhlau, 1998, 322–44.

Frevert, Ute, "Vom heroischen Menschen zum 'Helden des Alltags'," *Merkur* 63, 9/10 (2009), 803–12.

Froböse, Ingo, Bianca Biallas, and Birgit Wallmann-Sperlich, *Der DKV-Report 2018. Wie gesund lebt Deutschland?*, https://www.ergo.com/de/DKV-Report (accessed September 20, 2018).

Frommeld, Debora, "'Fit statt fett': Der Body-Mass-Index als biopolitisches Instrument," *Curare* 36, 1–2 (2013), 5–16.

Frothingham, Richard, "The Sam Adams Regiments in the Town of Boston," *Atlantic Monthly* 10, 58 (1862), 179–203.

Gambacchini, Peter, "The Bottom Line on Fitness. Corporate Fitness Programs Are Enhancing Employee Health, Happiness and

Productivity, and Saving Money in the Process," *Runner's World* 22, 7 (1987), 66–71.

Gamper, Michael, "Radrennfahrer," in: Netzwerk Körper (ed.), *What Can a Body Do? Praktiken und Figurationen des Körpers in den Kulturwissenschaften*. Frankfurt/M.: Campus, 2012, 197–202.

Ganahl, Simon, "Ist Foucaults dispositif ein Akteur-Netzwerk?," *foucaultblog*, April 1, 2013, http://www.fsw.uzh.ch/foucaultblog/featured/9/ist-foucaults-dispositif-ein-akteur-netzwerk (accessed November 29, 2016).

Gard, Michael, *The End of the Obesity Epidemic*. London: Routledge, 2011.

Gelz, Andreas, Katharina Helm, Hans W. Hubert, Benjamin Marquart, and Jakob Willis, "Phänomene der Deheroisierung in Vormoderne und Moderne," *helden.heroes.héros* 3, 1 (2015), 135–46.

Gems, Gerald R., "Welfare Capitalism and Blue-Collar Sport: The Legacy of Labour Unrest," *Rethinking History* 5, 1 (2001), 43–58.

Gerstle, Gary, *Liberty and Coercion. The Paradox of American Government: From the Founding to the Present*. Princeton, NJ: Princeton University Press, 2015.

Geyer, Christian, "'Fit statt fett': Bewegung, Bewegung, Bewegung!," *FAZ*, May 10, 2007, http://www.faz.net/aktuell/feuilleton/debatten/fit-statt-fett-bewegung-bewegung-bewegung-1434002.html (accessed May 12, 2016).

Gibson, James William, *Warrior Dreams. Violence and Manhood in Post-Vietnam America*. New York: Hill & Wang, 1994.

Gilbert, James, *Men in the Middle. Searching for Masculinity in the 1950s*. Chicago, IL: University of Chicago Press, 2005.

Gilman, Sander L., *Fat Boys. A Slim Book*. Lincoln, NE: University of Nebraska Press, 2004.

Gilman, Sander L., *Making the Body Beautiful. A Cultural History of Aesthetic Surgery*. Princeton, NJ: Princeton University Press, 1999.

Gilman, Sander L., *Obesity. The Biography*. Oxford: Oxford University Press, 2010.

Glick, Megan H., "Of Sodomy and Cannibalism: Dehumanisation, Embodiment and the Rhetorics of Same-Sex and Cross-Species Contagion," *Gender & History* 23, 2 (2011), 266–82.

Goltermann, Svenja, *Körper der Nation. Habitusformierung und die Politik des Turnens 1860–1890*. Göttingen: Vandenhoeck & Ruprecht, 1998.

Goltermann, Svenja, *Opfer. Die Wahrnehmung von Krieg und Gewalt in der Moderne*. Frankfurt/M.: S. Fischer, 2017.

Goodley, Dan, *Dis/Ability Studies. Theorising Disablism and Ableism*. London: Routledge, 2014.

Gosewinkel, Dieter, "Staatsbürgerschaft und Staatsangehörigkeit," *Geschichte und Gesellschaft* 21, 4 (1995), 533–56.

Graebner, William, "'The Man in the Water'. The Politics of the American Hero, 1970–1985," *The Historian* 75, 3 (2013), 517–43.

Graefe, Stefanie, *Resilienz im Krisenkapitalismus. Wider das Lob der Anpassungsfähigkeit*. Bielefeld: transcript, 2019.

Graefe, Stefanie, "Subjektivierung, Erschöpfung, Autonomie. Eine Analyseskizze," *Ethik und Gesellschaft* 2 (2015), www.ethik-und-ge sellschaft.de/ojs/index.php/eug/article/view/2-2015-art-3 (accessed May 7, 2018).

Graf, Simon, "Leistungsfähig, attraktiv, erfolgreich, jung und gesund: Der fitte Körper in post-fordistischen Verhältnissen," *Body Politics* 1, 1 (2013), 139–57.

Gramsci, Antonio, "Rationalization of Production and Work," in *The Gramsci Reader. Selected Writings 1916–1935*, ed. David Forgacs. New York: New York University Press, 2000, 289–94.

Gräser, Markus, *Wohlfahrtsgesellschaft und Wohlfahrtsstaat. Bürgerliche Sozialreform und Welfare State Building in den USA und in Deutschland 1880–1940*. Göttingen: Vandenhoeck & Ruprecht, 2009.

Greene, Jeremy A. and Elizabeth Siegel Watkins, "Introduction. The Prescription in Perspective," in: Jeremy A. Greene and Elizabeth Siegel Watkins (eds.), *Prescribed. Writing, Filling, Using, and Abusing the Prescription in Modern America*. Baltimore, MD: Johns Hopkins University Press, 2012, 1–22.

Greiner, Bernd, *War Without Fronts. The USA in Vietnam*, transl. by Anne Wyburd with Victoria Fern. New Haven, CT: Yale University Press, 2009.

Gruneau, Richard, *Sport & Modernity*. Cambridge: Polity, 2017.

Gumbrecht, Hans-Ulrich, "Modern, Modernität, Moderne," in: Reinhart Koselleck, Werner Conze, and Otto Brunner (eds.),

Geschichtliche Grundbegriffe. Historisches Wörterbuch zur politisch-sozialen Sprache, vol. 4. Stuttgart: Klett-Cotta, 1978, 93–131.

Gunkel, Henriette and Olaf Stieglitz, "Verqueerte Laufwege. Sport & Körper in Geschichtswissenschaften und Cultural Studies," *Body Politics* 2, 3 (2014), 5–20.

Gustav-Wrathall, John D., *Take the Young Stranger by the Hand. Same-Sex Relations and the YMCA*. Chicago, IL: University of Chicago Press, 1998.

Guthman, Julie, *Weighing In: Obesity, Food Justice, and the Limits of Capitalism*. Berkeley, CA: University of California Press, 2011.

Guthold, Regina, Gretchen A. Stevens, Leanne M. Riley, and Fiona C. Bull, "Worldwide Trends in Insufficient Physical Activity from 2001 to 2016. A Pooled Analysis of 358 Population-Based Surveys with 1.9 Million Participants," *Lancet Global Health*, September 4, 2018, http://dx.doi.org/10.1016/S2214-109X(18)30357-7 (accessed September 9, 2018).

Guttmann, Allen, *From Ritual to Record. The Nature of Modern Sports*. New York: Columbia University Press, 1978.

Haak, Sebastian, *The Making of the Good War. Hollywood, das Pentagon und die amerikanische Deutung des Zweiten Weltkriegs, 1945–1962*. Paderborn: Schöningh, 2013.

Hachtmann, Rüdiger, "'Bäuche wegmassieren' und 'überflüssiges Fett in unserem Volke beseitigen'. Der kommunale Breitensport der NS-Gemeinschaft 'Kraft durch Freude'," in: Frank Becker and Ralf Schäfer (eds.), *Sport und Nationalsozialismus*. Göttingen: Wallstein, 2016, 27–66.

Hachtmann, Rüdiger and Adelheid von Saldern, "Das fordistische Jahrhundert. Eine Einleitung," *Zeithistorische Forschungen* 6, 2 (2009), 174–85.

Hachtmann, Rüdiger and Adelheid von Saldern, "'Gesellschaft am Fließband'. Fordistische Produktion und Herrschaftspraxis in Deutschland," *Zeithistorische Forschungen* 6, 2 (2009), 186–208.

Hagemann, Karen, *Revisiting Prussia's Wars against Napoleon: History, Culture, and Memory*. Cambridge: Cambridge University Press, 2015.

Hagemann, Karen, "Tod für das Vaterland. Der patriotisch-nationale Heldenkult zur Zeit der Freiheitskriege," *Militärgeschichtliche Zeitschrift* 60, 2 (2001), 307–42.

Hale, E.E., "What Shall We Have for Dinner?," *Atlantic Monthly* 14, 83 (1864), 364–71.

Hales, Craig M., Cheryl D. Fryar, Margaret D. Carroll, et al., "Differences in Obesity Prevalence by Demographic Characteristics and Urbanization Level Among Adults in the United States, 2013–2016," *JAMA* 319, 23 (2019), 2419–29.

Hall, Stuart, "The West and the Rest. Discourse and Power," in: Stuart Hall and Bram Gieben (eds.), *Formations of Modernity*. Cambridge: Polity, 1992, 275–320.

Haller, Lea, Sabine Höhler, and Heiko Stoff, "Stress – Konjunkturen eines Konzepts," *Zeithistorische Forschungen* 11, 3 (2014), 359–81, https://www.zeithistorische-forschungen.de/3-2014/id%3D5136?language=en (accessed May 6, 2018).

Hanner, Richard, "Beginning Running," *Runner's World* 14, 7 (1979), 68–71.

Hannig, Nicolai and Malte Thießen (eds.), *Vorsorgen in der Moderne. Akteure, Räume und Praktiken*. Berlin: de Gruyter, 2017.

Haralambon, Olivier, *Der Radrennfahrer und sein Schatten. Eine kleine Philosophie des Straßenradsports*. Bielefeld: Covadonga, 2018.

Hargreaves, Jennifer, *Sporting Females. Critical Issues in the History and Sociology of Women's Sports*. London: Routledge, 1994.

Harrasser, Karin, *Körper 2.0. Über die technische Erweiterbarkeit des Menschen*. Bielefeld: transcript, 2013.

Harrasser, Karin, *Prothesen. Figuren einer lädierten Moderne*. Berlin: Vorwerk 8, 2016.

Harrasser, Karin, Henriette Gunkel, and Olaf Stieglitz, "Wieviel Technology ist im Laufschuh? – Ein Gespräch mit Karin Harrasser an der Schnittstelle von Kulturwissenschaft und Sportgeschichte," *Body Politics* 2, 3 (2014), 39–44.

Hartmann, Kathrin, "Kontinuität und Wandel von Männerbildern in den 90er Jahren am Beispiel sowjetischer und postsowjetischer Filme," Working papers of the Institute for East European Studies, Free University Berlin 39 (2002), http://www.oei.fu-berlin.de/politik/publikationen/AP39.pdf (accessed September 1, 2018).

Heater, Derek, *A Brief History of Citizenship*. New York: New York University Press, 2004.

Henderson, Joe, "The Year Running Became the Sport of the 70s," *Runner's World* 14, 1 (1979), 82–7.

Henderson, Joe, "Tips for the First-Time Marathoner," *Runner's World* 18, 10 (1983), 66–70.

Henne, Melanie, *Training Citizenship. Ethnizität und Breitensport in Chicago, 1920–1950*. Stuttgart: Steiner, 2015.

Herrera, Ricardo A., *For Liberty and the Republic: The American Citizen as Soldier, 1775–1861*. New York: New York University Press, 2015.

Heywood, Leslie, *Bodymakers. A Cultural Anatomy of Women's Body Building*. New Brunswick, NJ: Rutgers University Press, 1998.

Higdon, Hal, "A Race with Texture," *Runner's World* 12, 12 (1977), 44–7.

Higdon, Hal, "Is Running a Religious Experience? No One Seems to Have a Middle-of-the-Road Opinion as the Fanatic Fringe Builds," *Runner's World* 13, 5 (1978), 74–9.

Higdon, Hal, "The Master Plan. You Can Run Fast after 40. Here's How," *Runner's World* 26, 8 (1991), 66–9.

Hildebrandt, Tina, "Stups zum Glück: Warum Regierungen sich nicht anmaßen sollten, bis ins Letzte zu bestimmen, was gut für ihre Bürger ist," *Die Zeit* 1 (2015), December 30, 2014, http://www.zeit. de/2015/01/glueck-merkel-muttikratie (accessed May 12, 2016).

Hoberman, John, *Mortal Engines: The Science of Performance and the Dehumanization of Sport*. New York: Free Press, 1992.

Hoberman, John, *Testosterone Dreams. Rejuvenation, Aphrodisia, Doping*. Berkeley, CA: University of California Press, 2005.

Hodenberg, Christina von, *Das andere Achtundsechzig. Gesellschaftsgeschichte einer Revolte*. Munich: Beck, 2018.

Hoff, Ralf von den, Ronald G. Asch, Achim Aurnhammer, et al., "Helden – Heroisierungen – Heroismen. Transformationen und Konjunkturen von der Antike bis zur Moderne. Konzeptionelle Ausgangspunkte des Sonderforschungsbereichs 948," *helden.heroes. héros*. 1, 1 (2013), 7–14.

Hogan, Candace L., "Total Fitness '89: Off & Running, Ironmania, Real Life Experiments," *Runner's World* 24, 5 (1989), 46–50.

Hoganson, Kristin L., *Fighting for American Manhood: How Gender Politics Provoked the Spanish-American and Philippine-American Wars*. New Haven, CT: Yale University Press, 1998.

Honisch, Richard, "Wirtschaft und Leibesübungen," *Die Leibesübungen* 3, 22 (1927), 532.

Honneth, Axel, *Anerkennung: Eine europäische Ideengeschichte*. Berlin: Suhrkamp, 2018.

Horning, Dave, "Cold, Wet and Wild: Triathlon: Racing's Triple Threat: The Proper Mix of Three Disciplines Becomes the Greatest Challenge," *Runner's World* 17, 11 (1982), 32–9, 73–5.

Houchin Winfield, Betty and Janice Hume, "The American Hero and the Evolution of the Human Interest Story," *American Journalism* 15, 2 (1998), 79–99.

Hultling, C., "Partners' Perceptions of the Efficacy of Sildenafil Citrate (Viagra) in the Treatment of Erectile Dysfunction," *International Journal of Clinical Practice*, Supplement 102 (1999), 16–18.

Humphreys, A.R., "'The Eternal Fitness of Things': An Aspect of Eighteenth-Century Thought," *Modern Language Review* 42, 2 (1947), 188–98.

Hunt, Lynn, *Inventing Human Rights: A History*. New York: Norton, 2007.

Hutchinson, Woods, "The Physical Basis of Brain-Work," *North American Review* 146, 378 (1888), 522–31.

Isenmann, Moritz, "Die langsame Entstehung eines ökonomischen Systems. Konkurrenz und freier Markt im Werk von Adam Smith," *Historische Zeitschrift* 307 (2018), 655–91.

Jackson, Derrick Z., "All Quiet on the Fat Front," *Boston Globe*, October 11, 2002.

Jackson, Mark, *The Age of Stress: Science and the Search for Stability*. Oxford: Oxford University Press, 2013.

Jagose, Annamarie, *Orgasmology*. Durham, NC: Duke University Press, 2013.

Jagose, Annamarie, *Queer Theory: Eine Einführung*. Berlin: Querverlag, 2001.

Jarvis, Christina S., *The Male Body at War. American Masculinity during World War II*. DeKalb, IL: Northern Illinois University Press, 2004.

Jeffords, Susan, *Hard Bodies. Hollywood Masculinity in the Reagan Era*. New Brunswick, NJ: Rutgers University Press, 1994.

Jeffords, Susan, *The Remasculinization of America. Gender and the Vietnam War*. Bloomington, IN: Indiana University Press, 1989.

Jones, Max, "What Should Historians Do with Heroes? Reflections on Nineteenth- and Twentieth-Century Britain," *History Compass* 5, 2 (2007), 439–54.

Journal of Sport History, "One Hundred Years of 'Muscular Judaism': Sport in Jewish History and Culture," 26, 2 (Special issue) (1999).

Jünger, Ernst, *Storm of Steel* (1920), transl. by Michael Hofmann. New York: Penguin, 2016.

Kasson, John F., *Houdini, Tarzan, and the Perfect Man: The White Male Body and the Challenge of Modernity in America*. New York: Hill & Wang, 2002.

Keith, Alison, "The Economics of Viagra," *Health Affairs* (March/April 2000), 147–57.

Kienitz, Sabine, *Beschädigte Helden. Kriegsinvalidität und Körperbilder 1914–1923*. Paderborn: Schöningh, 2008.

Kienitz, Sabine, "Der Krieg der Invaliden. Helden-Bilder und Männlichkeitskonstruktionen nach dem Ersten Weltkrieg," *Militärgeschichtliche Zeitschrift* 60, 2 (2001), 367–402.

Kienitz, Sabine, "Körper – Beschädigungen. Kriegsinvalidität und Männlichkeitskonstruktionen in der Weimarer Republik," in: Karen Hagemann and Stefanie Schüler-Springorum (eds.), *Heimat-Front: Militär und Geschlechterverhältnisse im Zeitalter der Weltkriege*. Frankfurt/M.: Campus, 2002, 188–207.

Kienitz, Sabine, "Schöner gehen? Zur technischen Optimierung des kriegsinvaliden Körpers im frühen 20. Jahrhundert," *Body Politics* 3, 6 (2015), 235–59.

Kieran, David and Edwin A. Martini (eds.), *At War. The Military and American Culture in the Twentieth Century and Beyond*. New Brunswick, NJ: Rutgers University Press, 2018.

Kim, Tae-Jun and Olaf von dem Knesebeck, "Income and Obesity: What Is the Direction of the Relationship? A Systematic Review and Meta-Analysis," *BMJ OPEN* 8, 1 (2018), doi: 10.1136/bmjopen-2017-019862.

Kim, Tae-Jun, Nina Roesler, and Olaf von dem Knesebeck, "Causation or Selection – Relation between Education and Overweight/Obesity in Prospective Observational Studies. A Meta-Analysis," *Obesity Review* 18, 6 (2017), 660–72.

Kimmel, Michael, *The Gendered Society*. New York: Oxford University Press, 2000.

King, Rufus, "The Pioneers of Ohio," *Atlantic Monthly* 62, 372 (1888), 559–64.

Kingsolver, Barbara, *Animal, Vegetable, Miracle. A Year of Food Life*. New York: HarperCollins, 2007.

Kläber, Mischa, *Doping im Fitness-Studio. Die Sucht nach dem perfekten Körper*. Bielefeld: transcript, 2010.

Kleeberg, Bernhard (ed.), *Schlechte Angewohnheiten: Eine Anthologie, 1750–1900*. Berlin: Suhrkamp, 2012.

Kleeberg, Bernhard, "Schlechte Angewohnheiten. Einleitung," in: Bernhard Kleeberg (ed.), *Schlechte Angewohnheiten: Eine Anthologie, 1750–1900*. Berlin: Suhrkamp, 2012, 9–63.

Kleeberg, Bernhard, *Theophysis: Ernst Haeckels Philosohie des Naturganzen*. Cologne: Böhlau, 2005.

Kline, Wendy, *Bodies of Knowledge. Sexuality, Reproduction, and Women's Health in the Second Wave*. Chicago, IL: University of Chicago Press, 2010.

Kocka, Jürgen, *Angestellte zwischen Faschismus und Demokratie. Zur politischen Sozialgeschichte der Angestellten: USA 1890–1940 im internationalen Vergleich*. Göttingen: Vandenhoeck & Ruprecht, 1977.

Koedt, Ann, "The Myth of the Vaginal Orgasm," in: Shulamit Firestone and Ann Koedt (eds.), *Notes from the Second Year: Women's Liberation*. New York: Radical Feminism, 1970, 37–41.

Koehler, Herman J., *Manual for Physical Training for Use in the United States Army*. New York: Military Publishing Company, 1914.

Koehler, Herman J., *Manual of Gymnastic Exercises: Prepared for Use in Service Gymnasiums*. Washington, DC: Government Printing Office, 1904.

Kowalchick, Claire and Mark Will-Weber, "Extraordinary People," *Runner's World* 25, 8 (1990), 84.

Kracauer, Siegfried, *The Salaried Masses: Duty and Distraction in Weimar Germany* (1930). New York: Verso, 1998.

Krämer, Felix, *Moral Leaders. Medien, Gender und Glaube in den USA der 1970er und 1980er Jahre*. Bielefeld: transcript, 2015.

Krämer, Felix, "'Playboy tells his story': Krisenszenario um die hegemoniale US-Männlichkeit der 1970er Jahre," *Feministische Studien* 27, 1 (2009), 83–96.

Krasmann, Susanne, "Regieren über Freiheit. Zur Analyse der Kontrollgesellschaft in Foucaultscher Perspektive," *Kriminologisches Journal* 31 (1999), 107–21.

Kraus, Hans and Ruth P. Hirschland, "Minimum Muscular Fitness Tests in School Children," *Research Quarterly* 25 (1954), 178–88.

Kraus, Hans and Ruth P. Hirschland, "Muscular Fitness and Orthopedic Disability," *New York State Journal of Medicine* 54 (1954), 212–15.

Kreisky, Eva, "Fitte Wirtschaft und schlanker Staat. Das neoliberale Regime über die Bäuche," in: Henning Schmidt-Semisch and Friedrich Schorb (eds.), *Kreuzzug gegen die Fette: Sozialwissenschaftliche Aspekte des gesellschaftlichen Umgangs mit Übergewicht und Adipositas*. Wiesbaden: VS Verlag für Sozialwissenschaften, 2008, 143–61.

Kreuzenbeck, Nora, "Nothing to Lose. Fat Acceptance-Strategien und Agency als Widerstand und Unterwerfung in den USA von der Mitte der 1960er bis in die frühen 1980er Jahre," *Body Politics* 3, 5 (2015), 111–34, http://bodypolitics.de/de/wp-content/uploads/2016/01/Heft_5_print_End.pdf (accessed November 18, 2018).

Krüger, Michael, *Körperkultur und Nationsbildung: Die Geschichte des Turnens in der Reichsgründungsära – eine Detailstudie über die Deutschen*. Schorndorf: Hofmann Verlag, 1996.

Kugelmass, Jack (ed.), *Jews, Sports, and Rites of Citizenship*. Urbana, IL: University of Illinois Press, 2007.

Kühl, Stefan, *Die Internationale der Rassisten. Aufstieg und Niedergang der internationalen eugenischen Bewegung im 20. Jahrhundert*, 2nd edn. Frankfurt/M.: Campus, 2014.

Kunkel, Rolf, "'Die dreifache totale Fitneß'. Spiegel-Reporter Rolf Kunkel über die Triathlon-Weltmeisterschaft auf Hawaii," *Der Spiegel* 42 (1982), 264–9.

Kury, Patrick, *Der überforderte Mensch. Eine Wissensgeschichte vom Stress zum Burnout*. Frankfurt/M.: Campus, 2012.

Kury, Patrick, "Von der Neurasthenie zum Burnout – eine kurze Geschichte von Belastung und Anpassung," in: Sighard Neckel and Greta Wagner (eds.), *Leistung und Erschöpfung: Burnout in der Wettbewerbsgesellschaft*. Berlin: Suhrkamp, 2013, 107–28.

Kwolek-Folland, Angel, *Engendering Business. Men and Women in the Corporate Office, 1870–1930*. Baltimore, MD: Johns Hopkins University Press, 1998.

Langewiesche, Dieter, *Liberalism in Germany*. Princeton, NJ: Princeton University Press, 1999.

Latour, Bruno, *Reassembling the Social: An Introduction to Actor-Network-Theory*. Oxford: Oxford University Press, 2005.

Lears, T.J. Jackson, *Rebirth of a Nation: The Making of Modern America, 1877–1920*. New York: HarperCollins, 2009.

Lee, Jennifer A. and Cat J. Pausé, "Stigma in Practice: Barriers to Health for Fat Women," *Frontiers in Psychology* 7 (2016), https://www.frontiersin.org/articles/10.3389/fpsyg.2016.02063/full (accessed November 15, 2018).

Lehmann, Hans-Thies, "Wunsch nach Bewunderung. Das Theater um den Helden," *Merkur* 63, 9/10 (2009), 772–81.

Lengwiler, Martin and Jeannette Madarász, "Präventionsgeschichte als Kulturgeschichte der Gesundheitspolitik," in: Martin Lengwiler and Jeannette Madarász (eds.), *Das präventive Selbst. Eine Kulturgeschichte moderner Gesundheitspolitik*. Bielefeld: transcript, 2010, 11–28.

Lessenich, Stephan, *Die Neuerfindung des Sozialen. Der Sozialstaat im flexiblen Kapitalismus*, 3rd edn. Bielefeld: transcript, 2013.

Levenstein, Harvey, *Fear of Food: A History of Why We Worry about What We Eat*. Chicago, IL: University of Chicago Press, 2012.

Levenstein, Harvey, *Paradox of Plenty. A Social History of Eating in Modern America*. Berkeley: University of California Press, 2003 (1993).

Levy, Ariel, "Pill Culture Pops," *New York Magazine*, June 9, 2003, http://nymag.com/nymetro/news/features/n_8763/index2.html (accessed November 17, 2016).

Lewis, Barry, "Mapping the Way," *Runner's World* 27, 7 (1992), 94.

Lewis, Dio, "The New Gymnastics," *Atlantic Monthly* 10, 58 (1862), 129–48.

Lewis, Sinclair, *The Job*. New York: Harper & Brothers, 1917.

Lexchin, Joel, "Bigger and Better: How Pfizer Redefined Erectile Dysfunction," *PLoS Medicine* 3, 4 (2006) doi: 10.1371/journal.pmed.0030132.

Lindenberger, Thomas, "Eigen-Sinn, Herrschaft und kein Widerstand," Version: 1.0, in: *Docupedia-Zeitgeschichte*, September 2, 2014, http://docupedia.de/zg/Eigensinn?oldid=108792 (accessed July 8, 2016).

Linek, Jenny, *Gesundheitsvorsorge in der DDR zwischen Propaganda und Praxis*. Stuttgart: Steiner, 2016.

Linker, Beth, *War's Waste, Rehabilitation in World War I America*. Chicago, IL: University of Chicago Press, 2011.

Loe, Meika, *The Rise of Viagra. How the Little Blue Pill Changed Sex in America*. New York: New York University Press, 2004.

Lombard, Anne, *Making Manhood: Growing Up Male in Colonial New England*. Cambridge, MA: Harvard University Press, 2003.

Lorenz, Maren, *Leibhaftige Vergangenheit. Einführung in die Körpergeschichte*. Tübingen: Edition discord, 2000.

Lorenz, Maren, *Menschenzucht: Frühe Ideen und Strategien 1500–1870*. Göttingen: Wallstein, 2018.

Luciano, Lynne, *Looking Good: Male Body Image in Modern America*. New York: Hill & Wang, 2001.

Lüdtke, Alf, "'Deutsche Qualitätsarbeit' – ihre Bedeutung für das Mitmachen von Arbeitern und Unternehmern im Nationalsozialismus," in: Aleida Assmann, Frank Hiddemann, and Eckhard Schwarzenberger (eds.), *Firma Topf & Söhne. Hersteller der Öfen für Auschwitz: ein Fabrikgelände als Erinnerungsort?* Frankfurt/M.: Campus, 2002, 123–38.

Lüdtke, Alf, *Eigen-Sinn: Fabrikalltag, Arbeitererfahrungen und Politik vom Kaiserreich bis in den Faschismus* (1993). Münster: Verlag Westfälisches Dampfboot, 2015.

Lüdtke, Alf, "'Helden der Arbeit' – Mühen beim Arbeiten. Zur mißmutigen Loyalität von Industriearbeitern in der DDR," in: Hartmut Kaelble, Jürgen Kocka, and Hartmut Zwahr (eds.), *Sozialgeschichte der DDR*. Stuttgart: Steiner, 1994, 188–213.

Ludwig, Lisa, "Selbstliebe reicht nicht: Im Gespräch mit einer Fettaktivistin (Magda Albrecht)," *Broadly*, January 15, 2018, https://broadly.vice.com/de/article/vbyx5m/selbstliebe-reicht-nicht-im-ges praech-mit-einer-fettaktivistin (accessed November 15, 2018).

Luh, Andreas, *Betriebssport zwischen Arbeitgeberinteressen und Arbeitnehmerbedürfnissen. Eine historische Analyse von der Kaiserzeit bis zur Gegenwart*. Aachen: Meyer & Meyer, 1998.

Lupton, Deborah, "Self-Tracking Citizenship," *This Sociological Life. A Blog by Sociologist Deborah Lupton*, https://simplysociology.wordpress.com/ 2016/04/24/self-tracking-citizenship/ (accessed May 11, 2016).

Lupton, Deborah, *The Quantified Self. A Sociology of Self-Tracking.* Cambridge: Polity, 2016.

Lüthi, Barbara, *Invading Bodies. Medizin und Immigration in den USA 1880–1920.* Frankfurt/M.: Campus, 2009.

Lutz, Tom, *American Nervousness, 1903. An Anecdotal History.* Ithaca, NY: Cornell University Press, 1993.

Lynch, Jerry, "Mind Over Marathon. The Marathon Is Probably 5 Percent Physical and 95 Percent Psychological. If You Think You Can, You Can," *Runner's World* 25, 10 (1990), 36–42.

Macdonald, Charlotte, *Strong, Beautiful, and Modern: National Fitness in Britain, New Zealand, Australia and Canada, 1935–1960.* Vancouver: University of British Columbia Press, 2011.

MacDonogh, Giles, "Helden und Patrioten," *Merkur* 63, 9/10 (2009), 782–92.

McKendrick, Neil, John Brewer, and J.H. Plumb, *The Birth of a Consumer Society: The Commercialization of Eighteenth-Century England.* Bloomington, IN: Indiana University Press, 1982.

McKenzie, Shelly, *Getting Physical: The Rise of Fitness Culture in America.* Lawrence, KS: University of Kansas Press, 2013.

Mackert, Nina, "Feeding Productive Bodies: Calories, Nutritional Values and Ability in Progressive Era US," in: Peter-Paul Bänziger and Martin Suter (eds.), *Histories of Productivity. Genealogical Perspectives on the Body and Modern Economy.* London: Routledge, 2016, 117–35.

Mackert, Nina, "'I Want to Be a Fat Man / And with the Fat Men Stand'. US-Amerikanische Fat Men's Clubs und die Bedeutungen von Körperfett in den Dekaden um 1900," *Body Politics* 2, 3 (2014), 215–43.

Mackert, Nina, "Kimberlé Crenshaw: Mapping the Margins (1991), oder: Die umkämpfte Kreuzung," in: Olaf Stieglitz and Jürgen Martschukat (eds.), *Race & Sex: Eine Geschichte der Neuzeit.* Berlin: Neofelis, 2016, 50–6.

Mackert, Nina, "Writing the History of Fat Agency," *Body Politics* 3, 5 (2015), 13–24.

Mackert, Nina and Jürgen Martschukat, "Introduction: Critical Ability History," *Rethinking History* 23, 2 (2019), 131–7.

Mackert, Nina and Jürgen Martschukat, "Introduction: Fat Agency," *Body Politics* 3, 5 (2015), 5–11.

McLaren, Angus, *Impotence: A Cultural History*. Chicago, IL: University of Chicago Press, 2007.

McMahon, Darrin M., *Happiness: A History*. New York: Grove Press, 2006.

McRuer, Robert, "Compulsory Able-Bodiedness and Queer/Disabled Existence," in: Rosemarie Garland-Thomson (ed.), *Disability Studies: Enabling the Humanities*. New York: Modern Language Association of America, 2002, 88–99.

McRuer, Robert, *Crip Theory: Cultural Signs of Queerness and Disability*. New York: New York University Press, 2006.

Madarász-Lebenhagen, Jeannette, "Geschlechterbilder in Präventionskonzepten: Männer- und Frauenherzen im deutsch-deutschen Vergleich, 1949–1990," in: Sylvelyn Hähner-Rombach (ed.), *Geschichte der Prävention. Akteure, Praktiken, Instrumente*. Stuttgart: Steiner, 2015, 73–105.

Mailer, Norman, "Superman Comes to the Supermarket," *Esquire*, November 1960, https://www.esquire.com/news-politics/a3858/superman-supermarket/ (accessed June 11, 2017).

Mailer, Norman, "The White Negro," *Dissent*, Autumn 1957, https://www.dissentmagazine.org/online_articles/the-white-negro-fall-1957 (accessed June 11, 2017).

Mamo, Laura and Jennifer R. Fishman, "Potency in All the Right Places: Viagra as a Technology of the Gendered Body," *Body & Society* 7, 4 (2001), 13–35.

Mangan, J.A. (ed.), *Shaping the Superman. Fascist Body as Political Icon – Aryan Fascism*. London: Frank Cass, 1999.

Marcuse, Julian, *Körperpflege durch Wasser, Luft und Sport. Eine Anleitung zur Lebenskunst*. Leipzig: J.J. Weber, 1908.

MarketsandMarkets, "Weight Loss Management Market Worth $206.4 Billion by 2019 – New Report by MarketsandMarkets," *PRweb*, March 9, 2015, http://www.prweb.com/releases/weight-loss/management-market/prweb12542655.htm (accessed June 9, 2016).

Markula, Pirrko, "Firm but Shapely, Fit but Sexy, Strong but Thin. The Postmodern Aerobicizing Female Bodies," in: Andrew Yiannakis and Merrill J. Melnick (eds.), *Contemporary Issues in the Sociology of Sport*. Champaign, IL: Human Kinetics, 1994, 237–57.

Marshall, Barbara L., "'Hard Science': Gendered Constructions of

Sexual Dysfunction in the 'Viagra Age'," *Sexualities* 5, 2 (2002), 131–58.

Marshall, Barbara L. and Stephen Katz, "Forever Functional: Sexual Fitness and the Ageing Male Body," *Body & Society* 8, 4 (2002), 43–70.

Martin, Douglas, "Thanks a Bunch, Viagra; The Pill That Revived Sex, Or at Least Talking About It," *New York Times*, May 3, 1998, 3.

Martschukat, Jürgen, *American Fatherhood. A History*, transl. by Petra Goedde. New York: New York University Press, 2019.

Martschukat, Jürgen, *Die Ordnung des Sozialen: Väter und Familien in der amerikanischen Geschichte seit 1770*. Frankfurt/M.: Campus, 2013.

Martschukat, Jürgen, "'His Chief Sin is Being a Negro. Next He Whipped a White Man. Next He Married a White Woman.' Sport, Rassismus und die (In)Stabilität von Grenzziehungen in den USA um 1900," *Historische Anthropologie* 15, 2 (2007), 259–80.

Martschukat, Jürgen, "On Choice," *Food, Fatness and Fitness: Critical Perspectives*, March 1, 2016, http://foodfatnessfitness.com/2016/03/01/onchoice/ (accessed August 25, 2020).

Martschukat, Jürgen, "'The Necessity for Better Bodies to Perpetuate Our Institutions, Insure a Higher Development of the Individual, and Advance the Conditions of the Race.' Physical Culture and the Formation of the Self in the Late Nineteenth and Early Twentieth Century USA," *Journal of Historical Sociology* 24, 4 (2011), 472–93.

Martschukat, Jürgen, "The Pursuit of Fitness. Von Freiheit und Leistungsfähigkeit in der Geschichte der USA," *Geschichte und Gesellschaft* 42, 3 (2016), 409–40.

Martschukat, Jürgen, "'What Diet Can Do': Running and Eating Right in 1970s America," in: Jürgen Martschukat and Bryant Simon (eds.), *Food, Power and Agency*. London: Bloomsbury, 2017, 129–45.

Martschukat, Jürgen and Olaf Stieglitz, *Einführung in die Geschichte der Männlichkeiten*, 2nd edn. Frankfurt/M.: Campus, 2018.

Martschukat, Jürgen and Olaf Stieglitz, "Race & Sex: Eine Geschichte der Neuzeit, oder: Grenzüberschreitungen einer kritischen Geschichtswissenschaft," in: Olaf Stieglitz and Jürgen Martschukat (eds.), *Race & Sex: Eine Geschichte der Neuzeit*. Berlin: Neofelis, 2016, 13–24.

Mayer, Andreas, *Wissenschaft vom Gehen. Die Erforschung der Bewegung im 19. Jahrhundert*. Frankfurt/M.: S. Fischer, 2013.

Megroz, Gordy, "Down and Dirty," *Runner's World*, June 20, 2012, https://www.runnersworld.com/trail-running/a20816363/down-and -dirty-mud-runs/ (accessed December 18, 2018).

Melosh, Barbara, *Engendering Culture. Manhood and Womanhood in New Deal Public Art and Theater*. Washington, DC: Smithsonian Press, 1991.

Melzer, Scott, *Gun Crusaders. The NRA's Culture War*. New York: New York University Press, 2009.

Meranze, Michael, *Laboratories of Virtue: Punishment, Revolution, and Authority in Philadelphia, 1760–1835*. Chapel Hill, NC: University of North Carolina Press, 1996.

Merwin, H.C., "The Ethics of Horse-Keeping," *Atlantic Monthly* 67, 403 (1891), 631–40.

Metzl, Jonathan M. and Anna Kirkland (eds.), *Against Health: How Health Became the New Morality*. New York: New York University Press, 2010.

Meusel, Waltraud, *Trimm Dich im Büro!* (1971), 4th edn. Frankfurt/M.: Deutscher Sportbund, 1975.

Meuser, Michael, "Hegemoniale Männlichkeit im Niedergang? Anmerkungen zum Diskurs der Krise des Mannes," in: Claudia Mahs, Barbara Rendtorff, and Anne-Dorothee Warmuth (eds.), *Betonen-Ignorieren-Gegensteuern: Zum pädagogischen Umgang mit Geschlechtstypiken*. Weinheim: Beltz Juventa, 2015, 93–105.

Mickel, Howard A., "The True Runner Becomes Hooked on a Feeling," *Runner's World* 14, 4 (1979), 30.

Mill, John Stuart, *On Liberty / Über die Freiheit* (1859). Stuttgart: Reclam, 2009.

Mill, John Stuart, *Principles of Political Economy* (1848). London: Augustus M. Kelley, 1985.

Miller, Arthur, *Death of a Salesman*. New York: Viking, 1949.

Mills, Charles W., *The Racial Contract*. Ithaca, NY: Cornell University Press, 1997.

Mills, C. Wright, *White Collar: The American Middle Classes* (1951). Oxford: Oxford University Press, 1969.

Mirzoeff, Nicholas, *Bodyscape: Art, Modernity and the Ideal Figure*. New York: Routledge, 1995.

Mitchell, Gordon R. and Kathleen M. McTigue, "The US Obesity

'Epidemic': Metaphor, Method, or Madness?," *Social Epistemology* 21, 4 (2007), 391–423.

Möhring, Maren, "Der moderne Apoll," *WerkstattGeschichte* 29 (2001), 27–42.

Möhring, Maren, "Ethnic Food, Fast Food, Health Food. Veränderung der Ernährung und Esskultur im letzten Drittel des 20. Jahrhunderts," in: Anselm Doering-Manteuffel, Lutz Raphael, and Thomas Schlemmer (eds.), *Vorgeschichte der Gegenwart: Dimensionen des Strukturbruchs nach dem Boom*. Göttingen: Vandenhoeck & Ruprecht, 2016, 309–32.

Möhring, Maren, *Marmorleiber. Körperbildung in der deutschen Nacktkultur (1890–1930)*. Cologne: Böhlau, 2004.

Møller, Verner, *The Doping Devil*. Books on Demand, 2008.

Mollow, Anna, "Disability Studies Gets Fat," *Hypathia: A Journal of Feminist Philosophy* 30, 1 (2015), 199–216.

Mollow, Anna and Robert McRuer, "Fattening Austerity," *Body Politics* 3, 5 (2015), 25–49.

Moran, Rachel L., *Governing Bodies: American Politics and the Shaping of the Modern Physique*. Philadelphia, PA: University of Pennsylvania Press, 2018.

Mörath, Verena, *Die Trimm-Aktionen des Deutschen Sportbundes zur Bewegungs- und Sportförderung in der BRD 1970 bis 1984*. Berlin: Wissenschaftszentrum Berlin für Sozialforschung, 2005.

Morley, Christopher, *Kitty Foyle*. Philadelphia, PA: Lippincott, 1939.

Moskowitz, Eva S., *In Therapy We Trust: America's Obsession with Self-Fulfillment*. Baltimore, MD: Johns Hopkins University Press, 2001.

Mosse, George L., *The Image of Man: The Creation of Modern Masculinity*. Oxford: Oxford University Press, 1999.

Müller, Johann P., *Mein System: 15 Min. täglicher Arbeit für die Gesundheit*. Leipzig: Grethlein, 1904.

Müllner, Rudolf, "Sich in Form bringen: Historische Aspekte der körperlichen (Selbst-)Verbesserung im und durch Sport seit 1900," in: Stefan Scholl (ed.), *Körperführung. Historische Perspektiven auf das Verhältnis von Biopolitik und Sport*. Frankfurt/M.: Campus, 2018, 41–70.

Mumford, Kevin, "'Lost Manhood' Found: Male Sexual Impotence and Victorian Culture in the United States," *Journal of the History of Sexuality* 3, 1 (1992), 33–57.

Münch, Philipp, *Bürger in Uniform: Kriegserfahrungen von Hamburger Turnern 1914 bis 1918*. Freiburg: Rombach, 2009.

Münkler, Herfried, *Kriegssplitter: Die Evolution der Gewalt im 20. und 21. Jahrhundert*. Reinbek: rororo, 2017.

Muttarak, Raya, "Normalization of Plus Size and the Danger of Unseen: Overweight and Obesity in England," *Obesity* 26 (2018), 1125–9.

Nelson, Dana D., *National Manhood: Capitalist Citizenship and Imagined Fraternity of White Men*. Durham, NC: Duke University Press, 1998.

Nelson, Paul D., "Citizen Soldiers or Regulars: The Views of American General Officers on the Military Establishment, 1775–1781," *Military Affairs* 43, 3 (1979), 126–32.

Netzwerk Körper (ed.), *What Can a Body Do? Figurationen und Praktiken des Körpers in den Kulturwissenschaften*. Frankfurt/M.: Campus, 2012.

Nolte, Paul, "Das große Fressen. Nicht Armut ist das Hauptproblem der Unterschicht. Sondern der massenhafte Konsum von Fast Food und TV," *Zeit Online*, December 17, 2003, https://www.zeit.de/2003/52/Essay_Nolte (accessed August 25, 2020).

Nordhausen, Richard, *Moderne Körperkultur: Ein Kompendium der gesamten modernen Körperkultur durch Leibesübung*. Leipzig: J.J. Arnd, 1909.

Nünning, Ansgar, "Krise als Erzählung und Metapher: Literaturwissenschaftliche Bausteine für eine Metaphorologie und Narratologie von Krisen," in: Carla Meyer, Katja Patzel-Mattern, and Jasper Schenk (eds.), *Krisengeschichte(n): "Krise" als Leitbegriff und Erzählmuster in kulturwissenschaftlicher Perspektive*. Stuttgart: Steiner, 2013, 117–44.

Nye, David E., *America's Assembly Line*. Cambridge, MA: MIT Press, 2013.

Offermann, Stefan, "On Responsibilization – Or: Why Missing the Bus Can Be Political," *Food, Fatness and Fitness: Critical Perspectives*, January 1, 2017, http://foodfatnessfitness.com/2017/01/01/responsibilization/ (accessed May 7, 2018).

Offermann, Stefan, "Socialist Responsibilization: The Government of Risk Factors for Cardiovascular Diseases in the German Democratic Republic in the 1970s," *Rethinking History* 23, 2 (2019), 210–32.

Office of the Surgeon General et al., *The Surgeon General's Call to Action to Prevent and Decrease Overweight and Obesity*. Rockville, MD: Office of the Surgeon General, 2001.

Osler, Tom, "The Easy Way to a 50-Miler," *Runner's World* 16, 8 (1981), 55, 80–4.

Owen, Robert, "A New View of Society, Or, Essays on the Principle of the Formation of the Human Character, and the Application of the Principle to Practice, 1813–16," McMaster University Archive for the History of Economic Thought, https://socialsciences. mcmaster.ca/~econ/ugcm/3ll3/owen/newview.txt (accessed April 1, 2018).

Page, William, "Our Artists in Italy," *Atlantic Monthly* 7, 40 (1861), 129–38.

Park, Roberta, "Biological Thought, Athletics and the Formation of a 'Man of Character': 1830–1900," in: Roberta Park, *Gender, Sport, Science. Selected Writings of Roberta J. Park*. London: Routledge, 2009, 43–68.

Park, Roberta, "Blending Business and Basketball: Industrial Sports and Recreation in the United States from the late 1800s to 1960," *Stadion* 31, 1 (2005), 35–49.

Park, Roberta, "Muscles, Symmetry, and Action: 'Do You Measure Up?' Defining Masculinity in Britain and America from the 1860s to the Early 1900s," *International Journal of the History of Sport* 22, 3 (2005), 365–95.

Parker, William, "The Freedman's Story, I," *Atlantic Monthly* 17, 100 (1866), 152–67.

Patel, Kiran K., *Soldiers of Labor: Labor Service in Nazi Germany and New Deal America, 1933–1945*. Cambridge: Cambridge University Press, 2003.

Patel, Kiran K., *The New Deal: A Global History*. Princeton, NJ: Princeton University Press, 2016.

Pateman, Carole, *The Sexual Contract*. Stanford, CA: Stanford University Press, 1988.

Peña, Carolyn T. de la, *The Body Electric. How Strange Machines Built the Modern American*. New York: New York University Press, 2003.

Pesavento, Wilma J., "Sport and Recreation in the Pullman Experiment, 1880–1900," *Journal of Sport History* 9, 2 (1982), 38–62.

Peters, Keith, "In America, Corporate Fitness is an Idea Whose Time is Now," *Runner's World* 16, 4 (1981), 55–9.

Pfister, Gertrud, "200 Jahre Turnbewegung – von der Hasenheide bis heute," *Aus Politik und Zeitgeschichte* (APuZ) 16–19 (2011), http://www.bpb.de/apuz/33345/200-jahre-turnbewegung-von-der-hasenheide-bis-heute?p=all (accessed August 28, 2018).

Pfister, Gertrud, "'Stählung der Arbeiterschaft ist Stählung der Wirtschaft'? Zur Organisation und Ideologie des Betriebssports in Berlin (1880 bis 1933)," in: Gertrud Pfister (ed.), *Zwischen Arbeitnehmerinteressen und Unternehmenspolitik. Zur Geschichte des Betriebssports in Deutschland*. Sankt Augustin: Academia, 1999, 18–44.

Pfister, Gertrud, "The Role of German Turners in American Physical Education," *International Journal of the History of Sport* 26, 13 (2009), 1893–925.

Pfütsch, Pierre, "Zwischen Gesundheit und Schönheit. Fitness als biopolitische Praktik zur Modellierung des Körpers in bundesrepublikanischen Gesundheitspublikationen der 1970er und 1980er Jahre," in: Stefan Scholl (ed.), *Körperführung. Historische Perspektiven auf das Verhältnis von Biopolitik und Sport*. Frankfurt/M.: Campus, 2018, 265–90.

Pilcher, James E., "The Building of the Soldier," *The United Service Magazine* 4 (April 1892), 336.

Pinkerton, Elaine, "Running Can Be Your Substitute: If You Are Going to Be Addicted, Then Run," *Runner's World* 14, 5 (1979), 105–10.

Planert, Ute, "Der dreifache Körper des Volkes: Sexualität, Biopolitik und die Wissenschaften vom Leben," *Geschichte und Gesellschaft* 26 (2000), 539–76.

Plumb, J.H., "Disappearing Heroes," *Horizon* 16, 4 (1974), 48–51.

Plymire, Darcy C., "Positive Addiction: Running and Human Potential in the 1970s," *Journal of Sport History* 31, 3 (2004), 297–315.

Pollack, Andrew, "A.M.A. Recognizes Obesity as a Disease," *New York Times*, June 18, 2013.

Pollan, Michael, *The Omnivore's Dilemma. The Search for a Perfect Meal in a Fast-Food World* (2006). London: Bloomsbury, 2011.

Poole, Ralph J., "Männer im Pelz. Entblößungen und Verhüllungen des natürlichen Körpers um 1900," in: Jürgen Martschukat and Olaf Stieglitz (eds.), *Väter, Soldaten, Liebhaber. Männer und Männlichkeiten in der nordamerikanischen Geschichte – ein Reader*. Bielefeld: transcript, 2007, 159–82.

Poole, Ralph J., "Preface," in: Ralph J. Poole, Florian Sedlmeier, and Susanne Wegener (eds.), *Hard Bodies*. Münster: LIT, 2011, 6–20.

Post, Marty, "The Corporate Cup Runneth Over with Talent," *Runner's World* 18, 5 (1983), 52–6.

Potts, Annie, "Deleuze on Viagra (Or, What Can a 'Viagra-Body' Do?)," *Body & Society* 10, 1 (2004), 17–36.

Potts, Annie, "'The Essence of the Hard On': Hegemonic Masculinity and the Cultural Construction of 'Erectile Dysfunction'," *Men and Masculinities* 3, 1 (2000), 85–103.

Potts, Annie, Nicola Gavey, Victoria M. Grace, and Tiina Vares, "The Downside of Viagra: Women's Experiences and Concerns," *Sociology of Health & Illness* 25, 7 (2003), 697–719.

Potts, Annie, Victoria M. Grace, Nicola Gavey, and Tiina Vares, "'Viagra Stories': Challenging 'Erectile Dysfunction'," *Social Science & Medicine* 59, 3 (2004), 489–99.

Potts, Annie, Victoria M. Grace, Tiina Vares, and Nicola Gavey, "'Sex for Life'? Men's Counter-Stories on 'Erectile Dysfunction', Male Sexuality and Ageing," *Sociology of Health & Illness* 28, 3 (2006), 306–29.

Probst, Maximilian, "Held auf dem Sprung. Das postheroische Zeitalter geht zu Ende. Die Verherrlichung des Kämpfers kehrt zurück – nicht nur am rechten Rand," *Die Zeit* 29 (July 12, 2018), https://www.zeit.de/2018/29/mut-postheroische-gesellschaft-heroismus-nationalismus-totalitarismus (accessed August 23, 2018).

Pumping Iron (George Butler/Robert Fiore, USA, 1977).

Purkiss, Ava, "'Beauty Secrets: Fight Fat': Black Women's Aesthetics, Exercise, and Fat Stigma, 1900–1930s," *Journal of Women's History* 29, 2 (2017), 14–37.

Putney, Clifford, *Muscular Christianity. Manhood and Sports in Protestant America, 1880–1920*. Cambridge, MA: Harvard University Press, 2001.

Rabinbach, Anson, *The Human Motor. Energy, Fatigue, and the Origins of Modernity*. New York: Basic Books, 1990.

Rader, Benjamin G., "The Quest for Self-Sufficiency and the New Strenuosity: Reflections on the Strenuous Life of the 1970s and the 1980s," *Journal of Sport History* 18, 2 (1991), 255–66.

Radkau, Joachim, *Das Zeitalter der Nervosität. Deutschland zwischen Bismarck und Hitler*. Munich: Carl Hanser, 1998.

Raine, William M., "Taming the Frontier. Bucky O'Neill," *Outing* 46 (1905), 292–5.

Ramsbrock, Annelie, *The Science of Beauty: Culture and Cosmetics in Modern Germany, 1750–1930*. New York: Palgrave, 2015.

Ramsbrock, Annelie, Thomas Schnalke, and Paula-Irene Villa, "Menschliche Dinge und dingliche Menschen. Positionen und Perspektiven," *Zeithistorische Forschungen/Studies in Contemporary History*, online edition, 13, 3 (2016), http://www.zeithistorische-forschungen.de/3-2016/id=5403 (accessed December 6, 2016).

Raphael, Lutz, "Die Verwissenschaftlichung des Sozialen als methodische und konzeptionelle Herausforderung für eine Sozialgeschichte des 20. Jahrhunderts," *Geschichte und Gesellschaft* 22 (1996), 165–93.

Reagan, Ronald, "How to Stay Fit. The President's Personal Exercise Program," *Parade Magazine*, December 4, 1983, 4–6.

Reagan, Ronald, "Inaugural Address, January 20, 1981," *The American Presidency Project*, https://www.presidency.ucsb.edu/documents/inaugural-address-11(accessed September 27, 2020).

Reckwitz, Andreas, *Das hybride Subjekt. Eine Theorie der Subjektkulturen von der bürgerlichen Moderne zur Postmoderne*. Weilerswist: Velbrück, 2006.

Reckwitz, Andreas, *Subjekt*. Bielefeld: transcript, 2008.

Reed, J.D., "America Shapes Up," *TIME Magazine* 118, 18 (November 2, 1981), 94–106.

Reichhardt, Sven, *Authentizität und Gemeinschaft: Linksalternatives Leben in den siebziger und achtziger Jahren*. Berlin: Suhrkamp, 2014.

Reichardt, Sven, "Klaus Theweleits 'Männerphantasien' – ein Erfolgsbuch der 1970er-Jahre," *Zeithistorische Forschungen* 3 (2006), 401–21.

Reinold, Marcel, *Doping als Konstruktion. Eine Kulturgeschichte der Anti-Doping-Politik*. Bielefeld: transcript, 2016.

Reynolds, David and Miranda Mirosa, "Want Amidst Plenty: Food Insecurity in Rich Liberal Democracies," in: Glenn Muschert, Kristen Budd, Michelle Christian, Brian V. Klocke, Jon Shefner, and Robert Perrucci (eds.), *Global Agenda for Social Justice: Volume One*. Bristol: Policy Press, 2018, 131–42.

Rheinberger, Hans-Jörg, *Experimentalsysteme und epistemische Dinge: Eine Geschichte der Proteinsynthese im Reagenzglas*. Frankfurt/M.: Suhrkamp, 2006.

Ribbat, Christoph, *Deutschland für eine Saison – Die wahre Geschichte des Wilbert Olinde jr.* Berlin: Suhrkamp, 2017.

Rich, Adrienne, "Compulsory Heterosexuality and Lesbian Existence," *Signs: Journal of Women in Culture and Society*, 5, 4 (1980), 631–60.

Riesman, David, *The Lonely Crowd. A Study of the Changing American Character*. New Haven, CT: Yale University Press, 1950.

Riis, Jacob A., "Reform by Humane Touch," *Atlantic Monthly* 84, 506 (1899), 745–53.

Riley, A., "The Role of the Partner in Erectile Dysfunction and Its Treatment," *International Journal of Impotence Research* 14, Supplement 1 (2002), S105–9.

Riley, A. and E. Riley, "Behavioural and Clinical Findings in Couples Where the Man Presents with Erectile Disorder: A Retrospective Study," *International Journal of Clinical Practice* 54, 4 (2002), 220–4.

Rippberger, Anna-Lena, "Fitness-Apps: Das gefährliche Geschäft mit den Daten," *Merkur*, March 30, 2016, https://www.merkur.de/leben/gesundheit/krankenkassen-fitness-apps-gefaehrliche-geschaeft-daten-6260226.html (accessed November 15, 2018).

Ritchie, Ian, "Understanding Performance-Enhancing Substances and Sanctions Against Their Use from the Perspective of History," in: Verner Møller, Ivan Weddington, and John Hoberman (eds.), *Routledge Handbook of Drugs and Sport*. New York: Routledge, 2015, 20–30.

Rödder, Andreas, *21.0. Eine kurze Geschichte der Gegenwart*. Munich: Beck, 2015.

Roediger, David, *Working Toward Whiteness: How America's Immigrants Became White. The Strange Journey from Ellis Island to the Suburbs*. New York: Basic Books, 2005.

Roosevelt, Theodore, *America and the First World War*. New York: Charles Scribner's Sons, 1915.

Roosevelt, Theodore, "The Strenuous Life" (April 10, 1899), *Voices of Democracy. The U.S. Oratory Project*, http://voicesofdemocracy.umd.edu/roosevelt-strenuous-life-1899-speech-text/ (accessed July 7, 2016).

Rorabaugh, William J., *The Alcoholic Republic: An American Tradition*. Oxford: Oxford University Press, 1981.

Rosa, Hartmut, *Beschleunigung. Die Veränderung der Zeitstrukturen in der Moderne*. Frankurt/M.: Suhrkamp, 2005.

Rose, Nikolas, "Governing the Enterprising Self," in: Paul Heelas and Paul Morris (eds.), *The Values of Enterprise Culture*. London: Routledge, 1992, 141–63.

Rose, Nikolas, "Molecular Biopolitics, Somatic Ethics, and the Spirit of Biocapital," *Social Theory and Health* 5 (2007), 3–29.

Rose, Nikolas, *Powers of Freedom: Reframing Political Thought*. Cambridge: Cambridge University Press, 1999.

Rose, Nikolas and Carlos Novas, "Biological Citizenship," in: Aihwa Ong and Stephen J. Collier (eds.), *Global Assemblages: Technology, Politics, and Ethics as Anthropological Problems*. Oxford: Wiley-Blackwell, 2004, 439–63.

Rosen, Raymond C., Alan Riley, Gorm Wagner, et al., "The International Index of Erectile Function (IIEF): A Multidimensional Scale for Assessment of Erectile Dysfunction," *Urology* 49 (1997), 822–30.

Rosen, Raymond C., Joseph C. Cappelleri, and N. Gendrano III, "The International Index of Erectile Function (IIEF): A State-of-the-Science Review," *International Journal of Impotence Research* 14 (2002), 226–44.

Rothblum, Esther and Sondra Solovay (eds.), *The Fat Studies Reader*. New York: New York University Press, 2009.

Rothman, David J., *The Discovery of the Asylum. Social Order and Disorder in the New Republic*. Boston, MA: Scott Foresman, 1971.

Rothstein, William G., *Public Health and the Risk Factor: A History of an Uneven Medical Revolution*. Rochester, NY: University of Rochester Press, 2003.

Rotteck, Carl von and Karl Welcker (eds.), *Staats-Lexikon oder Encyklopädie der Staatswissenschaften*, vol. 9. Altona: Hammerich, 1840.

Rowe, John W. and Robert L. Kahn, *Successful Aging*. New York: Pantheon, 1998.

Rubino, Daniel, "Microsoft Band: Read the Backstory on the Evolution and Development Microsoft's New Smart Device,"

Windows Central, October 29, 2014, https://www.windowscentral. com/microsoft-band-read-backstory-evolution-and-development-microsofts-new-smart-device (accessed November 10, 2018).

Ruthven, K.K., "Fielding, Square, and the Fitness of Things," *Eighteenth-Century Studies* 5, 2 (1971–2), 243–55.

Sachse, Carola, *Siemens, der Nationalsozialismus und die moderne Familie: Eine Untersuchung zur sozialen Rationalisierung in Deutschland im 20. Jahrhundert*. Hamburg: Rasch & Röhring, 1990.

Saguy, Abigail C., *What's Wrong With Fat?* Oxford: Oxford University Press, 2013.

Saldern, Adelheid von, *Amerikanismus. Kulturelle Abgrenzungen von Europa und US-Nationalismus im frühen 20. Jahrhundert*. Stuttgart: Steiner, 2013.

Sarasin, Philipp, *Darwin und Foucault. Genealogie und Geschichte im Zeitalter der Biologie*. Frankfurt/M.: Suhrkamp, 2009.

Sarasin, Philipp, *Reizbare Maschinen. Eine Geschichte des Körpers 1765–1914*. Frankfurt/M.: Suhrkamp, 2001.

Sarasin, Philipp and Jakob Tanner, "Physiologie und industrielle Gesellschaft. Bemerkungen zum Konzept und zu den Beiträgen des Sammelbandes," in: Philipp Sarasin and Jakob Tanner (eds.), *Physiologie und industrielle Gesellschaft. Studien zur Verwissenschaftlichung des Körpers im 19. und 20. Jahrhundert*. Frankfurt/M.: Suhrkamp, 1998, 12–43.

Sargent, Dudley A., "The Physical Development of Women," *Scribner's Magazine* 5, 2 (1889), 172–85.

Sargent, Dudley A., "The Physical Proportions of the Typical Man," *Scribner's Magazine* 2, 1 (1887), 3–17.

Scheller, Jörg, *No Sports! Zur Ästhetik des Bodybuildings*. Stuttgart: Steiner, 2010.

Schild, Georg, *Zwischen Freiheit des Einzelnen und Wohlfahrtsstaat: Amerikanische Sozialpolitik im 20. Jahrhundert*. Paderborn: Verlag Ferdinand Schöningh, 2003.

Schlechtriemen, Tobias, "The Hero and a Thousand Actors: On the Constitution of Heroic Agency," *helden.heroes.héros.* 4, 1 (2016), 17–32.

Schmedt, Michael, "Fitness-Tracker. Der Datenhunger wächst," *Deutsches Ärzteblatt* 113, 7 (2016), 257–8.

Schmincke, Imke, "Sexualität als 'Angelpunkt der Frauenfrage'? Zum Verhältnis von sexueller Revolution und Frauenbewegung," in: Peter-Paul Bänziger, Magdalena Beljan, Franz X. Eder, and Pascal Eitler (eds.), *Sexuelle Revolution? Zur Geschichte der Sexualität im deutschsprachigen Raum seit den 1960er Jahren.* Bielefeld: transcript, 2015, 199–222.

Schneider, Angela J., "The Concept of Doping," in: Verner Møller, Ivan Weddington, and John Hoberman (eds.), *Routledge Handbook of Drugs and Sport.* New York: Routledge, 2015, 9–19.

Scholl, Stefan, "Einleitung: Biopolitik und Sport in historischer Perspektive," in: Stefan Scholl (ed.), *Körperführung: Historische Perspektiven auf das Verhältnis von Biopolitik und Sport.* Frankfurt/M.: Campus, 2018, 7–39.

Scholl, Stefan, "Europäische Biopolitik? Das Sport-für-alle Paradigma des Europarats in den 1960er und 1970er Jahren," in: Stefan Scholl (ed.), *Körperführung: Historische Perspektiven auf das Verhältnis von Biopolitik und Sport.* Frankfurt/M.: Campus, 2018, 243–64.

Scholl, Stefan (ed.), *Körperführung. Historische Perspektiven auf das Verhältnis von Biopolitik und Sport.* Frankfurt/M.: Campus, 2018.

Schultz, Jamie, *Qualifying Times: Points of Change in U.S. Women's Sport.* Urbana, IL: University of Illinois Press, 2014.

Scott, Emmett J., "Leisure Time and the Colored Citizen (1925)," in: David K. Wiggins and Patrick B. Miller (eds.), *The Unlevel Playing Field: A Documentary History of the African American in Sport.* Urbana, IL: University of Illinois Press, 2003, 88–90.

Sennett, Richard, *The Corrosion of Character: The Personal Consequences of Work in the New Capitalism.* New York: Norton, 1999.

Sennett, Richard, *The Culture of the New Capitalism.* New Haven, CT: Yale University Press, 2007.

Serazio, Michael, "Ethos Groceries and Countercultural Appetites: Consuming Memory in Whole Foods' Brand Utopia," *Journal of Popular Culture* 44, 1 (2011), 158–77.

Shachak, Mattan and Eva Illouz, "The Pursuit of Happiness: Coaching and the Commodification of Well-Being," *Querformat* 3 (2010), 18–31.

Shaler, Nathaniel S., "European Peasants as Immigrants," *Atlantic Monthly* 71, 427 (1893), 646–55.

Shaler, Nathaniel S., "The Use and Limits of Academic Culture," *Atlantic Monthly* 66, 394 (1890), 160–70.

Shangold, Mona, "The Woman Runner: Her Body, Her Mind, Her Spirit," *Runner's World* 16, 7 (1981), 34–44, 88.

Sheehan, George, "Medical Advice," *Runner's World* 10, 3 (1975), 40.

Sherman, Carl, "Little Blue Miracle," *Playboy Magazine* (US edition) 45, 7 (1998), 125 and 178.

Simon, Bryant, "The Geography of Silence: Food and Tragedy in Globalizing America," in: Jürgen Martschukat and Bryant Simon (eds.), *Food, Power and Agency*. London: Bloomsbury, 2017, 83–102.

Simon, Bryant, *The Hamlet Fire: A Tragic Story of Cheap Food, Cheap Government, and Cheap Lives*. New York: New Press, 2017.

Singer, Stefanie, "Entstehung des Betrieblichen Gesundheitsmanagements," in: Adelheid S. Esslinger, Martin Emmert, and Oliver Schöffski (eds.), *Betriebliches Gesundheitsmanagement. Mit gesunden Mitarbeitern zu unternehmerischem Erfolg*. Wiesbaden: Gabler, 2010, 23–48.

Sloterdijk, Peter, *You Must Change Your Life: On Anthropotechnics*, transl. by Wieland Hoban. Cambridge: Polity, 2013.

Smith, Adam, *The Wealth of Nations* (1776). New York: Prometheus Books, 1991.

Snyder, R. Claire, *Citizen-Soldiers and Manly Warriors: Military Service and Gender in the Civic Republican Tradition*. Lanham, MD: Rowman & Littlefield, 1999.

Sombart, Werner, *Händler und Helden: Patriotische Besinnungen*. Munich: Duncker & Humblot, 1915.

Sontag, Susan, *Illness As Metaphor*. New York: Farrar, Straus & Giroux, 1978.

Sontowski, Claudia, *Viagra im Alltag: Praktiken der Männlichkeit, des Körpers und der Sexualität*. Wiesbaden: Springer, 2016.

Spangenberg, Petra, "Betriebssport. Der Chef turnt mit: Immer mehr Firmen verordnen ihren Mitarbeitern Gymnastik am Arbeitsplatz," *Die Zeit* 37 (September 7, 1973), https://www.zeit.de/1973/37/der-chef-turnt-mit (accessed May 1, 2018).

Spark, Richard F., Robert A. White, and Peter B. Connolly, "Impotence Is Not Always Psychogenic: Newer Insights into Hypothalamic-Pituitary-Gonadal Dysfunction," *Journal of the American Medical Association* 243, 8 (1980), 750–5.

Spencer, Herbert, *Die Principien der Biologie*. Authorized German edition after the second English edition, transl. by B. Vetter, vol. 1. Stuttgart: Schweizbart'sche Verlagsbuchhandlung, 1876.

Spencer, Herbert, *The Principles of Biology*. London: Williams and Norgate, 1864.

Spencer, Lyle M., *Youth Goes to War*. Chicago, IL: Science Research Associates, 1943.

Spiker, Ted, "The Mudder Report," *Runner's World*, December 7, 2011, https://www.runnersworld.com/training/a20849132/the-mudder-report/ (accessed September 1, 2018).

Spöhrer, Markus, "'Wie ich zum Cyborg wurde': Das Cochlea Implantat und die Übersetzungen des transhumanen Körpers," *Body Politics* 3, 6 (2015), 309–27.

Spreen, Dierk, *Upgradekultur: Der Körper in der Enhancement-Gesellschaft*. Bielefeld: transcript, 2015.

Stagner, Vannessa C., "Healing the Soldier, Restoring the Nation: Representations of Shell Shock in the USA During and After the First World War," *Journal of Contemporary History* 49, 2 (2014), 255–74.

Stearns, Peter, *Fat History: Bodies and Beauty in the Modern West*. New York: New York University Press, 1997.

Stedman, E.C., "Edwin Booth," *Atlantic Monthly* 17, 103 (1866), 585–94.

Steigerwald, David, "All Hail the Republic of Choice. Consumer History as Contemporary Thought," *Journal of American History* 93, 2 (2006), 385–403.

Steiner, Reinhard, "Heldenposen," *Merkur* 63, 9/10 (2009), 925–33.

Steuben, Friedrich Wilhelm von, *Regulations for the Order and Discipline of the Troops of the United States* (1779). Philadelphia, PA: Eleazer Oswald at the Coffee-House, 1786.

Stewart, Tiffany M., "Why Thinking We're Fat Won't Help Us Improve Our Health: Finding the Middle Ground," *Obesity* 26, 7 (2018), 1115–16.

Stieglitz, Olaf, *100 Percent American Boys: Disziplinierungsdiskurse und*

Ideologie im Civilian Conservation Corps, 1933–1942. Stuttgart: Steiner, 1999.

Stieglitz, Olaf, "'A Man of Your Years Shouldn't Expect to Be Able to Do Those Things'. Älter werden in Bernarr Macfaddens Physical Culture-Welt," in: Stefan Scholl (ed.), *Körperführung: Historische Perspektiven auf das Verhältnis von Biopolitik und Sport.* Frankfurt/M.: Campus, 2018, 99–130.

Stieglitz, Olaf, "The American Crawl – Praktiken von Geschlecht und Moderne in US-amerikanischen Schwimmbecken, 1900–1940," *Gender: Zeitschrift für Geschlecht, Kultur und Gesellschaft* 10, 1 (2018), 63–80.

Stieglitz, Olaf and Jürgen Martschukat (eds.), *Race & Sex: Eine Geschichte der Neuzeit.* Berlin: Neofelis, 2016.

Stieglitz, Olaf, Jürgen Martschukat, and Kirsten Heinsohn, "Sportreportage: Sportgeschichte als Kultur- und Sozialgeschichte," *H-Soz-Kult,* May 28, 2009, http://hsozkult.geschichte.hu-berlin.de/forum/2009-05-001 (accessed July 8, 2016).

Stoff, Heiko, "Das Leistungsprinzip in der Wettbewerbsgesellschaft, 1960–1980," in: Frank Becker and Ralf Schäfer (eds.), *Die Spiele gehen weiter: Profile und Perspektiven der Sportgeschichte.* Frankfurt/M.: Campus, 2014, 277–305.

Stoff, Heiko, "Degenerierte Nervenkörper und regenerierte Hormonkörper: Eine kurze Geschichte der Verbesserung des Menschen zu Beginn des 20. Jahrhunderts," *Historische Anthropologie* 11, 2 (2003), 224–39.

Stoff, Heiko, "Der erfolgreiche Mensch: Ludwig Lewins transatlantisches Projekt, 1928," in: Stephanie Kleiner and Robert Suter (eds.), *Guter Rat: Glück und Erfolg in der Ratgeberliteratur, 1900–1940.* Berlin: Neofelis, 2015, 135–59.

Stoff, Heiko, *Ewige Jugend. Konzepte der Verjüngung vom späten 19. Jahrhundert bis ins Dritte Reich.* Cologne: Böhlau, 2004.

Stoff, Heiko, "Janine. Tagebuch einer Verjüngten.' Weibliche Konsumkörper zu Beginn des 20. Jahrhunderts," in: Claudia Bruns and Tilmann Walter (eds.), *Von Lust und Schmerz. Eine historische Anthropologie der Sexualität.* Cologne: Böhlau, 2004, 217–38.

Strange, Lisa S. and Robert S. Brown, "The Bicycle, Women's Rights, and Elizabeth Cady Stanton," *Women's Studies* 31, 5 (2002), 609–26.

Sutton, Nikki, "First Lady Michelle Obama: 'Making the Healthy Choice the Easy Choice'," September 15, 2011, https://www.whitehouse.gov/blog/2011/09/15/first-lady-michelle-obama-making-healthy-choice-easy-choice (accessed May 12, 2016).

Suzik, Jeffrey Ryan, "'Building Better Men': The CCC Boys and the Changing Social Ideal of Manliness," in: Roger Horowitz (ed.), *Boys and Their Toys? Masculinity, Class, and Technology in America*. New York: Routledge, 2001, 111–38.

Swan, Melanie, "The Quantified Self: Fundamental Disruption in Big Data Science and Biological Discovery," *Big Data* 1 (2013), 85–99.

Tanrisever, Ahu, *Fathers, Warriors, and Vigilantes: Post-Heroism and the US Cultural Imaginary in the Twenty-First Century*. Heidelberg: Winter, 2016.

Taylor, Frederick Winslow, *The Principles of Scientific Management*. New York: Harper & Brothers, 1911.

Taylor, Sonya Renee, *This Body Is Not an Apology. The Power of Radical Self-Love*. Oakland, CA: Berrett-Koehler, 2018.

Teleky, Richard, "Post-Heroism?," *Queen's Quarterly* 124, 1 (2017), 35–45.

Terzian, Tamar V., "Direct-to-Consumer Prescription Drug Advertising," *American Journal of Law & Medicine* 25 (1999), 149–67.

Tetzlaff, Sven, "Wie Jugendliche heute Helden sehen. Über den Geschichtswettbewerb des Bundespräsidenten," *Merkur* 63, 9/10 (2009), 813–20.

Thaler, Richard H. and Cass R. Sunstein, *Nudge: Improving Decisions about Health, Wealth, and Happiness*. New Haven, CT: Penguin Books, 2008.

Thayer, James B., "The Dawes Bill and the Indians," *Atlantic Monthly* 61, 365 (1888), 315–23.

Theberge, Nancy, "A Critique of Critiques. Radical and Feminist Writings on Sport," *Social Forces* 60, 2 (1981), 341–53.

Theiss, Louis E., "Measuring Physical Fitness," *Outing* 56 (1910), 344–50.

Theweleit, Klaus, *Male Fantasies* (1977/78), transl. by Stephen Conway. Minneapolis, MN: University of Minnesota Press, 1987–9.

Thorpe, Holly and Rebecca Olive (eds.), "Forum: Feminist Sport

History in the Past, Present, and Future," *Journal of Sport History* 39, 3 (2012), 373–486.

Tiefer, Leonore, "Doing the Viagra Tango: Sex Pill as Symbol and Substance," *Radical Philosophy* 92 (1998), 2–5.

Tiefer, Leonore, "Sexology and the Pharmaceutical Industry: The Threat of Co-optation," *Journal of Sex Research* 37, 3 (2000), 273–83.

Timmermann, Carsten, "Risikofaktoren. Der scheinbar unaufhaltsame Erfolg eines Ansatzes aus der amerikanischen Epidemiologie in der deutschen Nachkriegsmedizin," in: Martin Lengwiler and Jeanette Madarász (eds.), *Das präventive Selbst. Eine Kulturgeschichte moderner Gesundheitspolitik*. Bielefeld: transcript, 2010, 251–77.

Toufexis, Anastasia, "It's Not All in Your Head. New Therapies Keep Impotence from Being a Hopeless Condition," *TIME Magazine*, December 5, 1988, http://content.time.com/time/magazine/arti cle/0,9171,956444,00.html (accessed December 17, 2018).

Tovar, Virgie, *Hot & Heavy. Fierce Fat Girls on Life, Love and Fashion*. Berkeley, CA: Seal Press, 2012.

Tovar, Virgie, "Lose Hate Not Weight," *TED Talks*, July 19, 2017, https://www.youtube.com/watch?v=hZnsamRfxtY (accessed November 15, 2018).

Tovar, Virgie, *You Have the Right to Remain Fat*. New York: Feminist Press at CUNY, 2018.

Trebay, Guy, "Longer Harder Faster," *Village Voice*, October 26, 1999, https://www.villagevoice.com/1999/10/26/longer-harder-faster/ (accessed December 17, 2018).

Triggle, Nick, "Sugar Tax: How Will It Work?," *BBC News Health*, March 16, 2016, http://www.bbc.com/news/health-35824071 (accessed May 15, 2016).

Tuck, Stephen, "Introduction: Reconsidering the 1970s – the 1960s to a Disco Beat?," *Journal of Contemporary History* 43, 4 (2008), 617–20.

Tucker, William H., *The Science and Politics of Racial Research*. Champaign, IL: University of Illinois Press, 1994.

Tuma, Thomas, "Körperkult: 'Das kann auch geil sein'. Fitness-Studios entfernen sich immer mehr vom Klischee der muffeligen Muckibude im Hinterhof," *Der Spiegel* 38 (1999), 134–9.

Turse, Nick, *Kill Anything That Moves: The Real American War in Vietnam*. New York: Henry Holt and Company, 2013.

Tymn, Mike, "Trauma of Turning Forty," *Runner's World* 12, 9 (1977), 36–9.

Underhill, Jane, "Converting the Non-Runner," *Runner's World* 10, 4 (1975), 26–9.

Unger Hahn, Jane, "Heroes of Running 2005. Every Reason to Run Is a Good One," *Runner's World*, September 22, 2006, https://www.run nersworld.com/races-places/a20829842/heroes-of-2005/ (accessed July 4, 2018).

van Dyk, Silke, *Soziologie des Alters*. Bielefeld: transcript, 2015.

van Dyk, Silke, "Was die Welt zusammenhält. Das Dispositiv als Assoziation und performative Handlungsmacht," *Zeitschrift für Diskursforschung* 1, 1 (2013), 46–66.

van Dyk, Silke and Stefanie Graefe, "Fit ohne Ende – gesund ins Grab? Kritische Anmerkungen zur Trias Alter, Gesundheit, Prävention," *Jahrbuch für kritische Medizin und Gesundheitswissenschaften* 46, 3 (2013), 96–121.

Vatin, François, "Arbeit und Ermüdung: Entstehung und Scheitern der Psychophysiologie der Arbeit," in: Philipp Sarasin and Jakob Tanner (eds.), *Physiologie und industrielle Gesellschaft: Studien zur Verwissenschaftlichung des Körpers im 19. und 20. Jahrhundert*. Frankfurt/M.: Suhrkamp, 1998, 347–68.

Veit, Helen Z., *Modern Food, Moral Food: Self-Control, Science, and the Rise of Modern American Eating in the Early Twentieth-Century*. Chapel Hill, NC: University of North Carolina Press, 2013.

Verbrugge, Martha H., *Active Bodies: A History of Women's Physical Education in Twentieth-Century America*. Oxford: Oxford University Press, 2012.

Verheyen, Nina, *Die Erfindung der Leistung*. Berlin: Hanser, 2018.

Vertinsky, Patricia, "Feminist Charlotte Perkins Gilman's Pursuit of Health and Physical Fitness as a Strategy for Emancipation," *Journal of Sport History* 16, 1 (1989), 5–26.

Vertinsky, Patricia, "'Weighs and Means': Examining the Surveillance of Fat Bodies through Physical Education Practices in North America in the Late 19th and Early 20th Centuries," *Journal of Sport History* 35, 3 (2008), 449–68.

Vester, Katharina, *A Taste of Power: Food and American Identities*. Berkeley, CA: University of California Press, 2015.

Vester, Katharina, "Regime Change: Gender, Class, and the Invention of Dieting in Post-Bellum America," *Journal of Social History* 44, 1 (2010), 39–70.

Villa, Paula-Irene, "Einleitung – Wider die Rede vom Äußerlichen," in: Paula-Irene Villa (ed.), *schön normal. Manipulationen am Körper als Technologien des Selbst*. Bielefeld: transcript, 2009, 7–18.

Villa, Paula-Irene, "Habe den Mut, Dich Deines Körpers zu bedienen! Thesen zur Körperarbeit in der Gegenwart zwischen Selbstermächtigung und Selbstunterwerfung," in: Paula-Irene Villa (ed.), *schön normal. Manipulationen am Körper als Technologien des Selbst*. Bielefeld: transcript, 2009, 245–72.

Volkwein, Karen, "Introduction. Fitness and the Cross-Cultural Exchange," in: Karen Volkwein (ed.), *Fitness as Cultural Phenomenon*. Münster: Waxmann, 1998, ix–xxvi.

Voß, G. Günter and Hans J. Pongratz, "Der Arbeitskraftunternehmer: Eine neue Grundform der Ware Arbeitskraft," *Kölner Zeitschrift für Soziologie und Sozialpsychologie* 50 (1998), 131–58.

Wacquant, Loïc J.D., "Why Men Desire Muscles," *Body & Society* 1, 1 (1995), 163–79.

Warde, Robert, "Coming On Strong after 50," *Runner's World* 12, 11 (1977), 43–4.

Warren, Robert Penn, "A Dearth of Heroes," *American Heritage* 23, 6 (1972), 4–7 and 95–9.

Warren, Stephen, "US Special Forces: An Other Within the Self," *Critical Military Studies* 5, 1 (2019), 40–62.

Waters, Brent, "Defining the Runner's Personality," *Runner's World* 16, 6 (1981), 48–51.

Wayland, Francis, Jr., "An American in the House of Lords," *Atlantic Monthly* 12, 70 (1863), 137–53.

Weber, Max, *The Protestant Ethic and the Spirit of Capitalism* (1904/05). New York: W.W. Norton, 2009.

Wecter, Dixon, *The Hero in America. A Chronicle of Hero-Worship*. New York: Scribner, 1972.

Weeks, Jeffrey, "The Sexual Citizen," *Theory, Culture & Society* 15, 3–4 (1998), 35–52.

Weingarten, Susanne, "Ein Lob dem Mann, der nicht kann. Der

Potenzwahn in der Gesellschaft und seine bizarren Folgen," *Der Spiegel* 21 (May 18, 1998), 118–19.

Wellman-Stühring, Annika, "Silber-Sex. Von der Pathologisierung zur Aktivierung des gealterten Geschlechtskörpers," in: Peter-Paul Bänziger, Magdalena Beljan, Franz X. Eder, and Pascal Eitler (eds.), *Sexuelle Revolution? Zur Geschichte der Sexualität im deutschsprachigen Raum seit den 1960er Jahren*. Bielefeld: transcript, 2015, 303–22.

Wells, D. Colin, "Social Darwinism," *American Journal of Sociology* 12, 5 (1907), 695–716.

Wendt, Simon, "Introduction: Reconsidering Military Heroism in American History," in: Simon Wendt (ed.), *Warring over Valor. How Race and Gender Shaped American Military Heroism in the Twentieth and Twenty-First Centuries*. New Brunswick, NJ: Rutgers University Press, 2018, 1–19.

Wendt, Simon (ed.), *Warring over Valor. How Race and Gender Shaped American Military Heroism in the Twentieth and Twenty-First Centuries*. New Brunswick, NJ: Rutgers University Press, 2018.

Werber, Niels, "Soldaten und Söldner. Krieg, Risiko und Versicherung in der 'postheroischen' Epoche," *Merkur* 63, 9/10 (2009), 793–802.

Wheeler, Claude L., *The American Diseases – Neurasthenia*. New York: Bauer Chemical, 1909.

White, Kevin, *The First Sexual Revolution. The Emergence of Male Heterosexuality in Modern America*. New York: New York University Press, 1993.

Whyte, William H., *Is Anybody Listening? How and Why U.S. Business Fumbles When It Talks with Human Beings*. New York: Simon and Schuster, 1952.

Whyte, William H., *The Organization Man*. New York: Simon and Schuster, 1956.

Wiebe, Robert H., *The Search for Order, 1877–1920*. New York: Hill & Wang, 1967.

Wildmann, Daniel, *Begehrte Körper. Konstruktion und Inszenierungen des "arischen" Männerkörpers im "Dritten Reich."* Wurzburg: Königshausen & Neumann, 1998.

Wildt, Michael, *Am Beginn der "Konsumgesellschaft." Mangelerfahrung, Lebenshaltung, Wohlstandshoffnung in Westdeutschland in den fünfziger Jahren*. Hamburg: Ergebnisse Verlag, 1994.

Wildt, Michael, *Volk, Volksgemeinschaft, AfD*. Hamburg: Hamburger Edition, 2017.

Wildt, Michael, "Volksgemeinschaft," Version: 1.0, in: *Docupedia-Zeitgeschichte*, June 3, 2014, http://docupedia.de/zg/Volk sgemeinschaft?oldid=106491 (accessed July 8, 2016).

Wilkerson, Abby, "From the Land of the Fat to the Fat of the Land: The Thin Contract, Food Cultures, and Social Justice," in: Sofie Vandamme, Suzanne van de Vathorst, and Inez de Beaufort (eds.), *Whose Weight Is It Anyway? Essays on Ethics and Eating*. Leuven/The Hague: Acco, 2010, 143–57.

Wilkerson, Abby, "'Obesity,' the Transnational Plate, and the Thin Contract," *Radical Philosophy Review* 13, 1 (2010), 43–67.

Willard, Frances E., *A Wheel within a Wheel: A Woman's Quest for Freedom*. Bedford, MA: Applewood Books, 1997 (1895).

Wiltse, Jeff, *Contested Waters: A Social History of Swimming Pools in America*. Chapel Hill, NC: University of North Carolina Press, 2007.

Wirtz, Mica, "'Fit statt fett' und 'in Form'. Ein kritischer Blick auf aktuelle Programme zur Bevölkerungsgesundheit," *Sozial Extra* 34, 3–4 (2010), 46–9.

Wischnin, Bob, "Alex Ratelle Wants to Go Forever," *Runner's World* 14, 7 (1979), 84.

Woitas, Melanie, "'Go for the burn!' Jane Fondas Aerobic-Videos und die Entstehung des Aerobic Body," in: Stefan Scholl (ed.), *Körperführung: Historische Perspektiven auf das Verhältnis von Biopolitik und Sport*. Frankfurt/M.: Campus, 2018, 291–312.

Woitas, Melanie, "Vom männlichen Elitetraining zum weiblichen Breitensport: Aerobic im Spannungsfeld geschlechtlicher Aneignungsprozesse in den USA," *Ariadne* 69 (2016), 34–41.

Wolfe, Tom, "The 'Me' Decade and the Third Great Awakening," *New York Magazine*, August 23, 1976, http://nymag.com/news/fea tures/45938/ (accessed June 9, 2016).

Womack, James P., Daniel T. Jones and Daniel Roos, *The Machine That Changed the World*. New York: Free Press, 2007.

Zeithistorische Forschungen/Studies in Contemporary History, Themenheft, Die 1970er-Jahre – Inventur einer Umbruchzeit, online edition, 3 (2006) https://zeithistorische-forschungen.de/3-2006.

Zimmermann, Moshe, "Muskeljuden versus Nervenjuden," in: Michael

Brenner and Gideon Reuveni (eds.), *Emanzipation durch Muskelkraft. Juden und Sport in Europa*. Göttingen: Vandenhoeck & Ruprecht, 2006, 15–28.

Zink, Vivian, "At Texas Instruments, Fitness ls Good Business," *Runner's World* 16, 4 (1981), 58.

Zukin, Sharon, *Naked City. The Death and Life of Authentic Urban Places*. Oxford: Oxford University Press, 2009.

Zweiniger-Bargielowska, Ina, *Managing the Body: Beauty, Health and Fitness in Britain, 1880s–1939*. Oxford: Oxford University Press, 2010.

INDEX